# James Joyce and His Contemporaries

*Edited by*
## Diana A. Ben-Merre
*and*
## Maureen Murphy

*Prepared under the auspices of Hofstra University*

Contributions to the Study of World Literature, Number 30

Greenwood Press
New York • Westport, Connecticut • London

PR
6019
09
Z63366
1989

Joseph Astman
In Memory

**Library of Congress Cataloging-in-Publication Data**

James Joyce and his contemporaries.

(Contributions to the study of world literature,
0-738-9345 ; no. 30)
"Prepared under the auspices of Hofstra University."
Includes index.
1. Joyce, James, 1882-1941—Criticism and inter-
pretation. 2. English literature—Irish authors—
History and criticism. 3. English literature—20th
century—History and criticism. 4. Ireland—
Intellectual life—20th century. I. Ben-Merre, Diana A.-
II. Murphy, Maureen, 1940-  . III. Series.
PR6019.09Z63366 1989    823'.912    88-32789
ISBN 0-313-26667-0 (lib. bdg. : alk. paper)

British Library Cataloguing in Publication Data is available.

Library of Congress Catalog Card Number: 88-32789
ISBN: 0-313-26667-0
ISSN: 0-738-9345

First published in 1989

Greenwood Press, Inc.
88 Post Road West, Westport, Connecticut 06881

Printed in the United States of America

The paper used in this book complies with the
Permanent Paper Standard issued by the National
Information Standards Organization (Z39.48-1984).

10 9 8 7 6 5 4 3 2 1

Janet Egleson Dunleavy, ''The Ectoplasmic Truthtellers of 'The Dead' '' and Maria Tymoczko, ''Symbolic Structures in *Ulysses* from Early Irish Literature'' in *James Joyce Quarterly*, reprinted by permission;

''Francis and Hanna Sheehy Skeffington,'' from *Joyce and Feminism*, reprinted by permission of Indiana University Press.

# Contents

# Abbreviations

Note:    We have adopted the James Joyce Quarterly's system of abbrevia-
         tions for references to Joyce's works or to the Ellmann biog-
         raphy.

CP                Joyce, James. Collected Poems. New York: Viking
                  Press. 1957.

CW                Joyce, James. The Critical Writings of James Joyce,
                  ed. Ellsworth Mason and Richard Ellmann. New
                  York: Viking Press, 1959.

D                 Joyce, James. "Dubliners": Text, Criticism and
                  Notes, ed. Robert Scholes and A. Walton Litz.
                  New York: Viking Press, 1969.

E                 Joyce, James. Exiles, New York: Viking Press, 1951.

FW                Joyce, James. Finnegans Wake, New York: Viking
                  Press, 1939 and London: Faber and Faber, 1939.

GJ                Joyce, James. Giacomo Joyce, ed. Richard Ellmann.
                  New York: Viking Press, 1968.

JJ                Ellmann, Richard. James Joyce, New York: Oxford
                  University Press, 1959.

JJII              Ellmann, Richard. James Joyce, rev. ed., New York:
                  Oxford University Press, 1982.

L I, II, II       Joyce, James. Letters of James Joyce, Vol. I, ed.
                  Stuart Gilbert. New York: Viking Press, 1966.
                  Vols. II and III, ed. Richard Ellmann. New York:
                  Viking Press, 1966.

P                 Joyce, James. "A Portrait of the Artist as a Young
                  Man": Text, Criticism and Notes, ed. Chester G.
                  Anderson. New York: Viking Press, 1968.

SH                    Joyce, James.  Stephen Hero, ed. John J. Slocum and
                      Herbert Cahoon.  New York:  New Directions, 1963.

SL                    Joyce, James.  Selected Letters of James Joyce, ed.
                      Richard Ellmann.  New York:  Viking Press, 1975.

U                     Joyce James.  Ulysses.  New York:  Random House, 1934
                          ed., reset and corrected 1961.

# Preface

This collection of essays, an outgrowth of a conference on James Joyce
and his contemporaries, focuses on Joyce's work from significant points
of view and places Joyce in the context of the Ireland of his time.
The first part, Joyce's canon, deals with central problems of interpretation in his fiction.   Janet Egleson Dunleavy, Joseph Bentley, and
Suzette Henke treat problems of narrative, Maria Tymoczko and Julienne
H. Empric, problems of characterization.
     Dunleavy, examining the problematic nature of the narrative voices
in "The Dead," identifies four different narrative voices and their
places in the story.   In a similar vein, Henke's identification of
ALP's narrative language in Finnegans Wake helps to delineate character
and theme.   Dealing with the central problem of narrative unity in
Ulysses, Bentley finds that Jean Piaget's theory of child development
offers a pattern by which disparate narrative elements can be understood.   Tymoczko, demolishing the view that the trio of characters in
Ulysses is European, demonstrates that figures from early Irish sagas
served as models for characterization in Ulysses, while Empric en-
larges the rather static view of feminine characterization in A Portrait of the Artist as a Young Man.
     The second part, "The Rhetoric of Joyce's World," explores Joyce's
belief that literature in any form tends to structure consciousness and
that popular literature, indeed all forms of popular culture, does so
more insidiously and on a grander scale than any other.   R. B. Kershner, Jr., develops this idea in his discussion of the strange conjunction of Maria Corelli and Stephen Dedalus in Ulysses.   The influence of
popular literature also is evident in Cheryl Herr's essay that describes the complex mixture of Roman Catholic doctrine and economics in
Jaun's sermon in Finnegans Wake (III, ii).   Jeanne A. Flood and Bonnie
Kime Scott analyze the rhetoric of nationalist politics and social reforms, showing how these are reflected in "The Dead" and in Stephen
Hero and Portrait.
     "Joyce's Connections to the Writers of His Time," part III, tells
something about the continuities of literary influences.   Dominic Manganiello demonstrates that Joyce's connection with Oscar Wilde is deeper than the shared theme of the betrayed artist; Rhoda B. Nathan reveals affinities between Joyce's and Shaw's dramatic interests and influences, and Michael Kenneally describes the way Sean O'Casey measured
himself against Joyce in the writing of his own Autobiographies.

Joyce's influence on the Irish writers of today is the subject to the fourth part. Modern Irish prose writers, as Joseph Browne's essay on Flann O'Brien suggests, are often ambivalent about their relationship to Joyce; however, the poets seem to find him a fairly straightforward and a rather benign presence. If Joyce truly told Yeats, "I have met with you too late," he has had a good deal to teach modern Irish poets. Perhaps, ironically, his most important function is to serve as an alternative to Yeats. Robert F. Garratt's essay illuminates this aspect of Joyce's influence; Lucy McDiarmid shows specifically how this "familiar ghost" has been an enabling presence for Seamus Heaney.

Richard Ellmann tells us that Joyce, fond of coincidences, was pleased to share his birthdate with James Stephens and his birth year with Eamon de Valera [JJI, 22]. The final group of essays are devoted to other 1982 Irish centenarians: Pádraic Ó Conaire, James Stephens and Eamon de Valera. Philip O'Leary describes Pádraic Ó Conaire's pioneering efforts to provide a modern urban voice for literature in the Irish language, while Brendan O'Grady compares the work of James Stephens with that of another contemporary, Seumas O'Kelly, author of The Weaver's Grave.

Eamon de Valera, one of Joyce's models for Shaun in Finnegans Wake, is the subject of the last essay: Francis M. Carroll's analysis of de Valera's part in the Irish Bond-Certificates Drive of 1919-1921.

Irish history and an awareness of the Irish past informed the work of Joyce and his generation. This past has continued to enlarge not only our understanding of Joyce, but also the director of modern Irish and, through Joyce, modern European literature.

# Part I

# Joyce's Canon:
# Style and Structure

# The Ectoplasmic Truthtellers of "The Dead"

*Janet Egleson Dunleavy*

As Hugh Kenner and John Kelleher have established, James Joyce's "The Dead" is not just a story about Gabriel Conroy's progression from self-absorption to self-awareness during an evening begun at the annual Christmas dance given by his aunts and concluded at the side of his sleeping wife in a room in the Gresham Hotel.(1)   It is also a ghost story, featuring a veritable Who's Who of Irish dead who walk unseen through the substructure, perceived only in the subconscious minds of the Misses Morkan's living guests, and manifest only to readers guided through allusion and analogue by such a Dante as Professor Kelleher. These spirits are perversely unwilling to reveal themselves that they may be given their due, yet they become malevolent when treated with disrespect.  Gabriel Conroy is their chief target.  Socially inept among both the living and the dead, he unwittingly exhibits symptoms of hoof-in-mouth disease in the company of Lily, the caretaker's daughter and Miss Ivors, his old schoolmate—with almost everyone, in fact, including his own good wife, Gretta.  The indignant spirits of the dead have the last word.

Professor Kelleher identifies the narrative level on which Joyce's story is a ghost tale.  His evidence is irrefutable and his conclusions are supported by (as we ought to know from Henry James) the long-established custom in England and Ireland of telling ghost stories at Christmas time.   Moreover, Professor Kelleher's explanation of how the ghost story is woven together with the other narrative levels fabricated by Joyce gives both depth and texture to "The Dead."  But in both explication and explanation Professor Kelleher concerns himself only with the better class of Irish ghost, the spirits of the Irish dead who so distinguished themselves in myth, legend, or history as to be celebrated by living compatriots in song, story, and statuary.  Yet also unseen but not unheard at the Misses Morkan's annual dance are a number of lesser-known ghostly guests.  About the evening's event, we are told that "everyone who knew them came to it."  They came, too, these unidentified spirits, and if we read carefully we see that they knew not only their hostesses, but their hostesses' nephew as well—better, in all probability, than the luminaries spotted by Professor Kelleher. Very much at home in the Morkan household, they are not unlike the living among whom they walk unseen but in whom they maintain a lively interest.

How, then, have these ghosts gone unnoticed for so long?  Very easily:  after all, they are ghosts; their stock-in-trade is to go unnoticed.  In addition, trends in literary criticism since "The Dead" was first published have also conspired to keep them (and therefore Joyce's readers) in the dark.  In the early years of the century, for example, it was the fashion to attribute the shrewd observations and pithy comments for which the ghosts should have received credit to the author himself, James Joyce.  A few years later, when the author was banished from the text to do his work offstage while paring his finger-nails, these same remarks were credited to that ubiquitous observer of fictional events, the omniscient narrator.  And then, just when their cover was nearly blown by investigators searching for point- of-view narrators (who work together, like the Lavender Hill Mob, rather than alone, like Willy Sutton), all narrators were declared redundant, sup-planted (appropriately in this age of automation) by a more efficient literary device, narrative mode.

As things have turned out, this latest shift in literary fashion has proved a lucky turn of events.  Had it not occurred when it did, bounty- seeking critics surely would have accused our ghosts of con-trolling the text through conspiratorial point-of-view narration.(2) However, the evidence necessary to support the conspiracy theory does not exist:  our ghosts do not work together; they are not the Lavender Hill Mob.  Rather, like the members of the chorus of T. S. Eliot's Mur-der in the Cathedral, they are a pick-up group of observers and curio-sity-seekers, minor characters who perform an important role within the narrative framework, ghostly guests whose gossip we are privileged to overhear.

To better understand how these ghosts function in the structure of "The Dead," let us go back to why for so long their voices were con-fused with those of others--first the author, then an omniscient nar-rator, then a narrative team.  In "The Dead," wherever the action is--downstairs, where the guests enter; upstairs, where the Misses Morkan's annual dance is in progress; in Gabriel's mind (or memory), crossing the O'Connell Street Bridge; in a room at the Gresham Hotel -- there a voice intermittently joins the narrative to report on what may be seen, heard, thought, remembered.  These narrative accounts link with dialo-gue, descriptive connectives, and dramatic episodes to provide the lin-ear structure of the story.  The linear structure carries the action through time, from after 10:00 p.m., when Gabriel and Gretta arrive at the "dark, gaunt house on Usher's Island," until the early morning hour when, the Christmas party over, Gabriel and his wife are alone together in the Gresham Hotel.  With its perceivable beginning, middle, and end, the story offered within the linear structure affirms the finiteness of the visible world, the contrarieties of human life.  At the same time, the linear structure serves as the skeleton of the story, the unique-ness of which depends upon other narrative levels and fictional devices --much as the uniqueness of a human being is perceived not just from hip bone connected to the thigh bone but from a web of other physiolog-ical and social characteristics.

If this were all that was true of the narrative accounts of "The Dead," they might yet serve readers who prefer to get their story from an author persona, omniscient narrator, or team of narrators--their raison d'etre within the telling of the story could be regarded as con-ventional, and the manner in which they function with other narrative elements would be both apparent and easily described.  That something more is happening, however, in these narrative accounts of "The Dead" --something that distinguishes the narrative mode--is strongly sug-gested by the fact that they are not presented in camera-eye or report-orial style, or through one single distinctive narrative voice, or through a well-drilled team of narrative voices.  What we seem to have instead is a story filtered in part through at least four different and distinctive personalities who cannot be ranked as multiple point-of-view narrators, because they are not given full responsibility for telling the tale, but who can be described as characters, so fully are they developed on at least one narrative level and so specific are their roles.

We first meet these four characters within the first few pages of "The Dead." Voice I (how else shall we distinguish them?) opens the story with "Lily, the caretaker's daughter, was literally run off her feet." Voice II introduces the passage that begins "It was always a great affair, the Misses Morkan's annual dance." Voice III reveals a poetic perspective as it heralds Gabriel's arrival: "A light fringe of snow lay like a cape on the shoulders of his overcoat and like toecaps on the toes of his goloshes; and, as the buttons of his overcoat slipped with a squeaking noise through the snow-stiffened frieze, a cold fragrant air from out-of-doors escaped from crevices and folds." Voice IV provides more pedestrian details: "He was a stout, tallish young man. The high colour of his cheeks pushed upwards even to his forehead where it scattered itself in a few formless patches of pale red; and on his hairless face there scintillated restlessly the pol-ished lenses and the bright gilt rims of the glasses which screened his delicate and restless eyes."

The distinguishing feature of each of these four voices, dominant rhythm, is insistently evident when these lines are read aloud; it reg-isters subtly even when they are read silently (as the author, of course, intended and expected). "Lily, the caretaker's daughter" has a three-syllabled dactyllic pattern that is sustained whenever this voice is heard. "It was always a great affair, the Misses Morkan's annual dance" is predominantly iambic. "A light fringe of snow lay like a cape on the shoulders of his overcoat and like toecaps on the toes of his goloshes" has the slow, stately dignity of the spondaic. "He was a stout, tallish young man" is as prosy in rhythm as its message is pro-saic. Moreover, Voice I and Voice II are conversational in both tone and language; Voice III employs metaphor, simile, poetic diction, pitch, stress, consonance, assonance, and alliteration; and Voice IV offers a catalogue of visual detail. These and other characteristics of our four ghosts (who are never seen but are often heard throughout the evening) remain consistent throughout the story.

When Voice I enters the narrative, it is a little after ten o'clock, just about the time when the Misses Morkan are growing anxious because neither Freddy nor the Conroys have yet arrived. Voice II fol-lows with an account from a different perspective of exactly the same time span. The simultaneity of these two passages is emphasized by the identical observations, from downstairs and upstairs, with which they end. The Conroys arrive, and the two aunts escort Gabriel's wife to the ladies dressing room, while the reader and at least three of the ghosts remain downstairs in the cloakroom with Gabriel and Lily. Voice I falls silent, possibly discomfited by Lily's aberrant behavior (the Misses Morkan, if they ever knew, certainly would not tolerate such back talk). Voice III probes the mood and mind of Gabriel. Voice IV glosses over the embarrassing episode between Gabriel and Lily by con-centrating on other visual details. Each voice reacts differently to what has happened. Meanwhile, leaning over to hide his flushed face, Gabriel flicks at his shoes. Then, accompanied by the ghosts (of whom he is unaware), he joins the other guests upstairs. There he suppres-ses his somber mood, regains his poise, and greets his aunts affably. Voice IV, condescending and slightly sardonic, but also articulate and observant, remarks Gabriel's behavior. Thereafter, Voice IV and Voice III continue to hover around Gabriel, on whom the narrative focuses, while Voice II comes and goes, interjecting an occasional word about others, until the guests sit down to dinner. During dinner, Voice II becomes almost garrulous, rambling on in the clichés we have come to expect from this one of the four: carving is "hot work"; Aunt Kate and Aunt Julia toddle around the table "on each other's heels"; the dessert is praised "from all quarters"; and so forth. As the last glasses are filled and the small talk ceases, Voice III underscores Gabriel's antithetical mood and thoughts. Gabriel delivers his speech without revealing his inner gloom to the others, and following a row of asterisks indicating the lapse of time between the end of dinner and the end of the party, Voices II, III, and IV are next heard between lines of dialogue, speeding the guests on their way. In the carriage en route to the Gresham, the Conroys are accompanied by Voice III and Voice IV; these two even go up with the Conroys to their room. There, "the time had come," observes Voice III, for Gabriel "to set out on his journey westward."

The word "west," with its double meaning in Irish usage of "world of the dead," establishes the true course of this journey. Outside the snow continues to fall, and Gabriel imagines it falling, too--not only there in Dublin, but also on the Bog of Allen and the "dark mutinous Shannon waves." Suspended between not only the worlds of the waking and the sleeping, so like the worlds of the living and the dead, but also the world perceived and the world imagined--closer now than at any other time to all the spirits, unknown and famous, kindly and malevolent, that have been with him throughout the story--Gabriel senses himself journeying through the void that has separated him not only from others but also from himself. On this metaphoric journey will he achieve at last the integration of self he has sought without success in his self-constructed, self-important image? Is Gabriel capable of such drastic change? Ghosts and mirrors are the truthtellers; ghosts and mirrors always reflect the true self in all good ghost stories.

The text suggests (but does not state) that in "The Dead" significant evidence concerning Gabriel Conroy's true nature, its potential and its limitations, may be compiled from both ghosts and mirrors. The reader is left, not with answers, but with questions: Is the true Gabriel Conroy inalterably that twice-mirrored man caught once by the chevalglass and once before, in Lily's--the caretaker's daughter's-- eyes? Is this Joyce's final irony (consistent with that other much-discussed level of "The Dead," the naturalistic), that what Gabriel will awake to is the same self-deception that has characterized him in the past? Out of all the lovely poetry of the last lines of Joyce's story does there come only a new prose for that "pitiable fatuous fellow" described so accurately, from different perspectives, by ectoplasmic characters perceived in the printed word but imaged only in the mirror of the reader's mind?

Close analysis of specific passages in which these four unidentified ghosts may be perceived affirms their presence, distinguishes them as characters, and contributes to an understanding of their different roles. Voice I trips, skips, and scampers from word to word, as Lily herself scampers along the bare hallway, unimpeded for the most part by voiced consonant stops or by intricately articulated consonant clusters. Nearly three-quarters of the vowels in the passage ending "calling down to Lily to ask her who had come" are either neutral or nearly so (cf. the predominance of the vowel sounds of "pat," "pet," "pit," "pot," "put"). In stressed syllables vowels often are framed by sibilants, fricatives, or nasals. When consonant stops do occur, they are found with but few exceptions (a) in unstressed words (e.g., "to," "had"); (b) in consonant combinations where they are wholly or partly elided in normal speech (e.g., "ground," "behind"); (c) at the end of syllables that precede syllables beginning with a vowel (e.g., "let in"); or (d) at the end of a statement, in which case syntax, not sound, dictates the full stop. Throughout the paragraph as a whole, however, syntax dictates few stops: the entire passage consists of 129 words arranged in five sentences consisting of coordinate clauses or propositional phrases requiring but five commas in all and no other internal punctuation. Social position and educational background are indicated by diction: all those who arrive at the hall door are described, collectively, as "guests"; upstairs, respectfully referred to, but with a familiarity that permits omission of their surname, are "Miss Kate" and "Miss Julia." Metaphoric language is homely: Lily scampers; the hall-door bell is wheezy. "Literally" is used colloquially, as an intensive.

Voice II moves more sedately than Voice I, walking like the Misses Morkan rather than scampering like Lily. Continuants rather than consonant stops still frame most vowels, providing effortless transitions from word to word, but an increased alternation of front and back vowels and open and closed vowels requires more movement of speech articulators, and those consonant stops that do occur are found in stressed syllables in midstatement (e.g., "splendid style") as well as in unstressed syllables. Moreover, although but four sentences are formed by the first 128 words of the passage beginning "It was always a great affair, the Misses Morkan's annual dance," appositional phrases, comma clauses, and even a semicolon dictate more pauses than are found in the passage narrated by Voice I. Social position and educational background also are different: guests and family members are referred to familiarly by first names (e.g., "Julia," "Kate," "Mary Jane," "Pat," "Gabriel," "Freddy"); "everyone" is used to mean not everyone in fact but everyone of the Misses Morkan's social circle; the "modest" life of the Misses Morkan, which provides them with diamond-bone siroins, three-shilling tea, and the best bottled stout, is clearly modest only by their standards (to Lily it must seem very grand indeed). Diction used by Voice II to refer to Freddy Malins's drinking problem is later repeated in dialogue ascribed to one of the sisters, strengthening the suggestion that Voice II emanates from a spirit who once enjoyed, in the world of the living, a similar background, education, and social standing. An impression of banality, derived from the content of the narrative account, is reinforced by the use of such cliches as "fallen flat" and "main prop."

Voice III, by contrast, moves haltingly, with measured cadence, not only because (in the passages beginning "He stood on the mat" and "He continued scraping his feet vigorously") 97 words form two sentences broken by six commas and a semicolon, but also because these sentences contain words and word clusters in which several syllables in succession are stressed (e.g., "light fringe of snow," "snow-stiffened frieze," "cold fragrant air"). Moreover, a significant increase indicated in these phrases in rounded, open vowels and related diphthongs framed by consonant stops requires even greater movements of speech articulators, while highly alliterative syllable sequences also slow the pace at which these passages may be read. Social position is similar to that of Voice II, Lily is "the girl," the Misses Morkan are "Aunt Kate" and "Aunt Julia," family friends are referred to by first name. Yet diction is much less conversational, much more formal, than that of Voice I or Voice II, figurative language is more imaginative, more poetic, and a rhythmic use of repetition, of whole words as well as specific sounds, enhances the poetic quality. Social position seems to match that of Gabriel Conroy, who regards himself as superior in education and intellect to most other guests at the dance. Indeed, Voice III focuses almost exclusively on Gabriel, especially on what he must be thinking and feeling, as if he were the only one present with whom Voice III can find rapport, while the other ghostly voices concern themselves also with the attitudes and actions of other characters.

Voice IV shares many characteristics of Voice III:  syntax, clusters of stressed syllables, formality of diction, impression of social class and superior education.  It lacks, however, the poetic quality of Voice III:  it is neither as alliterative nor as rhythmic.  In tone it is less somber, more sardonic.  The adjectives Voice IV employs suggest that this spirit is tuned to the visible and social rather than to the audible and individual world.  Despite its obvious acquaintance with all the people in the story and its familiarity with all the events, persons, and places to which they refer, Voice IV assumes a posture that is aloof, uninvolved.  Like Voice II and Voice III, however, it refers to the Misses Morkan as "Aunt Kate" and "Aunt Julia" and calls Gabriel Conroy and Freddy Malins by their first names.  Curiously (possibly a reason for identifying Voice IV as male) it refers to Gabriel's wife not as Gretta but as "Mrs. Conroy."

Who are these disembodied speakers of "The Dead," with their expressive distinctions and individualized perceptions?  In mood and manner they seem (again, like the chorus of T. S. Eliot's Murder in the Cathedral) people of the city, other Lilys and Julias and Kates and Gabriels who once lived out their lives in the same houses and streets, ectoplasmic voices of a Dublin spirit underworld who comment from different perspectives on the events of the story, not only through what they say but also through the background music provided by the varying rhythms of their narrative accounts.  Never malevolent, like those other famous ghosts identified by Professor Kelleher, they are agreeable if invisible guests at the Misses Morkan's annual dance.  Voice I is sympathetic with hard-working Lily at the start of the story, but it withdraws (in silent disapproval?) when she takes the liberty of replying bitterly to Gabriel's well-meaning sally.  Voice IV seems to relish his position as uninvolved observer, but when Gabriel reacts with embarrassment to Lily's retort, he tactfully draws attention away from the crimson Gabriel, who has taken momentary refuge in attending to the luster of his shoes.  Such actions and attitudes characterize Voices I, II, III, and IV and they provide each with a unique role in the story.  Like the named and more clearly defined characters, all of the voices come and go in time and place; they shift from overview to close-up and back again; they respond to (rather than report) what is going on in each episode.  They are the dead who live the life of the living in a story in which the living live the lives of the dead.

Those of us who often read ghost stories know how to prove the existence of a ghost:  the trick is to trap it into revealing itself in a mirror.  To catch a ghost that exists only in an idea evoked by words on a printed page is a more difficult problem, but an analogous method may serve.  In the following passages transcribed from Joyce's "The Dead," conventional spelling and punctuation have been changed to reflect what might be "heard" by an implied reader engaged in a silent reading of the text.  The implied reader postulated may be either one whose own spoken language contains dialectic variables similar to those that would have been "heard" by Joyce himself, as he wrote the text, or one sufficiently familiar with such dialectic variables as to expect and therefore "hear" them, given clues imbedded in the text.  It is understood that individual phrasing may differ somewhat among readers who match this description (cf. Gertrude Stein's experiments with verbal portraits in "Ada" and "Picasso" and her emphasis on dialogue as a method of characterization in "In Circles"). But stress patterns and rhythms imbedded in the dialect should not be affected significantly. It is further understood that readers with no familiarity with the variables implied in the text may not have the same aural experience as an implied reader, and consequently, may not perceive, unaided, the same patterns of sound and rhythm. While it is interesting to speculate on the nature of the variables these readers might introduce and how such variables might result in differences in interpretation, this is a subject unrelated to the question of the ghostly presences introduced by Joyce, and therefore such speculation has not been attempted here.

Changes in conventional spelling and punctuation used in the following transcriptions to indicate aural factors (e.g., rhythm, rhyme, alliteration, and intonation pattern) that impinge on the consciousness of an implied reader are in part logical, in part arbitrary. Logically, consonants not ordinarily sounded (e.g., the "d" of "behind" in the phrase"'behind the") are dropped, and eclipsed syllables (e.g., the second and third syllables of "literally") are rewritten to represent the pronunciation the implied reader would expect to hear. Spelling is revised to offer a rough approximation of phonation (e.g., "kum" for "come"), but fine distinctions of limited significance within the parameters essential to this study (e.g., the difference between the "a" of "caretaker" and the "a" of "ladies" are not attempted. Nor have IPA (International Phonetic Alphabet) symbols been employed to render the text phonetically--partly because interpretation of the data presented here is not dependent upon fine discriminations, but also because an IPA transcription would limit access to the data base to those who read IPA with ease. Arbitrarily, commas, colons, and semicolons are used to represent pauses, which are regarded as unuttered syllables (as spaces between words are included in a printer's character count).

The following key to the transcribed passages provides more specific information about both methodology and symbol system:

Syllable: letter or letters between space marks.
Phrasing: syllable(s) between any two punctuation marks.
Statement (affirmative, negative, interrogative): syllable(s) between any two end-punctuation marks.
Pause, mid-sentence: comma = one unuttered syllable; colon/semicolon = two unuttered syllables. (Note: Unuttered syllables are here regarded as unstressed. Arguments for counting some unuttered syllables as stressed might be made but would not substantially change conclusions.)
Pause, end of statement: period/question mark/exclamation mark = two unuttered syllables.
Stressed and unstressed syllables: superscript and text. (Note: Finer distinctions between stressed and unstressed syllables, showing comparative degrees of stress, can be indicated through use of a musical staff--or, a little less subtly, through use of superscript, base line, and subscript--rather than merely by means of these two alternatives; such finer distinctions improve the perception of intonation pattern, to be sure, but do not alter significantly either the argument or the conclusions presented here.)
Intonation pattern: the result of a combination of factors--syntax and meaning, juxtaposition of stressed and unstressed syllables, phrasing, type of end punctuation.
Vowels: "long" vowels are indicated by uppercase letters; "ah," "aw," "ow," by these phonetic spellings; "short" vowels by lowercase letters; neuter vowels (schwa) by an apostrophe.
Text: D 175-78.

## Voice 1

"Lily, the caretaker's daughter . . . to ask her who had come."

li $_{lE}$ th' $^{kAr}$ tAk 'rz $^{daw}$ t'r, w'z $^{li}$ tr' lE $^{run}$ nof

'r $^{fEt}$. hahrd $_{dlE}$ h'd shE brawt $^{wun}$ jen t'l m'n

'n t' th' li $_{t'l}$ $^{pan}$ tri bu $^{hIn}$ dth' o f's 'n th' $^{grown}$

flawr $_{'n}$ helpt $_{'m}$ $^{of}$ w' thiz $^{O}$ v'r kOt, than th'

hwEz $_{E}$ hawl dawr bel klangd $_{a}$ $^{gen}$, 'n shE had tu

skam $_{p'r u}$ $_{long}$ $_{th'}$ bAr hawl wA $_{t'}$ let $_{'n u}$ nuth $_{r}$ gest.

it w'z $^{wel}$ f'r $^{hur}$ shE h'd $^{not}$ tu ' ten t' th' $^{lA}$ $_{dEz}$

awl $_{sO}$; but m's $^{kAt}$ 'n m's $^{jUl}$ yud $^{thawt}$ 'v that

'n had kun $^{v'r}$ t'd th' $^{bath}$ $_{rUm}$ up stArz in tu u $^{lA}$ $_{dEz}$

dres $_{s'ng}$ $_{rUm}$. m's $^{kAt}$ 'n m's $^{jUl}$ yu w'r $^{thAr}$,

gos'p $_{ing}$ 'n laf $_{ing}$ 'n fus $_{ing}$; $^{waw}$ king $^{af}$ t'r Etch

u th'r t' th' $^{hed}$ 'v th' $^{st^rz}$; pEr $_{'ng}$ down $_{,}$ $^{O}$ v'r

th' $^{ban}$ n's t'rz, 'n $^{kawl}$ $_{'ng}$ $^{down}$ tU $^{li}$ $_{lE}$ tu as $_{k'r}$ $^{hU}$ h'd $^{kum}$.

## Voice 2

"It was always a great affair . . . on the ground floor."

't w'z $^{awl}$ w'z u $^{gran}$ $_{d'}$ $^{fAr}$ th' $^{mis}$ 's $^{mawr}$ k'nz an

yU 'l $^{dans}$. ev $_{ri}$ bah $_{di}$ hU $^{nyU}$ them $^{kAm}$ tU 't:

mem $_{b'rz}$ 'v th' $^{fam}$ $_{lE}$, Old frenz 'v th' $^{fam}$ lE, th'

mem $_{b'rz}$ 'v $^{jyUl}$ yiz kwI 'r, $^{e}$ nE 'v $^{kAts}$ pyU p'lz that w'r

grOn up $_{E}$ $^{nuf}$, and $^{E}$ vin sum $_{'v}$ $^{mA}$ $_{rE}$ jAnz pyU p'lz

tU. ne $_{v'r}$ wuns h'd it $^{fawl}$ in $^{flat}$. f'r $^{yErz}$ 'n $^{yErz}$ it

'd gon of 'n splen $_{d'd}$ $^{stIl}$, 'z long 'z en i w'n $^{kud}$

ri $^{mem}$ b'r; $^{e}$ v'r sins $^{kAt}$ en $^{jyUl}$ yu: af t'r th' $^{deth}$ 'v

thAr $^{bruth}$ er $^{pat:}$ h'd $^{left}$ th' hows in $^{stO}$ $_{nE}$ $^{bat}$ t'r

an $^{tA}$ kin $^{mA}$ $_{rE}$ $^{jAn}$, thAr $^{On}$ li $^{nEs}$, t' $^{liv}$ wi them

in th' $^{dahrk gawnt hows}$ $_{in}$ $^{ush}$ erz $^{I}$ l'n, th' $^{u}$ p'r

pahrt $_{'v}$ $^{hwitch}$ thA h'd $^{ren}$ t'd fr'm $^{mis}$ t'r $^{ful}$ 'm, th' kOrn fak <sub>t'r 'n th'</sub> grown flOr.

## Voice 3

"A light fringe of snow . . . crevices and folds."

u lIt frinj '<sub>v</sub> snO lA <sub>lIk</sub> ' kAp '<sub>n</sub>

th' <sup>shOl</sup> d'rz 'v iz <sup>O</sup> v'r kOt en lIk <sup>tO</sup> kaps on th'

tOz '<sub>v</sub> iz gu <sup>losh</sup> iz; <sup>and,</sup> az th' <sup>but</sup> tinz 'v iz <sup>O</sup> v'r kOt

slipt <sub>wi th'</sub> <sup>skwE</sup> king <sup>noyz</sup> thrU th' <sup>snO</sup>

stif <sub>ind</sub> <sup>frEz,</sup> <sub>u</sub> kOld frA <sub>grint</sub> <sup>Ar</sup> frum <sup>ow</sup> t'v <sup>dOrz,</sup> is

kApt <sub>frum</sub> kre vis is <sub>an</sub> fOldz

## Voice 4

"He was a stout, tallish young man . . . left by his hat."

hE w'z u <sup>stowt tawl</sup> <sub>ish</sub> yung man. th' <sup>hI ku</sup> l'r

'v iz <sup>tchEks pusht up</sup> w'rdz, <sup>E</sup> vin tu iz <sup>fahr</sup> hed,

wAr it <sup>skat</sup> 'rd it self in u <sup>fyU fawrm</sup> lis <sup>pat</sup> chiz 'v

pAl red; <sub>en on iz</sub> <sup>hAr</sup> lis <sup>fAs,</sup> thAr <sup>sin</sup> t'l lA tid <sup>res</sup>

lis lE th' <sup>po</sup> lisht <sup>lenz</sup> iz en th' <sup>brIt gilt rimz</sup> '<sub>v</sub>

th' <sup>glas</sup> iz witch <sup>skrEnd</sup> iz <sup>del</sup> i kut 'n <sup>res</sup> lis

Iz. <sub>hiz</sub> <sup>glo</sup> <sub>sE</sub> blak hAr <sub>w'z</sub> <sup>pahrt</sup> tid 'n th' <sup>mid</sup> dul an

brusht <sub>in u</sub> <sup>long k'rv</sup> be <sup>hIn</sup> <sub>diz</sub> <sup>Erz</sup>, wAr 't <sup>k'rld</sup>

slIt <sub>li bi</sub> <sup>nEth</sup> <sub>th'</sub> <sup>grUv left</sup> <sub>bI iz</sub> <sup>hat.</sup>

Preliminary investigation of this subject was reported at the 1975 James Joyce Symposium in Paris in a short essay entitled "The Ectoplasmic Voices of 'The Dead': Some Suggestions for Further Study of Narrative Structure." Revised conclusions based on computer analysis of relevant data were presented at "James Joyce and His Contemporaries: A Centenary Tribute" under the title "More Ghosts in 'The Dead.'" I am indebted to Hofstra University students John Walsh, John Leone, Janet Van Albert, and Karen Perry who, under the supervision of Professor Miriam Tulin, performed the parts of Voices I, II, III, and IV described below to provide "living footnotes" to my text. The essay was subsequently published in the James Joyce Quarterly 21, 4: Summer, 1984, 307-19.

NOTES

1.    See Hugh Kenner, <u>Dublin's Joyce</u> (Boston:    Beacon Press,
1962), 62-68; John Kelleher, <u>Irish History and Mythology</u> in James
Joyce's "The Dead" (Chicago:    American Committee for Irish Studies,
1971), reprinted from <u>The Review of Politics</u> 27, no. 3 (July 1965):
414-33.    These and subsequent studies of tone, levels of meaning, and
structure in "The Dead" follow an earlier analysis of agons by David
Daiches; see <u>The Novel and the Modern World</u> (Chicago:    University of
Chicago Press, 1939), 91-100.    As Robert Scholes and A. Walton Litz
have pointed out in their "Editors' Introduction to Criticism Section,"
while general agreement concerning the unity of <u>Dubliners</u> has been conceded and the structural unity of this last story has been linked to
that of the collection as a whole, the conclusion of "The Dead" has
generated a wide range of critical interpretations <u>DCE</u> 303.

2.    Indeed, this was one of the conclusions tested in my essay
presented at the 1975 James Joyce Symposium.    Further analysis, as
noted, led to its rejection.

## 2

# The Mediation of the Woman and the Interpretation of the Artist in Joyce's *Portrait*

### Julienne H. Empric

In offering interpretations of Joyce's A Portrait of the Artist as a Young Man, critical opinion suggests that, except for the image of the birdgirl who is tied to Stephen's redemption in the fourth part, other portrayals of women characters are rather negative. They are associated with the guilt that forms the net--one might say the "snood"--of imprisonment for Stephen, the would-be flier. When viewed in greater detail, however, the figure of the woman in successive character formulations serves to mediate Stephen's experiences in a way similar to the Virgin Mary's mediation to Christ in the Roman Catholic tradition, or to Beatrice's in Dante's Divine Comedy. And ultimately, in Portrait the woman comes to symbolize not only Ireland and the Roman Catholic Church, but also the magnetic force of that sensual creativity an artist must both court and reject in order to accomplish his purpose.

Since Stephen's father, the priests, and the boys he encounters play more important roles throughout the book, they are presented more fully and more realistically than the female characters. The women share in the same shadowy, ambiguous role that Stephen later comes to associate with the primal, irrational, compelling, and mysterious forces. The movement in Portrait away from the detailed autobiographical third-person characterization of Stephen Hero is particularly apparent in the increasingly shadowy presentation of the women: Stephen's mother and Emma Clery (here distilled to "E-- C--" and the personal feminine pronoun in most of the book), and in the complete elimination of Stephen's sister Isabelle, her dramatic illness and death. On the other hand, increased attention is accorded to the Blessed Virgin (both directly and indirectly through Stephen's interaction with Eileen, his Protestant childhood playmate), to the Irish peasant women, and to street ladies, showing that Joyce chose to amplify the more representative and symbolic value of the women figuring in Stephen's developing artistic consciousness.

A full study of the women throughout the novel would require a lengthy essay; however, the first part of Portrait affords rich enough examples of the range and purpose of the women characters as they affect Stephen. In the first two or three pages, which have been cause for so much critical attention, Joyce plots his architectural design for the symbol of woman throughout the book.

Stephen's mother, Mary Dedalus, and Dante, his aunt and tutor (note the immediate relation of the names "Mary" and "Dante" to the forms of mediatrix just mentioned), are the initial mediators between

Stephen and his "worlds": they catalyze the development of conscience. His mother introduces the internal, personal, sensual, and affective world. She has a "nicer smell" than his father, plays for him to dance, is associated with freely rendered and as yet unexamined affection ("the kiss"), is tearful and protective at his departure for boarding school, and is his confidante for illness and homesickness. It is wholly appropriate to this characterization and its consistency that in one of her last appearances in the novel "he allowed his mother to scrub his neck and root into the folds of his ears and into the interstices at the wings of his nose" [175].

Dante has her sensual aspects as well, but she employs these primarily to initiate Stephen into the external world of politics, civil and ecclesiastical, in the maroon and green velvet-backed brushes and later in her maroon and green mourning costume in Stephen's hallucination of the burial of Parnell [27]. It is hardly accidental that the sketch of the world and the clouds in Stephen's geography book should be colored maroon and green [15].

Both Dante and Mary Dedalus precipitate the development of conscience and the awareness of the "other" that Stephen is to explore through the rest of the work. The stage of toilet-training (the feel of the oilcloth that "when you wet the bed first . . . is warm then . . . gets cold" [7]), more than a documentation of tactile sensations to recur and pattern the rest of the book, presents a foretaste of other social regulations and repressions through which Stephen will be constrained. It is his mother who puts the oilsheet on, as it is his mother and Dante who make him "apologize" and threaten him with fantastic punishment should he refuse:

> The Vances lived in number seven. They had a different father and mother. They were Eileen's father and mother. When they were grown up he was going to marry Eileen. He hid under the table. His mother said:
> --O, Stephen will apologize.
> Dante said:
> --O, if not, the eagles will come and pull out his eyes. [8]

In the "Epiphanies" Joyce had ascribed these chastizing words to Mr. Vance, Eileen's father;(1) therefore, it is a clearly defined artistic choice that in Portrait he assigns them to Mary Dedalus and Dante Riordan. Because the prose in this passage attempts to imitate the disconnected narrative of a child's memory, there is a rather obscure connection of cause and effect between Stephen's proposed marriage to Eileen and his hiding under the table and need for apology. Later in the narrative, this link--Eileen--marriage-guilt-blindness, even castration--is, in retrospect, strengthened.(2) But even here, Stephen's early association of Eileen with feelings of guilt and difference (she is female and she is Protestant) emerges with clarity. Again, the awakening of the religio-social conscience is a task appropriated by (and accepted as appropriate to) the women, and one aspect of their success in this task is Stephen's growing sense of prohibition about the peer-aged "other."

Beyond mediating these initiations, the women in the first part of Portrait establish their range of control: they are linked irrefutably with the status quo, with Ireland and the Roman Catholic religion. The fecund Clane peasant women standing at half doors of cottages with children in their arms [18-20] recollect for Stephen the comfort of mother and home, the security of an unquestioning acceptance of life and order. Dante represents "a clever woman, a well-read woman" [11],

but she too is one whose commitment to the hierarchical authority of
the Church has to tally colored her ability to think freely in the
political structure of another age.  For all her education she is, like
all the other women in the novel, absolute in her acceptance of the old
way:  "God and religion before everything!  Dante cried.  God and religion before the world!" [39].  What Mr. Dedalus had called the "spoiled
nun" in her is really a vestigial aspect of the Clane peasantry:  the
blind spot of an unquestioning acceptance of authority and tradition.
These first important women, then, provide appropriate cultural and
ethical regulation of Stephen's exposure and experience.  They represent Catholic Ireland as she was—compelling both as mythic birthing
ground and as prospective redemptress, the devouring womb.  The shaping
of Stephen's consciousness through the early narrative leaves little
question that adult women reinforce a social pattern that will result
in Stephen's subjugation or rejection.  Their mediation is toward order
rather than risk, stability and protection rather than innovation,
replication and safety rather than individuation and transcendence.
This repressive attitude is something the child Stephen tolerates much
more passively than the adolescent of the later chapters, or than the
spitting and embittered misogynist of _Stephen Hero_.

Ironically, because unknown to Stephen and veiled even from the
reader at this point, these restrictive tendencies the women embody are
nonetheless instrumental in kindling the soul of the artist:  restric-
tion creates the artistic temperament, as the mysteries of the litany
of the Blessed Virgin initiate Stephen's primary involvement with metaphor and symbol.  While Mary Dedalus and Dante, mother and tutor, represent the legitimate "other" to which Stephen is born and bred,
Eileen, the little Protestant girl Stephen thinks he will marry, is
beyond the limits of legitimate acceptability. After he is directed to
apologize, Stephen speculates on Dante's attitude toward Eileen:

> she did not like him to play with Eileen because Eileen
> was a protestant and when she [Dante] was young she knew
> children that used to play with protestants and the
> protestants used to make fun of the litany of the
> Blessed Virgin. _Tower of Ivory_, they used to say, _House_
> _of Gold!_  How could a woman be a tower of ivory or a
> house of gold? [35]

Later, during what might be called his first "escape" from home, his
"mental" retreat from the political problems around the Christmas dinner table, Stephen works out his own answers to this conundrum, and he
does so through a process of personal imaginative synthesis one might
call a protoartistic act.  This passage also serves as a prototypic
epiphany:

> Eileen had long thin cool white hands too because she
> was a girl.  They were like ivory; only soft.  That was
> the meaning of _Tower of Ivory_ but protestants could not
> understand it and made fun of it.  One day . . . she had
> put her hand into his pocket where his hand was and he
> had felt how cool and thin and soft her hand was.  She
> had said that pockets were funny things to have:  and
> then all of a sudden she had broken away and had run
> laughing down the sloping curve of the path.  Her fair
> hair had streamed out behind her like gold in the sun.
> _Tower of Ivory_. _House of Gold_. By thinking of things
> you could understand them. [42–43]

While Stephen's mother and Dante precipitate the awakening of Stephen's consciousness and conscience, Eileen and the Virgin Mary present Stephen with the raw materials for his first epiphanic recognition: direct sensual experience (Eileen), and indirect symbolic experience (the Blessed Virgin), each puzzling, but together leading to the need for mental integration.(3)  The sensations of Eileen's physical loveliness--the touch of the skin and structure of the insinuate hand, the subtle invasion of his pocket, the probably innocent but exciting discovery of the concept "pocket" (likely an adaptation of the recurrent marsupial image for woman in Stephen Hero), the comet-like suddenness of this experience and its recession--lead Stephen to cosmic but apparently satisfying conclusions about the validity of Church mysteries.

The intensity of the narration in attempting to remain true to the young boy's discovery heightens the warm humor of the passage:  that the symbolic "mystery" should be so simply unravelled; that Stephen should bask in such complete conviction; that such prepubescent sensual experience should pretend to clarify the highly rarified symbolization of Church doctrine; that it should be a Protestant girl (already forbidden fruit) named Eileen (a name ironically as well as appropriately meaning "the light") who should illuminate for Stephen's imagination what the Roman Catholic Church had set forth for acceptance, and what, to his thinking, no Protestant might come to understand!  Instead, the mystery of these epithets for the Virgin Mary engages his mind as the mystery of Eileen's loveliness had engaged his senses, so that he comes to appreciate the beauty of this spontaneous moment with Eileen, recollected in tranquillity and through the words of the litany, "ivory" and "gold," and he transfers his responses to these metaphoric vehicles (Eileen's hands and hair) to what he assumes must, then, be the positive and pleasant attributes of the metaphoric tenor, the Blessed Virgin.(4)  Here the symbolic dimensions of liturgical metaphor are validated only through the personal intuition of an artistic psyche.

Eileen, the Protestant girl-child, becomes the mediatrix to the Blessed Virgin, as E-- C-- and her sign of womanhood will later enable him to approach the Blessed Virgin, herself mediatrix to Christ, the mediator to God.  Seen from this perspective, Stephen seems to be no more than a Pip at the end of a line of go-betweens.  However, it is not so much position as activity that redeems him.  He comes to appreciate and be content with an understanding of the Virgin Mary through a sensually gratifying experience with Eileen.  More important, he is not satisfied to rest in the physical and tangible loveliness of the experience with Eileen; he is compelled to solve mysteries of metaphor if not religion, and to resolve the distance between the sensual and the spiritual.  He accomplishes the solution and resolution by an artistic synthesis.  Not only is Eileen mediatrix to the Mediatrix Mary, but the two representations of woman occasion Stephen's first artistic act, in which he takes on the role of mediator between matter and spirit.  At this point the women relinquish their mediating function to serve more clearly as muse.  Stephen unlocks the gates of heaven with a newly discovered earthly key, but his heaven, even this early in the novel, is an aesthetic one.  Stephen has encompassed neither the conundrum of the opposite sex nor the mystery of the Church, but his puzzlement has led to a vacuum in which the sacred and the mundane can interpenetrate. And it is owing to this achieved synthetic perspective that, from this early moment, we can mark the development of his personal hermeneutics.

Stephen's position in the society of Catholic Ireland, so firmly established by the adult women, enables him to trust his own interpretation.  This membership has, from the start, afforded him an identification with the elect; he comes to expect that his explanations are

characterized by a privileged validity.  Frank Kermode clarifies the
importance of such a perspective in a recent work on interpretation:

> To divine the true, the latent sense, you need to be of
> the elect, of the institution.  Outsiders must content
> themselves with the manifest, and pay a supreme penalty
> for doing so.  Only those who know the mysteries--what
> the stories really mean--can discover what the stories
> really mean . . . There is seeing and hearing, which are
> what naive listeners and readers do; and there is per-
> ceiving and understanding, which are in principle re-
> served to an elect.(5)

It is the women who initiate Stephen into knowing what the stories
really mean.  They legislate knowledge of "the stories" and they present new experiences which must be reconciled to or integrated with the
old "stories."  While later Stephen will come to employ his interpre-
tive talents to divorce himself from the structures to which he was
born, his security and self-esteem are nurtured amidst the maze-like
patterns of control in which he grows.  The women who spin about him
the webs of the society of Catholic Ireland mediate this security and
self-esteem.  Their power is countered by a call to the individual self
provided by Eileen (and later Mercedes, E-- C--, and the birdgirl).
Stephen's early satisfaction with what he perceives to be his valid
interpretation of Tower of Ivory and House of Gold will foster a growing and self-engendered confidence.
    The symbolic function women serve in Joyce's novel allows a com-
plex vision of Stephen's experience.  From the background established
by the archetypal Irish woman and mother figure, Stephen takes his primary form; but in the process of development occasioned by woman as
"others" he asserts himself and moves toward the freedom both permitted
and necessitated by his exile.

## NOTES

1.     Robert Scholes and Richard M. Kain, The Workshop of Deadalus:
James Joyce and the Raw Materials for "A Portrait of the Artist as a
Young Man" (Evanston:  Northwestern University Press, 1965), 11.

2.     The reason for Stephen's guilt is never made clear.  As
Marvin Magalaner notes, it is "possibly related to sex (. . . he was
going to marry Eileen) or to religion (Eileen is Protestant) or simply
to disobedience to constituted authority (his mother and his gover-
ness)"; see Marvin Magalaner and Richard M. Kain, Joyce:  The Man, the
Work, the Reputation (New York:  New York University Press, 1956), 112.

3.     See Dorothy Van Ghent, The English Novel:  Form and Function
(New York:  Rinehart and Company, 1953), 266-67.  Van Ghent not only
gives a definition for "epiphany" that many critics have found work-
able, she also makes a useful distinction between major and minor epiphanies, the former referring to important accretive syntheses at the
end of chapters of Portrait, the latter "marking all stages of
Stephen's understanding" [267].

4.     Hugh Kenner believes that "the instant of insight depends on
a re-shaping of association, a sudden conviction that the Mother of
God, and the symbols appropriate to her, belong with the cold, the
white, the unpleasant in a blindfold morality of obedience"; see Dub-

lin's Joyce (Bloomington:   Indiana University Press, 1956), 117.   I
agree instead with John B. Smith, among others, who sees images in Portrait as transcending static assignments to attain a "dynamic associa-
tive development"; he, too, reads the passage as affirmative in tone.
See John B. Smith, Imagery and the Mind of Stephen Dedalus:  A Comput-
er-Assisted Study of Joyce's "Portrait of the Artist as a Young Man"
(Lewisburg, PA.:  Bucknell University Press, 1980), 15, 64.

    5.   Frank Kermode, The Genesis of Secrecy:  On the Interpretation
of Narrative (Cambridge:  Harvard University Press, 1979), 3.

# 3

# Symbolic Structures in *Ulysses* from Early Irish Literature

## *Maria Tymoczko*

Symbolic structures in Ulysses—the phrase conjures up images of a wily battle-scarred veteran of Troy afoot in Dublin, a woman weaving and un-weaving a tapestry of thoughts, a son looking for (or perhaps not look-ing for) a father,(1) bronze-by-gold sirens, a surly nationalist of a cyclops, and all the rest of the determinations that go back to Joyce's old chapter headings for Ulysses and Stuart Gilbert's study. Gilbert's book was immensely useful in helping general readers and critics alike to understand Ulysses, but the view of Ulysses that Gilbert dissemi-nated and that Joyce fostered has narrowed critical investigation and interposed itself between readers and the text. The Homeric parallels popularized by Gilbert have served to restrict critical reception of Ulysses in no area more than that of its symbolic structures.

If we examine the commonly accepted symbolic values for Bloom, Stephen, and Molly, we see that they all come from European tradition as a whole. There is nothing particularly Irish about them. The es-tablished symbolic approach to Ulysses goes with the predilection of the critical establishment to see Joyce as a European writer rather than an Irish one. Accordingly, his cosmopolitan spirit is stressed, his disdain for the Irish Revival and Irish nationalism is celebrated, and his admiration for Ibsen is emphasized. We are told that Joyce's books "are of Irishmen and by an Irishman, but not for Irishmen."(2)

I do not wish to dispute Joyce's cosmopolitan spirit, his debt to Ibsen, or the established symbolic interpretations of Bloom, Stephen, or Molly. Instead I would like to suggest that they are incomplete. We must reconsider the notion that Joyce's books are not "for Irish-men," particularly in light of his advice to Arthur Power, given in 1921 while Joyce was finishing Ulysses: "You are an Irishman and you must write in your own tradition. Borrowed styles are no good. You must write what is in your blood and not what is in your brain." When Power objected "that he was tired of nationality and wanted to be in-ternational, like all the great writers," Joyce countered, "They were national first, and it was the intensity of their own nationalism which made them international in the end" [JJI 520]. European elements of Joyce's symbolism are correct as far as they go, but we will see that the European values for Leopold Bloom, Stephen Dedalus, and Molly Tweedy Bloom are harmonics. The dominant note of the symbolism behind their identities and their relationships is Irish and comes from the Irish tradition.

It has become a commonplace to observe that one can see in Joyce's writings the melding of nineteenth-century naturalism and the symbolist reaction to naturalism.  To generalize crudely, if we accept the prevailing critical view that the symbolism in Ulysses is European, particularly Greek, then the Irish elements in the book presumably must be naturalistic.  If Joyce's writings are to be set in the context of Irish tradition, the question of this balance of symbolism and naturalism in Ulysses must be reopened.  Why is the Irish Ulysses, Leopold Bloom, a Jew?  Why is his "son" a Greek named Stephen Dedalus?  Why is his wife Molly from Gibraltar?  In what sense are these three characters in James Joyce's tradition, of his "blood" rather than his "brain"?

The explanations of these apparent anomalies not covered by the Homeric parallels are usually made in terms of European symbol systems or an ingenuous naturalism.  It is said that Joyce's protagonist was modeled on specific Jews he had met in Dublin or elsewhere.(3)  Moreover, critics point out that the character evokes the legend of the Wandering Jew.  As a Jew, Bloom is a universal metropolitan hero "equally at home and ill at ease in any city of the world."(4)  Stephen Dedalus, on the other hand, is at once rational Greek, master artisan, Christian martyr, and emblem of Dublin.  His name is "the wedge by which symbolism enters" A Portrait of the Artist, and that symbolism carries over into Ulysses as well.(5)  Finally, Molly's youth in Gibraltar captures the ironic Irish contribution to the British army.  Her Mediterranean origin infuses passion and profusion, fertility and sensuality, into the clammy climate of Dublin.

Let us consider the naturalism in all of this.  Not one of these characters has a typical Irish name, not one is from the oldest native families of Ireland--families whose clan is signalled by "mac" or "o".  Why do the main characters of Ulysses, particularly Bloom as the Irish Everyman, not come from modern Irish stock with common Irish names?  Why is each alienated in some way from Irish culture?  Is this constellation of characters plausible in any naturalistic sense?(6)

Kenner notes, too, the incongruity in Bloom's coming from an immigrant family in a "country whose citizens characteristically emigrate."(7)  Joyce even signals the difficulty of accepting Leopold Bloom as an immigrant and a Jew in a naturalistic sense with Deasy's bigoted joke about why Ireland is the only country never to have persecuted the Jews: "Because she never let them in" [U 36].  We might pursue this by asking why Bloom's "Jewishness" causes relatively little comment within the framework of the book, and why Bloom knows relatively little about Jewish culture.  Indeed Bloom is so ignorant about "the faith of his fathers" that Jewishness becomes the decor rather than the substance of his world.

We see here some of the problems with the "naturalism" of Ulysses.  The fact that these questions are so seldom raised should remind us, however, of how strongly readers and critics of Joyce's work are influenced by the prevailing European symbolic interpretations of the identities of the main characters of Ulysses even when the symbolic values contravene naturalism.(8)

If we are to take Joyce seriously as an Irishman, we must consider that his primal symbol systems may be Irish.  In particular, we will want to examine native Irish literature for correlates to his work when naturalism breaks down, as it does in the case of the main characters in Ulysses.(9)  Taken one by one, Joyce's main characters in Ulysses are plausibly explained in terms of the shared symbolism of European literary tradition.  As a system, however, Joyce's three main characters have no parallel in European literature, but point to a more unified source than European literature can provide.  The interface of Stephen, Bloom, and Molly is Irish.  Joyce's constellation of

characters in Ulysses—a Greek, an ersatz-Jew, and a lady from Spain—
appears to be based on the mythic structures of Lebor Gabala Erenn,
"The Book of Ireland," generally known in English as The Book of Invasions.

The Book of Invasions contains the pseudo-history of Ireland, or
the traditional history of Ireland before 432 (which is the usual date
given for the coming of Patrick and the beginning of the written history of Ireland). Its prototype was probably composed in the seventh
century to fill in the gap for Ireland in such standard classical
histories as those by Origen and Eusebius. Though the story apparently
was originally restricted to the account of the history of the Milesians, supposed ancestors of the Goidelic stock in Ireland, it was
opened up at an early period to include bits of cosmogony and old myth.
Eventually it came to contain the "history" of Ireland since creation,
giving accounts of several conquests of Ireland and culminating in the
invasion of the sons of Mil.(10)

By the twelfth century The Book of Invasions and its associated
king list had become the matrix for the rest of Irish history and literature. It was the organizing referent for Irish tradition, and accordingly it stands in initial position in the great twelfth-century
manuscript, The Book of Leinster. By the seventeenth century the contents of The Book of Invasions were presupposed or distilled in most
native Irish historical materials from The Annals of the Four Masters
to Geoffrey Keating's History of Ireland. By 1861 Eugene O'Curry felt
obliged to spend little time explaining The Book of Invasions to his
Irish audience; he notes in his Lectures on the Manuscript Materials of
Ancient Irish History that "The Milesian history is pretty generally
known, and has been much canvassed by the writers of the last 150
years."(11)  In the nineteenth century the story of the Milesians was
promoted by both scholars and popularizers, from precursors of the
Irish Literary Revival such as Standish O'Grady to writers of school
history books. Elements of The Book of Invasions are still part of
popular history among the Irish and Irish-Americans alike.

There is ample evidence that James Joyce knew the main lines of
The Book of Invasions. Ulysses itself contains direct references to
the Milesians (including an allusion to the Milesian appreciation of
Hebrew) and to Balor [U 297, 328, 688]. In addition to the internal
evidence in Ulysses, numerous references to the framework of The Book
of Invasions occur in Joyce's critical writings, especially in his 1907
Trieste lecture, "Ireland, Island of Saints and Sages" [CW 153-74]. It
can be demonstrated that, along with popular and oral sources, Joyce
had several written sources for his material related to The Book of Invasions, including school histories such as those by P. W. Joyce and
William Francis Collier, as well as more scholarly sources such as
Henri D'Arbois de Jubainville's The Irish Mythological Cycle and Celtic
Mythology. (A discussion of Joyce's treatment of these and other written sources is beyond the scope of the present essay, however, and will
be treated in a future study).

The relevant features of The Book of Invasions for the symbolism
in Ulysses can be summarized as follows:

> There are six invasions of Ireland. The first two
> groups of invaders are wiped out and essentially leave
> no survivors. The third, fourth, and fifth groups—
> those of Nemed, the Fir Bolg, and the Tuatha De Danann,
> respectively—came from Scythian stock. The Nemedian
> invasion is eventually abandoned because of opposition
> and difficulties from the Fomorians, a chaotic and
> oppressive race of marauders. The Nemedian invasion is

succeeded by that of the Fir Bolg, who are in turn overcome by the Tuatha De Danann.  Though these three groups
are related genealogically, their characters and experiences differ widely.  The Fir Bolg are subjugated and
become laborers in Greece, while the Tuatha De Danann
become skilled in lore, crafts, and hidden knowledge.
The Tuatha De Danann become allies of the Athenians before departing for Ireland.

Meanwhile the Goidels, genealogical relations of their
predecessors in Ireland, settle in Egypt at the time of
the Pharaohs.  They become sympathizers of Moses and aid
the Israelites in their flight from Egypt.  Grateful for
their help, Moses offers the Goidels a place in the Promised Land should they care to accompany the Hebrews,
but the Goidels decline.  After some years the Goidels
are expelled from Egypt in revenge for aiding the Israelites.  They undertake various travels (including a second sojourn in Egypt during which their leader, Mil,
marries the Pharaoh's daughter).  Eventually they go to
Spain, where they make conquests, settle down, and take
wives.  While in Spain the Goidels see Ireland from a
high tower and decide to go there.  After various strug-
gles with their predecessors in Ireland (the Tuatha De
Danann), the Goidels, or Milesians, defeat the Tuatha De
and arrange a settlement with them--the Milesians get
the upper half of Ireland, and the Tuatha De get the
half below ground.

The Book of Invasions is in itself a fascinating subject.  It depends on the medieval circular map of the world, the medieval tradition
of the seven wonders of the world (which included the Roman pharos at
Corunna from which the Milesians sight Ireland), and much more.  It also cheerfully assumes that Ireland is the second promised land and that
the Irish language is second only to Hebrew in its sacredness.(12)
    To reassure those who might envision an Irish analogue of Gil-
bert's study of Ulysses, let me begin by saying that The Book of Invasions is used only in a partial way in Ulysses, in the manner that
Joyce uses mythic structures in general.  In his discussion of early
Irish mythological elements in "The Dead," John Kelleher cautions,

Everyone of course knows that Joyce was fond of weaving
into his work parallels with myth, saga, and epic.  It
is, however, a mistake to assume, when such a parallel
is identified, that it must be complete.  It rarely is.
Even Ulysses does not reflect the entirety of the Odyssey.  In Finnegans Wake wonders can be done with a mere
hint of resemblance.  Usually Joyce is content with a
few salient indications as, for example, in the well-
known sketch-parody of Dante's Divine Comedy in the
story "Grace."  The same, I think, holds for "The Dead"
and "The Destruction of Da Derga's Hostel."  The shadowy
similarity between Gabriel Conroy and Conaire Mar is
enough for Joyce's purposes which by their very nature
must be suggestive rather than explicit.(13)

The same method characterizes Joyce's use of The Book of Invasions
in Ulysses:  he refers to main points in the early Irish story rather
than giving point-by-point correspondences.  Though the references to

The Book of Invasions are incomplete, they are not insignificant.  In
the Irish story we find the unified source for the constellation of
main characters in Ulysses:  Greek, Jew, and Mediterranean woman.  The
Book of Invasions provides the scaffold for the relations of the central characters in Joyce's novel and supplies typologies for Joyce to
work with in developing his cast.  Let us turn to the relationship between Joyce's characters and their counterparts in The Book of Invasions.

Leopold Bloom can be seen as a counterpart to the Goidels--the
Irish invaders who could have been Jews because they were invited by
Moses to share in the Promised Land:  "'Come with us, with thy whole
people,' said Moses, 'if you will, and remain permanently with us, and
when we reach the land that God hath promised us, you will get a share
in it.'"(14)  The Goidels are confederates of Moses but not Hebrews,
sympathetic to Moses but not among the chosen people.  The Goidels
share Hebrew history but choose deliberately to go in a different direction.  In the same way, Bloom has Jewish sympathies and through his
father the potential of being a Jew, but his actual experience and
identity are not Jewish.  Because Jewish descent comes through the
mother's line and Bloom's mother and maternal grandmother both have
Irish names, Bloom appears not to be a Jew.  Moreover, Bloom is not
circumcised, and he has been officially baptized as a Christian twice.
We should also note Bloom's explicit statement that "in reality" he's
not a Jew [U 643].(15)  Bloom's mixed identity--his Jewish sympathies
and ancestry combined with his Irish actuality--mirrors the early history of the Goidels in The Book of Invasions more than a naturalistic
representation.  It is also possible that Bloom's preoccupation with
Egyptian and Turkish things is intended to reflect the Goidelic so-
journs in Egypt.  It brings to mind as well the Pharaoh's daughter who
becomes one of Mil's wives.

In the Stephen Dedalus of Ulysses we can see a representative of
the Irish invaders with a Greek heritage, particularly the Tuatha De
Danann.  We have seen that in The Book of Invasions the Tuatha De Danann are known for their learning and skills, even magical skills.  The
Tuatha De Danann "learned druidry and many various arts in [the northern islands of Greece] . . . till they were knowing, learned and very
clever . . . they considered their men of learning to be gods."(16)
Like the Tuatha De, Stephen Dedalus is schooled in ancient knowledge;
like them he has the richness of Western culture and its secret mysteries at his disposal; like them he can be as arrogant and aloof as a
divinity.  The Tuatha De Danann attitude toward artists also has an
amusing parallel in Stephen's aesthetic theory; following Flaubert,
Stephen believes that "the artist, like the God of the creation, remains within or behind or beyond or above his handiwork, invisible,
refined out of existence, indifferent, paring his fingernails" [P 215].
The identification of Stephen and the Tuatha De Danann is mediated as
well by the Athenian alliance of the Tuatha De Danann, since in some
versions of the classical myth Daedalus is an Athenian.  The chief hero
of the Tuatha De Danann is Lug, the samildánach, the "many-skilled,"
and Stephen, too, is many-skilled.  Teacher, bard, singer, potential
journalist--he is even urged to take up the professions of singer and
newspaperman on Bloomsday.

Molly appears to represent the recurrent Spanish connection in
Irish pseudo-history.  In her is embodied Mediterranean sensuality--but
a sensuality that is Ireland's legitimate heritage in The Book of Invasions.  Of the characters in The Book of Invasions, Molly calls to mind
Tailltiu, daughter of Magmor king of Spain, and wife to Eochaid son of
Erc, king of the Fir Bolg.  When Eochaid son of Erc is defeated, she
marries Eochaid the Rough son of Dul of the Tuatha De Danann.  Later

Tailltiu becomes foster mother of Lug, the young hero of the Tuatha De Danaan, and her memory comes to be celebrated with games at the site of her grave.(17)    Tailltiu is also credited with clearing one of Ireland's plains:

> Tailltiu (came) after the fighting of (the first) battle of Mag Tuired to Coill Chuan (Cuan's Wood); and the wood (was) cleared at her command, so that it was a clovery plain before the end of the year, and she inhabited it afterwards.(18)

Tailltiu's dwelling place brings to mind Molly's love of flowers and nature, a love of lushness appropriate to both women because of their Mediterranean origins.  Note, too, that both Bloom and Molly toy with the idea that Stephen might move into their home--become, as it were, their "fosterson."  Whatever her erotic fantasies about the situation, we might say that like Tailltiu, Molly almost becomes "fostermother" of a multitalented youth.

Tailltiu and the Spanish wives obtained by some of the Goidels after their conquest of Spain might have suggested to Joyce that Mediterranean passion enters Irish tradition through the distaff side-a-possible explanation for all the women with vigorous sexual appetites who people medieval Irish literature.  In terms of the scaffolding of Ulysses, we should also observe that Molly enjoys dalliance on hilltops and heights and places from which she has a large vista.  Her final thoughts of the day are memories in which her embraces of Mulvey on the rock of Gibraltar fuse with the memories of her lovemaking with Poldy on the Hill of Howth.  This may remind us of the Spanish tower from which the Goidels spot Ireland in The Book of Invasions.

The Book of Invasions also illuminates Joyce's portrait of the Citizen in the "Cyclops" episode of Ulysses.  Joyce's treatment of this character has been cited to show his disdain for the Irish cultural revival and for crude forms of insular nationalism.  Richard Ellmann indicates that the Citizen was modeled in particular on the founder of the Gaelic Athletic Association, Michael Cusack [JJI 62-63].(19)  The Book of Invasions adds resonance to these interpretations, for the Citizen can be seen as the representative of still another wave of invaders, the Fir Bolg.  In Irish typology the Fir Bolg are short, dark, ugly, crude people. They were laborers in Greece, and in Ireland, after the conquests of the Tuatha De Danann and the Goidels, they became the unfree, subjugated, non-noble populace.  The Fir Bolg typology--current in Joyce's time, and still in force today--is one element behind Joyce's construction of the Citizen.(20)

The Citizen is not only crude in his person and his thought, he is chaotic as well.  Kenner points out that Joyce could associate the nationalistic movement with destruction and chaos, particularly with the 1916 destruction of Dublin:  "When the biscuit-tin, by heroic amplification, renders North Central Dublin a mass of ruins we are to remember what patriotic idealism could claim to have accomplished by Easter 1916."(21)  The most chaotic figures in early Irish literature are the Fomorians, who are responsible for the failure of the Nemedian invasion and who fight against and for a time oppress the Tuatha De Danann.  The battle between the Fomorians and the Tuatha De Danann is a reflex of the Indo-European pattern of the battle of the gods of order with the gods of chaos. The Fomorians are often conflated with the Fir Bolg in the ancient texts:  each group opposes the Tuatha De Danann in a battle at a Mag Tuired; each group is defeated by the Tuatha De.  This conflation is reflected in Joyce's treatment of the Citizen, and it may explain why he is simultaneously an ordinary-sized person and a gigantic figure in the parodies paralleling the action of the chapter.

The most chaotic figure of all the Fomorians is Balor, the one-eyed figure who can turn men to stone with his gaze and who is killed in the Second Battle of Mag Tuired by Lug. Elsewhere the Fomorians in general have only one eye. As a group the Fomorians can be compared to the Cyclops, and we should remember that it is the narrator, not the Citizen, whose (single) eye is mentioned. The Citizen, then, represents two groups in The Book of Invasions—he is crude Fir Bolg and chaotic one-eyed Fomorian wrapped in one—and at the same time owes something to the specific characterization of Balor.

With this typology behind the Citizen, we would expect Stephen Dedalus rather than Bloom to oppose the Citizen, because Dedalus seems to represent Lug in particular and the Tuatha De Danann in general. It is the Tuatha De who fight both the Fir Bolg and the Fomorians at the battles of Mag Tuired, and Lug who slays Balor. It is suggestive that Joyce originally intended Stephen to be part of the "Cyclops" episode.(22) Since Bloom was apparently intended as the Citizen's victim from the very start,(23) the mythological structure of The Book of Invasions may offer some clue to Joyce's original plans for the chapter. As it stands, Joyce has bent the early Irish myth in having Bloom rather than Stephen oppose the Citizen. But The Book of Invasions explains why there is a typological as well as a personal contrast between Bloom and the Citizen: they represent the opposition of their races within Ireland.

We have already seen that from a naturalistic point of view it is an anomaly that the three main characters of Ulysses are in some way foreign and do not have Irish names; it is particularly paradoxical that Bloom's father is an immigrant in a nation whose people emigrate. The Book of Invasions helps to explain why the central characters in Ulysses are all outsiders, though they stand as universalized representations of Dubliners. The invasion theory of Irish history in The Book of Invasions is predicated upon the notion that there are no aboriginal inhabitants of the island. According to this view of things, everyone is an outsider, descended as it were from immigrants. From the perspective of Irish pseudo-history, the cultural alienation of Stephen, Bloom, and Molly mirrors the heritage of all of the island's inhabitants as descendants of invaders. Thus, within an Irish mythic framework, if not an Irish naturalistic context, the main characters of Ulysses are typical of the race.

In this light we see the ultimate irony of Deasy's joke about Ireland's having no Jews as well as the irony of the Citizen's xenophobia and his virulence against the Jews in particular [U 323, 338]. The Book of Invasions suggests that the Goidels of Ireland and their descendants should have a natural sympathy and affinity for the Jews, for the Goidels might well have joined Moses' band and shared in Jewish history. Indeed, the Goidels might be called an "Israelitish" race.(24) The Citizen betrays his base ancestry with his anti-Semitic views.

Much of the action of Ulysses takes place as the characters walk about Dublin. The path captures, in part, a walk Joyce took with his friend Byrne on the eve of his departure from Dublin in 1909 [JJI 299-300]. It also simulates the sea journeys of Ulysses as he attempts to return to Ithaca. However, the motif of a sea journey is not confined to the Odyssey: it is found as well in The Book of Invasions. The invasion framework of Irish history means that there is a great deal of journeying in Irish pseudo-history, and the Milesians in particular spend a long time in boats upon the sea. In the Irish story as in the Greek, the characters are not merely at sea for 7 Eccles Street, the

ultimate goal of Bloom's travels, has both Ithaca and Ireland as its
mythic counterparts.

Bloom and the Goidels, Stephen and the Tuatha De Danann, Molly and
Tailltiu, the Citizen and the Fomorians / Fir Bolgs—taken one by one
each correspondence between Ulysses and The Book of Invasions is of
little moment.  Taken together they carry weight.  Ireland's pseudo-
history, which shaped native Irish concepts of time and identity for
over a thousand years, finds its way into Ulysses and informs the relations of Joyce's main characters.

Joyce's use of elements from The Book of Invasions ·to structure
Ulysses is probably one reason why Joyce was attracted to Victor
Bérard's theory that the Odyssey was of biblical origin.  Bérard's
theory links Hebrew and Greek, a linkage we see in The Book of Invasions as well.  The similarity between The Book of Invasions and the
Odyssey, in Bérard's critical theory, would in turn legitimate Joyce's
own fusion in Ulysses of elements from both stories.

Joyce's choice of typologies from The Book of Invasions, particularly his decision to make the main character in Ulysses a Jew, was not
entirely arbitrary or simply literary.  The question of national traits
was of great interest to him.  He felt personal affinities to the Jews,
and he believed that in general the Irish and the Jews were similar and
their destinies alike.  In a letter to Carlo Linati accompanying his
scheme of classical and anatomical correspondences for the book, Joyce
referred to Ulysses as "an epic of two races (Israelite-Irish)."(25)
These apparently naturalistic observations were perhaps a conventional
product of the "two peoples" rhetoric of Irish nationalist politics, in
which Irish suffering under the English was compared to the Israelites'
bondage and captivity, but they receive their mythic justification in
The Book of Invasions.(26)

Recognition of the connection between The Book of Invasions and
the constellation of the main characters in Ulysses sheds light on a
critical bone of contention:  the level of irony and satire in Ulysses.
Ellmann has detailed Joyce's concept of Ulysses and shown how Bloom
fits these ideas -- like Ulysses Bloom is intelligent, prudent, sensitive, and of good will.  His broadmindedness, love of life, curiosity,
and kindliness mark him as special.  Kenner speaks of Bloom as "the
hidden hero," and shows that Bloom has the traits of a Homeric chief-
tain [JJI 370-74, 379, 382-83].(27)  Nonetheless, if Ulysses is considered primarily within the framework of classical myth and European symbolism, the constellation of Jewish father, Greek son, and Spanish wife
is at best bizarre and at worst a travesty.  If only the Homeric parallels are considered, the novel can be seen as mainly satiric or mock
heroic:  Molly becomes "faithful Penelope with a difference," and Bloom
is "a legendary hero fallen upon evil days."(28)  Levin notes that "the
Homeric overtones do contribute their note of universality . . . but in
doing so they convert a realistic novel into a mock-epic."(29)  In the
context of Irish pseudo-history as well as Greek myth, the constellation of the main characters is perfectly clear, indeed it is appropriate and almost natural.  And Molly, following in the footsteps of Tailltiu and other women in early Irish literature and myth, should not be
expected to limit herself to one man.  The great female figures of native Irish literature are sexually forthright rather than physically
chaste.

The thematic implications of the Irish scaffolding in Ulysses are
wide-ranging.  Paradoxically, Joyce's use of the Irish framework from
The Book of Invasions is part and parcel of his insistence that Ireland
must be European if Ireland is to be renewed.  (In Thomas Kettle's
words, "If Ireland is to become a new Ireland she must first become
European" [JJI 64].  The import of The Book of Invasions is that

Ireland, through its invasions, has inherited the best from Egypt, Israel, Greece, the North of Europe, Belgium, and Spain.  Ireland's people and culture are the distillation of Europe and the Mediterranean world.  In Ulysses this ideal is presented in a modern form.

Matthew Arnold's essay on Hebraism and Hellenism contends that the world moves between the two poles of Jew and Greek; and Joyce himself held this view [JJI 407].  Bloom and Dedalus represent these two types.  By suggesting the union of Hebraic Bloom and Hellenistic Dedalus through classical parallels and the Irish substructure, Joyce is suggesting that Ireland is heir to the whole range of human experience, valuation, and potential.  Elsewhere such temperaments might be opposed, but in Ireland they are fused: "Jewgreek is greekjew" [U 504].  The binding structure from The Book of Invasions helps to explain why Joyce believed that in Ireland at any rate those two temperaments could be reconciled:  Ireland's populace can be seen as heirs to both typologies because of successive waves of invasions and generations of intermarriage.  As early as his 1907 Trieste lecture, "Ireland, Island of Saints and Sages," Joyce wrote:

> Our civilization is a vast fabric, in which the most
> diverse elements are mingled, in which Nordic aggres-
> siveness and Roman law, the new bourgeois conventions
> and the remnant of a Syriac religion are reconciled.  In
> such a fabric, it is useless to look for a thread that
> may have remained pure and virgin without having under-
> gone the influence of a neighbouring thread.  What race,
> or what language . . . can boast of being pure today?
> And no race has less right to utter such a boast than
> the race now living in Ireland. [CW 165-66]

This theme is elaborated in Ulysses.

In Ulysses Joyce plays not only with the traditional view of Irish history but also with the traditional Irish concept of reincarnation.(30)  Metempsychosis, the word that reverberates through Ulysses like the thunderclap in Finnegans Wake, refers not only to the rebirth of Ulysses, Penelope, and Telemachus, but to the rebirth of Ireland's avatars from The Book of Invasions.  In Joyce's novel the types of Hebraic Milesian, Greek Tuatha De, and Spanish female reappear in contemporary Dublin.

Ulysses revives the Irish myth of The Book of Invasions in the context of detailed, contemporary realism.  Joyce thus suggests the applicability of that myth to twentieth-century life:  the myth is alive, universal, to be taken literally in the modern period.  Joyce also implies that Ireland's native populace will tend toward the characteristics embodied in the main characters of Ulysses:  Greek, Hebrew, sensual Mediterranean.  Implicitly we can see Joyce's nationalistic statement, albeit a statement repugnant to the Irish nationalists.  Joyce, the former Parnellite and later admirer of Griffith, puts forth a position reminiscent of both:  to cease being "an unfortunate priestridden race" and to escape the straitjacket of colonial morality—British Victorianism—Ireland needed spiritual "home rule," a return to its own past and heritage.  Paradoxically, Ireland could turn to a Continental outlook for help in accomplishing this return.

Joyce's use of The Book of Invasions in Ulysses suggests that cosmopolitanism is Ireland's heritage—a heritage obliterated by the twin conquests of Christianity and the Sassenach—as well as its goal.  The Irish mythic parallels for Ulysses imply that neither an inward-turning, insular mentality nor a stifling sexual asceticism is natural to Ireland.  In holding these positions, Joyce is at odds with the studied insularity of most other Irish Revival authors and their insistence that the peasantry of Ireland preserved a noble and natural moral purity that would redeem a corrupt English-speaking world.(31)   In turning to The Book of Invasions for his typologies of Irish character and experience, Joyce gives his perspective on the Irish Literary Revival: that the best of Ireland never was and never can be inward-turning. Ireland must reach out beyond Ireland and beyond England to the wisdom and experience and morality of all Europe and the wider world.

Joyce had a vision for Ireland that may still be relevant:   to transcend the crabbed, insular, prejudiced, political framework; to reach out to the world; to overcome priestly, puritanical morality; to assert the artistic and the rational and the moral rather than merely the pedestrian.  These things might be accomplished, he says, by reasserting the Greek, the Jewish, and the sensual Mediterranean elements of the Irish heritage--in a word, for the Irish to own themselves as Irish, not as Anglo-Saxons or West Britons.  The Irish mythic elements in Ulysses are part of Joyce's attempt to create "at last a conscience in the soul of this wretched race" [L II 311].

In 1906 Joyce wrote to his brother Stanislaus, "If the Irish programme did not insist on the Irish language I suppose I could call myself a nationalist" [L II 187].  Ulysses, written more than a decade later, is as nationalist as anything by Hyde or Gregory, Yeats or Synge.  Joyce must be seen in the context of the Anglo-Irish Literary Revival both in terms of his reuse of Irish literary and mythic material and in terms of the nationalist implications of his thematics.

Consonant with his aesthetic theories, Joyce does not present these views didactically.  He "seeks a presentation so sharp that comment by the author would be an interference" [JJI 88, cf. 61].  Bloom and Molly and Stephen speak in their own voices, the voices of Ireland's traditional history and mythic nature.  It is Molly who denigrates priestly morality in favor of nature and Bloom who has compassion and a large political outlook, and who hates xenophobia (the great vice both of classical literature and the Irish heroic age).  Joyce does not comment on these issues in his authorial voice.  Instead he "abandons himself and his reader to the material" [JJI 88].  Art, rather than nationalist polemic, is Joyce's goal.  Whatever nationalist message there is to be found in Ulysses, "the nation might profit or not from his experiment, as it chose" [JJI 68].(32)   By and large, Ireland has chosen not to profit from the lessons of Ulysses.

One of the reasons why the native Irish symbolic values for the main characters in Ulysses and the significance of their configuration--their debt to The Book of Invasions--have not been recognized is because of the dual isolation of the novel.  Though there was no customs exclusion order on Ulysses in Ireland after 1932 and though the book was never banned by the official Censorship Board, it remained isolated from the Irish reading public by less formal blacklisting, including clerical disapproval.(33)  The Irish reading public, steeped in native popular history, is the audience to whom the archetypes in Ulysses would speak most immediately and to whom they would be most apparent.  On the other hand, the vast majority of European and American readers and critics are isolated from native Irish literature.  This unfamiliarity with Joyce's own formative traditions has resulted as we have seen, in Joyce's being  treated as a European writer to the exclusion of his Irish sources, themes, symbols, and archetypes, including a major structural framework for Ulysses, The Book of Invasions.(34)

After Joyce's death, his brother Stanislaus recollected Joyce's methods of literary creation:  "In all Joyce's work, the architectonic plan is dominant.  He did not set to work until he had the plan clearly

in his mind."(35)  The architectonic structure of Ulysses has been primarily perceived in terms of its Homeric parallels and secondarily in
terms of Hamlet.  Kenner has suggested that one reason why Joyce described Ulysses in Homeric terms while the book was in progress was
that the Homeric scheme turned the book "into something that could be
talked about."   Still later the Homeric structure helped critics and
readers alike manage the amorphous text with its genre innovations.(36)

Stanislaus Joyce, who was more versed in Irish tradition than most
of his brother's Continental companions, wrote of Ulysses in 1941:
"Whoever studies it in detail will find that a number of generations of
Irish history have been superimposed one on another."(37)  Ulysses is a
roman à clef, though no one key fits it exactly.  To the Odyssey and
Hamlet, the books which are most widely acknowledged to have contributed to the architectonic structure of Ulysses, we should now add a
third:  The Book of Invasions.  One of the keys to Ulysses is Irish.

## NOTES

1.  For the argument that Stephen is trying to "get clear" of all
fathers see Hugh Kenner, "Ulysses" (London:  Allen and Unwin, 1980),
10-19.  This essay is the nucleus of the first chapter of a work in
progress, "Ulysses" and Early Irish Literature.   I am indebted to
Vivian Mercier and John V. Kelleher for their comments and suggestions
on a preliminary draft of this essay.

2.  Harry Levin, James Joyce, A Critical Introduction (Norfolk,
Conn.:  New Directions, 1941), 6.

3.  JJI, 204, 238-39, 385, 443; Louis Hyman, The Jews of Ireland
(Shannon:  Irish University Press, 1972), 167-92.

4.  Levin, James Joyce, 84.

5.  Ibid., 46.

6.  For some thematic values of the characters' alienation see
the discussion in Hyman, Jews of Ireland, 178-80, as well as the references cited there.

7.  Kenner, "Ulysses," p. 71.

8.  For a discussion of the naturalistic background of Irish Jews
see Hyman, Jews in Ireland.

9.  Throughout this essay I assume the distinction between native
Irish literature, which originated and was recorded in Irish, and Anglo-Irish literature, which is recorded in English and has its roots in
English literary tradition.  The distinction between native Irish and
the Anglo-Irish Ascendancy probably lies behind Joyce's characterization of his tradition as "divided against itself" [CW 81-82, 185].  In
Ulysses when Stephen speaks of Irish art as "The cracked lookingglass
of a servant" [6], he is probably to be understood as referring to contemporary Irish art emulating English standards rather than the native
tradition which writers like Yeats and Gregory were attempting to
revive.

10.  The Book of Invasions survives in four recensions which have
been edited in two series:  Leabhar Gabhala, The Book of Conquests of

Ireland, The Recension of Micheal O Cleirigh, eds. R. A. S. Macalister and John MacNeill, (Dublin:  Hodges, Figgis, 1916); and Lebor Gabala Erenn, The Book of the Taking of Ireland, ed. R. A. S. Macalister, 5 vols. (Dublin:  Irish Texts Society, 1938-1956.)

11.   Eugene O'Curry, Lectures on the Manuscript Materials of Ancient Irish History (Dublin:  James Duffy, 1861), 446.

12.   For a discussion of some of these elements, see John V. Kelleher, "Humor in the Ulster Saga" in Veins of Humor, ed. Harry Levin (Cambridge:  Harvard University Press, 1972), 35-38.

13.   John V. Kelleher, "Irish History and Mythology in James Joyce's 'The Dead,'" The Review of Politics 27, no. 3, (July 1965): 421.

14.   Macalister and MacNeill, Leabhar Gabhala, 198-99.

15.   For a full discussion of the question of Bloom's religion and ethnic affiliations, see Erwin R. Steinberg, "James Joyce and the Critics Notwithstanding, Leopold Bloom is not Jewish," Journal of Modern Literature 9 (1981-1982): 27-49.

16.   Macalister and MacNeill, Leabhar Gabhala, 142-43.

17.   Tailltiu is the modern Telltown, and under the Gaelic Athletic Association the old Telltown games were revived and continue to be observed to the present.  The irony of the nationalists' choice to celebrate the memory of a woman who goes from husband to husband cannot have escaped Joyce.  Note also that Tailltiu's "sensuality" here is part of her function as a Sovereignty figure.

18.   Macalister and MacNeill, Leabhar Gabhala, 150-51; I have made the spelling of names in this quotation consistent with the rest of this essay.

19.   See also Michael Groden, "Ulysses" in Progress (Princeton: Princeton University Press, 1977), 132ff.

20.   Oliver Gogarty accused Joyce of himself having Fir Bolg melancholy [JJI 122].

21.   Kenner, "Ulysses," 139, cf. 92-96.

22.   Groden, "Ulysses" in Progress, 133-37, cf. 149.

23.   Ibid., 132.

24.   Hyman (Jews of Ireland, 180) applies the term to the Goidels.

25.   On all these points, see JJI 383-84, 393, 407-8, 529, 535.

26.   For a discussion of the "two peoples" theme in Irish politics, see Kenner, "Ulysses," 137-39.  It may be, of course, that the political trope is itself based on The Book of Invasions scheme, which Irish audiences would have recognized.

27.   See Kenner, "Ulysses," ch. 5.

28.    Levin, James Joyce, pp. 68, 73.

29.    Ibid., 71. Note, however, the possibility that Joyce's work reflects back on the classical epic, suggesting that "Homer's heroes were not quite so heroic as he painted them, and that Penelope like Molly Bloom, was no better than she should be" (Vivian Mercier, The Irish Comic Tradition [1962; reprint, London:  Oxford University Press, 1969], pp. 213-14). Mercier also suggests that Joyce may have known an account of Penelope's infidelity.

30.    For a brief modern assessment of Celtic beliefs about reincarnation, including a discussion of Caesar's attribution to the Celts of the Pythagorean theory of metempsychosis, see Proinsias MacCana, Celtic Mythology (London:  Hamlyn, 1970), 123.

31.    See William Irwin Thompson, The Imagination of an Insurrection (1967; reprint, New York:  Harper and Row, 1972), 10ff.

32.    For other political aspects of Ulysses and the interaction of Joyce's politics and aesthetics, see Richard Ellmann, The Consciousness of Joyce (New York:  Oxford University Press, 1977), 73-95.

33.    Michael Adams, Censorship:  The Irish Experience (Alabama: University of Alabama Press, 1968), 31n.

34.    By and large those Irish citizens who have been most inclined to read Ulysses are cosmopolitan, and thus are familiar with the European and American literary establishments; they, like readers of Ulysses in general, come to the book preconditioned to perceive the established Homeric parallels.

35.    Stanislaus Joyce, Recollections of James Joyce, ed. Ellsworth Mason (1941; reprint, New York:  James Joyce Society, 1950), 19.

36.    Kenner, "Ulysses," 22-23.

37.    St. Joyce, Recollections, 19.

## 4

# The Stylistics of Regression in *Ulysses*

## *Joseph Bentley*

After six decades of argument the central question about Ulysses remains the same: What, if anything, gives organic justification to its sequence of styles, its apparently gratuitous shifts from one technical experiment to another? While it is unlikely that a final answer will ever be found, Jean Piaget's theory of child development may provide a way to clarify and justify the book's disparate array of themes. The impulse to recapture the infantile state, which can be seen as determining both content and technique in Ulysses, leads to a radically simple reading of the book. The theory has the further advantages of depending only on observations about the text and on relatively safe assumptions about psychology.

Before proceeding to a description of Piaget's infantile universe, it is useful to make two observations about Ulysses. First, the novel presents a set of tangential plots concerning people who feel dispossessed, usurped, or in some way robbed of what was once vitally important to them. Ireland's traditions, language, and independence Stephen's mother, religion, and home and Bloom's wife, son, and Jewish heritage are among the most prominent examples of what the characters have lost and sometimes wish to recapture. Since the present is experienced as a reality bereft of former sources of comfort and identity, all desirable futures are pictured as either real or symbolic regressions into the past. In this way Joyce actualizes the Ulyssean pattern of consciousness by making origins serve as ends. As Bloom puts it, "Think you're escaping and run into yourself" [U 377]. This fusion of past with future devalues the present and thus diminishes the clarity with which a self experiences its own identity. It imposes a psychic pressure toward loss of ego by insinuating the unreliability of what Jacques Derrida calls "the metaphysics of presence."

The second observation is less obvious. The series of stylistic experiments which begin in episode 10, "Wandering Rocks," provides the reader with an equivalent to the losses and usurpations that the characters have suffered. After gaining possession of the book's real events and ideas in the first two hundred pages--which Joyce in a letter to Harriet Weaver called "the initial style, or Rock of Ithaca"-- the reader is set adrift in the stylistic analogue of perilous seas, a verbal environment in which the meticulously detailed set of initial entities is constantly blurred, befogged, and diminished. Only in the final episode are we allowed to recapture a version of the original mode of presentation. Molly's monologue is conspicuously unlike those of Stephen and Bloom earlier in the book, but it is still a personal monologue, a return after more than four hundred pages to a known, single perspective. As such it is experienced as a return to the book's initial style, its home key.

These observations suggest a mechanically imposed unity of plot and technique. A book about displaced people is presented in verbal simulations of displacement and final restoration. Though this has been as far as most critics have been willing to go on the issue—Hugh Kenner in several books, for example, or Marilyn French in The Book as World—the answer remains unsatisfactory because of the artificial and distantly analogical nature of the harmony it claims. Those who try to discredit Joyce make the point that his structures are only clever contrivances with no grounding in deeply felt human experience. Without a coherent theory of the necessary relation of stylistic experiment and a plot tendency toward regression, even the friendliest treatments of Ulysses must create either fragmentary or factitious conceptions. We take a large step closer to a unifying theory when we hypothesize that the home from which Joyce's characters have been evicted is the original state of infancy. Many will find such an idea irritating because it has been so often overstated by followers of the Freudian and Rankian schools. Besides, the issues of birth trauma and return to the womb have become not only clichés but, more important, repellently vague and facile ideas. If, however, we give the infantile hypothesis another chance, using precise experimental models drawn from a rigorously descriptive scientist like Piaget, we will find that the emphasis on childbirth in Ulysses is the key not only to the book's meaning but also to the question of organic unity between plot and technique.

The twin facets of Ulysses—lost origins and alien syntaxes—imply states of existential disorientation or loss of a previously clear sense of identity. An assault on the integrity of an ego structure evokes an experience identical with the infantile state in which the subject has not yet learned how to know his own existence by contrasting it with other entities in his environment. It would seem, when its main attributes are noted, that residues of the infantile mind can function as a basis in reality for the artistic and existential coherence of Ulysses. The work of Piaget, especially his conclusions about the forms of childhood logic in The Construction of Reality in the Child, is useful here. His analysis of infantile epistemologies, taken as an aggregate of simultaneous patterns, seems strikingly like a description not only of Ulysses but also of most cubist art. Although there is no evidence that Piaget understands anything about modernist literature, he appears to have discovered its key. Piaget's descriptions clarify the role of those styles in Ulysses that create an increasing disjunction between reality and mind, between raw content and modes of presentation.

In the child's earliest phase, what Piaget calls the sensorimotor period of the first two years of life, the data of sensation are processed in a double way, first as flat image and second as rounded object. Children, the theory goes, perceive the world as both free-floating image and substantial object. When children see the world as a congeries of flat images—as they do exclusively in the first six months and intermittently during the remainder of their first two years—they are unable to conceive of themselves as objects among other objects occupying and thus creating space. They are so egocentric that their failure to perceive objects in their three-dimensionality prevents them from locating themselves as entities in a continuum. They are thus without a concept of self. The world is a kaleidoscope with an emptiness at its center where the self should be. Infants, incidentally, are an exception to the Cartesian cogito. They think—that is, they process information--but their kind of information does not permit them to know their existence.

The bizarre multiplicity of Ulysses--which reaches its highest degree of eccentricity in the obstetrical episode where a child is born and Bloom finally attaches himself to Stephen--harmonizes perfectly with the book's other aspects if we see the stylistic multiplicity as identical with the Ulyssean quest for the primal home. The primal home of all people who have ever lived, if Piaget is correct, consists of a world of flat images that block a clear sense of self, which gradually changes to a world of solid objects where the self can be experienced.

Piaget's description of this sensorimotor phase is reminiscent of some theoretical constructs in phenomenology. F. H. Bradley, Franz Brentano, Edmund Husserl, Martin Heidegger, and MerleauPonty suggest analogous schema for preconscious reality in the instants prior to perception. The value of Piaget, however, is that his primal cognitive models are derived from rigidly controlled experiments on actual subjects and that his findings have been verified by many psychologists since he published them in the 1930s. He is in no sense a metaphysician; his findings suggest a deep structure in the mind upon which all later mental structures depend. Further, this primal structure presents an exotic universe in which causation, space, time, and ego do not exist. As a result of this absense we can tentatively suppose that many religious, mystical, philosophical, and intuitive accounts of the soul, the ground of being, the void, and "the still point of the turning world" are based on, and even made imaginable, by residues of this phase.

Piaget also calls this phase "magico-phenomenalistic." From a spatial perspective it is phenomenalistic because it consists of qualities--free-floating adjectives--not yet configured into objects. From a temporal perspective it is magical because it consists of incoherent events. Magic is by definition the absence of imaginable causes. Sequences occur in coincidental order in such a universe. Piaget shows that the expectation of magic lasts far longer than the phenomenalistic mode of spatial arrangement in children. Some never entirely abandon the tendency to assume that events simply jump into reality in indeterminate relations. (Joyce scholars are well aware of his great fascination with coincidences, whether they come in the form of chance encounters or in the form of puns. "Divine coincidences!" was one of his favorite exclamations.)

Specific references to infancy and childbirth abound in Ulysses, but they are less important to this thesis than the alterations of space, time, causation, and selfhood created by the stylistic shifts. At the beginning Mulligan hails the sea as a mother and Stephen remembers his mother's death. At the same moment Bloom reads an ad for a Zionist colony, sees an old woman, and envisions the death of Israel as a mother land. In personal and ethnic terms the return is blocked. Later, Stephen imagines a telephone line made of navel cords stretching back to "smooth-bellied Eve," and much later Bloom goes to bed as the "childman weary, the manchild in the womb," reversed in relation to his wife in bed, head downward, in the position for rebirth. In a surreal episode Bloom becomes a baby himself, complete with bib and diaper, before giving birth out of his own androgynous body to eight sons. Scores of other passages can be cited; even the name Odysseus is etymologically linked to a Greek word for parturition.

The implications of Joyce's stylistic techniques are of primary importance to this argument. If his techniques are something more than factitious simulations of displacement from home, they must be united with the facts of lost origins and the experience of existential disorientation. In several ways they do add up to such an impression.

First, the book is divided into parts in which interior monologue is recorded and parts in which no subjective information is directly presented. In the first eleven episodes, in the second half of "Nausikaa," and in the final episode, the inner voices are rendered, reminding us of the constant narratization people use to construct conscious identities for themselves. Without such inner verbalizations, self-consciousness does not occur. In the other episodes, considerably more than half the book, unidentified narrators tell from external perspectives what is happening and what is being thought. Though we are often reminded of the subjective in these episodes, the characters' inner selves are not manifested directly. The most elementary fact about all but fifteen of the four hundred and forty-six pages between "Sirens" and "Penelope" is that they deny the interior monologue. The subjective is not denied, but it is removed into a vague area totally lacking the precise definition that it has in the book's other sections.

A second effect of the technical experiments is a deflection of focus from objects to words. The effect of such sentences as "Deshil Holles Eamus" [U 383] is the divorce of words from their meaning. The sentence means "Let's walk westward on Holles Street," but no immediate picture of walking on a street is provided. Similarly, the cinematic sequences of "Circe" overwhelm reality with exaggerated, self-conscious virtuosity. Objects, like persons, recede into a vague area where they lose spatial definition and temporal continuity.

A third effect is the experience of the kind of incoherence that Piaget calls magic. Narrators enter and depart from nowhere at unpredictable times in no clear sequence. They suggest social types or period styles, but they are disembodied and unidentified. Events are abrupt, uncaused, and seemingly random. These discontinuous presences dramatize the world of coincidence, acausality, or magic which motivates the decisions of the book's major characters. Virtually every turn of the action depends on an unforeseeable juxtaposition of events. For example, most of the book's action springs from a dream Haines had the night before. Stephen was awakened by his guest screaming the words "black panther" [4]. Stephen then slept again and dreamed of an exotic man, "Haroun al Raschid," who took him home from a street of harlots, offered him food, and said, "In. Come. Red carpet spread. You will see who" [47]. When he sees Bloom leaving the library [218], Stephen remembers the dream for a second time. When we discover that Stephen had met Bloom at least twice many years ago, we realize that the exotic man in Stephen's dream was Bloom in disguise. The "trigger" for Stephen's dream was the word panther, which suggests leopard and Leopold, and thus when Bloom attempts to penetrate Stephen's half-conscious state at the end of "Circe," Stephen mumbles, "Who? Black panther . . ." [608]. Coincidental word associations and coincidental encounters determine Stephen's behavior and reactions. When we recall that Bloom had also dreamed of the East, of himself as a sultan and of his wife as an odalisque, the coincidences seem even more improbable.

The most extraordinary coincidence is revealed in "Nausikaa." Bloom's dream actually contained the same message as Stephen's: "Come in. All is prepared. I dreamt" [370]. Joyce may or may not wish to suggest a telepathic exchange here, but when we relate these examples of synchronicity to the concept of coincidence as magic, we can see how they fit into a pattern of sequences which mimic the schema of reality found only in Piaget's sensorimotor or magico-phenomenalistic phase. Those who prefer a mystical explanation will deprive themselves of an answer that accounts for the regressive curve of the plot, the ego loss of the theme, and the spatiotemporal displacements of the style.

These technical experiments create three important effects: they

blur subjective time and thus diminish the experience of personal identity; they distort space by divorcing objects and actions from the
words that name them; and most significantly, they destroy continuity
and dramatize acausality. In effect, they create a world with the same
features that the real world had for each of us in infancy. It is a
world in which no space, time, causation, or selfhood exists, the warm
and secure world we have lost and which, like Ulysses, we need to recapture when the adult universe becomes unbearably threatening and
painful. The style is both search and discovery. From this perspective the diversity of Ulysses contains a profound unity which is motivated by intuitions of the primal reality that its characters seek and
its artistry provides.

However well the pieces fit together, caution is required of anyone advancing this kind of idea. Ulysses, true to its title, concerns
attempts to regain lost homes. Infancy is the only home we can call
universal. Joyce signals his concern with infancy by his pervasive use
of the motifs of maternity and child care. Most important, Piaget's
detailed account of infantile reality matches exactly the space, time,
cause, and ego transformations evoked by the series of styles that dominate most of the book. Nevertheless, the conclusion that Joyce's intuitions of his own lost infancy motivated what is unique in Ulysses
must remain tentative. The conclusion depends on two assumptions:
that the primal universe remains stored in the unconscious and that it
can impinge upon the adult mind and alter its sense of appropriate
form. Both assumptions seem sound, but remain forever unprovable.

We are left with a choice. We can suppose that Ulysses has no
organic unity, that its form is a masterpiece of architecture with no
necessary relation to its plot, or we can choose the perspective I have
offered. If we choose the latter, the advantages are considerable.
The Piaget thesis provides unity by presenting a viewpoint from which
such disparate elements as paranormal coincidence, loss of self, distortion of language, phenomenological reductions, surrealist attacks on
the substantial world, and even pedantic exuberance are seen as effects
of the one central theme in the book no one can deny—its evocation of
loss and its determined effort to regain the security of safe harbor
and home. When we realize that, the book's ultimate message is the
same as T. S. Eliot's:

> We shall not cease from exploration
> And the end of all our exploring
> Will be to arrive where we started
> And know the place for the first time.
> ["Little Gidding," in The Complete Poems and Plays,
> 1909-1950, 145]

Piaget's models will make us certain, despite the lack of final proof,
that Ulysses is grounded in the non-Euclidean geometries that prevail
in the place where we all began.

# 5

# Anna the ''Allmaziful'': Toward the Evolution of a Feminine Discourse

*Suzette Henke*

## FEMININE NARRATIVE

On a panel dealing with "Political Perspectives on Joyce's Work" at the Fifth International James Joyce Symposium in Paris, Philippe Sollers rose to speak waving a bright red copy of Finnegans Wake. "Voilà!" he declared triumphantly. Je vous donne une révolution! Sollers was assuming, of course, that linguistic and aesthetic revolution constitutes a political act. Later, he explained: "It is this saturation of the polymorphic, polyphonic, polygraphic, polyglotic, varieties of sexuality, this unsetting of sexuality, this devastating ironicalization of your most visceral, repeated desires which leaves you . . . troubled when faced with Joyce. Freud, Joyce: another era for manwomankind."(1)

As literary critics, we may find it difficult to comprehend the double linguistic and political revolution to which Sollers so gleefully alludes. Only now are we beginning to acknowledge the radically "destructive" and decentering impact that Joyce's text could have on literature and culture alike. Certainly, as Margot Norris has argued, encoded in the obvious linguistic subversiveness of the Wake is an implicit challenge to the patriarchal culture that it parodically replicates and defies.

But what, precisely, is the nature of the verbal revolution that Joyce perpetrates, and what is its relationship to the "feminist" sex-role revolution that Sollers describes? In February 1982, at a centenary conference at the State University of New York at Purchase, Judith Johnston offered a feminist critique of the Wake, challenging Joyce's masterwork as a lexical playfield ultimately glorifying the "sameold gamebold adamic structure" [FW 615.6] of androcentric language and history. Phallic power, she argued, is still the name of Joyce's raucous atomic/Adamic game of linguistic punning that reduces to mockery Anna Livia's continuous, run-on "feminine" language and makes women little more than marginal figures in a male-dominated society.(2) In contrast, the French feminist Julia Kristeva has expressed glowing admiration for what she interprets as Joyce's defiance of patriarchal authority "not only ideologically, but in the workings of language itself, by a return to semiotic rhythms connotatively maternal."(3)

In James Joyce and the Revolution of the Word, Colin MacCabe marshals evidence from psycholinguistics that suggests the radical development of what he terms a nonphallocentric feminine discourse:

> If the "masculine monosyllables" [190.35] serve as the
> fixed point around which the rhythm flows, it is the
> feminine stream which provides the movement.  Language
> is a constant struggle between a "feminine libido" which
> threatens to break all boundaries and a "male fist"
> which threatens to fix everything in place.(4)

Asserting the priority of "grandma's grammar," the language learned by
Issy and articulated by Anna, MacCabe concludes that:  "It is the impact of this discourse on the phallocentric male discourse which produces Finnegans Wake."(5)

MacCabe's ideas are provocative but a little troubling.  What,
precisely, is "phallocentric" discourse?  And if we accept MacCabe's
premise that "to speak is to have accepted a symbolic castration,"(6)
then we must conclude, as he does, that women cannot "master" language
at all, but must utter a separate discourse that proves impenetrable to
the male analytical mind.  Nevertheless, I suspect that Kristeva and
MacCabe have sown semiotic seeds that may prove both controversial and
seminal to future literary criticism.

If we seriously examine the notion of a nonphallocentric language,
we begin to move in the direction of elucidation.  The problem is, of
course, that the term itself is a metaphor that figuratively suggests
an aggressive "will to power" evident in both language and culture.  It
is a neologism that posits a genital model for a univocal and exclusive
worldview.  If we consider the origins of a logocentric culture founded
on the word and the law--on logic, mastery, and cognitive cohesion--
then we can trace the history of Western patriarchy back to its origins
in the Greek city-state.  Aristotelian logic is based on a rational
discourse that excludes, both conceptually and politically, the recognition of irrational, subversive modes of thought such as the Eleusinian mystery cults and Dionysiac rites.  Anyone who has taken "Philosophy 1" knows that the very foundation of Western logic is the premise
that a thing cannot be true and not true at the same time--unless, of
course, one is either a madman or a poet.

A "nonphallocentric" language that refuses to ascribe univocal
truth-value to a single word, phrase, sentence, or proposition need not
be either "vaginocentric" or "uterocentric."  It could embrace, instead, an anarchic and polymorphous model structured around the bisexual organization of the psyche originally posited by Freud.  As MacCabe
suggests, the Wake introduces into language "an ineradicable and inex-
haustible bisexuality, a constant process."(7)

In Finnegans Wake Joyce makes an intuitive and metonymic leap into
the void of incertitude by celebrating the prolific possibilities of a
"feminine" or bisexual and polymorphous discourse--protoform, lyrical,
rhythmic, and cyclical.  If the world is a Derridean text, then the
text of Finnegans Wake offers a Derridean supplement to the text of the
world by creating a polysemic playfield, a palimpsest of multiple meanings that are both magical and metaphorical.  Joyce reduces the linguistic sign to its formal components, and through puns, neologisms,
portmanteau words, and linguistic ruptures creates a textual universe
of polymorphous perversity.

As Paul Ricoeur points out, the use of poetic metaphor involves a
"creative use of polysemy" that allows us to "experience the metamor-
phosis of both language and reality."(8)  By collapsing metaphor and
metonymy into a single linguistic unit, Joyce achieves a unique deraci-
nation of poetic language from surrounding and definitive context.
Whereas a single word usually takes its connotation from the context of
a larger discourse, Joyce refuses us the certitude of contextual veri-
fication.  He instantiates in the text an infinite regression of

possible meanings. And, in so doing, he displaces onto a traditional sign-system a polysemic discourse that moves in the direction of idiolectical creativity.

Once again, we return to the fundamental premise that a thing cannot be and not be at the same time. For Joyce, of course, it can. We are always of "twosome twiminds" about any particular linguistic unit because we have been denied the logocentric closure of direct statement. At every point, Joyce violates the primary rule of Aristotelian logic and denies the univocal perspective of rational intellection. We are thrust into the world of primary process, where the "truth" of every linguistic sign becomes a function of multiple contexts, defined in binary opposition to "signs on a white field" that seem to take on a will of their own.

What we should keep in mind is that encoded into this anarchic project is a revolutionary refusal to accept the logocentric authority embedded in the Father as thunderbearer, hammer-hurler, judge, priest, lawmaker, and linguistic word-giver. Finnegans Wake is a unique work of art that subverts the linguistic code of a logocentric culture at the same time that it calls into question the "universal" assumptions of phallocentric social organization.

What does all this have to do with Anna Livia Plurabelle? As early as Joyce-Again's Wake, Bernard Benstock speculated that the Anna Livia sections of the Wake provide a paradigm for "feminine" discourse by "combining the musical with the prosaic, sound with sense, to produce words-made-flesh and flesh-made-words that are . . . both pure and multiple in meaning."(9) Benstock suggests, furthermore, that

> Anna Livia dominates the entire book, both in poetic measure and in structural balance. Her flowing style serves for much of the metrics of the Wake's language, . . . while her "mamafesta" chaper, the washerwomen chapter, and the final soliloquy are in many ways lyrical highlights in the Wake.(10)

If we take the notion of a polymorphous language seriously, we might conclude that the elusive "dreamer" of the Wake (if there is, indeed, a dreamer) is neither male nor female, but a bisexual representative of the new "manwomankind" that Sollers invokes in defense of Joyce's revolutionary text.

## ANNA LIVIA PLURABELLE

In Finnegans Wake Joyce makes use of a uniquely feminine or bisexual discourse to celebrate Anna Livia Plurabelle as archetypal female principle. The two old washerwomen who tell us the tale of ALP see her through an overlay of gossip and popular cliche. They view the world through "Gerty MacDowell eyes" and impose a soap-opera vision of reality onto their sudsy, soporific story. At the same time, however, Joyce seems to be suggesting that the only way to learn about Anna is to immerse oneself "in the swim" of her hindmoist waters—to become a part of the subject described. Knowledge of the unknowable "other" demands empathy and an exercise in personal identification that may mean getting wet from frequent splashes in the waters of life. "Are you in the swim or are you out? O go in, go on, go an!" [204.27]. The tripartite invocation suggests ritual immersion and baptism, a knowledge that comes through imaginative assimilation.

Like characters in a Beckettian drama, the washerwomen feel convinced that "talk" can "save us" [215.34]. So long as they continue to narrate a story, to articulate the stirrings of consciousness in oral history and myth, they remain part of a "tale told of Shaun or Shem"—

a tale of waking and resurrection, of "teems of times and happy returns. The seim anew. Ordovico or viricordo" [215.22-23]. Like the river itself, the narrative of ALP must "never stop" and demands "continuarration"—a nonstop discourse of female fertility. "You're not there yet. I amstel waiting. Garonne, garonne!" [205.14-15].

Anna Livia Plurabelle emerges in Finnegans Wake as Joyce's all-including, most farraginous feminine archetype. The earth-mother of Ulysses, the mythic Gea-Tellus, gives way to the more primal forces of flowing water symbolic of a mysterious, protean unconscious. As womb of the world, Anna Livia absorbs both squalor and sentiment, reality and dream. She is the mysterious river-woman, an eternal source of vitality flowing out of the depths of the earth and carrying the leaves, flowers, and sediment of life in the wake of her shifting shoreline.

Whereas the principal male persona, Humphrey Chimpden Earwicker, is identified in terms of an ancient Irish giant buried in the rocks of Howth and Chapelizod, Anna Livia embodies a fluid, ever-elusive reality. She captures the Heraclitean flux that fascinated her creator, and she forever changes in the context of a changeless biological cycle. In Finnegans Wake the obsessive, logocentric power of the male, along with the idée fixe of patriarchal authority, has been ossified into stony impotence. The compulsive desire for mastery has hardened into the rocky sensibility of Finn MacCool, an ancient Irish giant helplessly shaking a "meandering male fist" [123.10]. The masculine persona is paralyzed in intractable patriarchy. The female, in contrast, remains fluid and free. The traditional hero, dead and outmoded from the beginning of the book, has to be dreamt into waking, into "array surrection," by Anna's life-giving riverrun. Even more than Molly Bloom, Anna Livia captures the semiotic rhythms of the capacious unconscious. She is open, fluid, and forever "yea-saying" to the rushing torrent of temporal phenomena that characterizes the "given" moment of cosmic experience.

"Allalivial, allalluvial!" [213.32]. All alive are part of that divine being Allah, here "done" by Joyce in a feminine mode. Unlike the Judeo-Christian deity, omnipotent and omniscient, the female mother-goddess is immanent in the world of nature. Her "omni" qualities are less than plenipotentiary and manifest an all-encompassing alliance with life and love, rather than with the knowledge and power traditionally ascribed to a male deity. If old father ocean, an angry Poseidon, manifests himself as a wrathful Jehovah, Mother Anna flows through the land rejuvenating all her daughter / sons without the acerbic sting characteristic of her salt-sea father.

Wishing us "Teems of times and happy returns," Joyce celebrates Anna the "Almaziful": "Anna was, Livia is, Plurabelle's to be" [215.24]. Playing the "trinity scholard," he feminizes and Latinizes the eternal Trinity of Catholicism. His invocation resurrects a three-personed mother-goddess who is both Catholic and Freudian. In her ancient identity as Anna, ALP evokes an archetypal matriarch who wields atavistic powers worshipped of old by prehistoric, pagan cultures. She is the great earth-mother, the maternal deity that preceded Hera and Zeus in the Greek pantheon and later functioned as the Ceres figure of Eleusinian cults. Simultaneously, however, she represents woman as Cybele, destructive moon-goddess and proverbial temptress. And she reflects, as well, the subterranean libido that Freud described in his analysis of the id. The primordial Anna symbolizes both primitive rites and a more modern recognition of the powerful forces of the unconscious.

Like Molly Bloom, the "matronly" Anna is definitely male-identified. In an effort to please her irascible spouse, Anna works her fin-

gers (and knees) to the bone.  For the pleasure / plaisir of her greedy
partner, she labors "for to plaise that man hog . . . till her pyrrak-
nees shrunk to nutmeg graters while her togglejoints shuck with goyt"
[199.22].   Such feminine altruism is ill-rewarded by a husband who
refuses to be satisfied.  At every lifegiving favor "my hardey Hek he'd
kast them frome him, with a stour of scorn" [199.24].

   In a letter written to lighten her heart, Anna complains of her
partner's impotence and gives voice to a sense of insecurity about ag-
ing and the loss of her figure: "By earth and the cloudy but I badly
want a brandnew bankside, bedamp and I do, and a plumper at that!"
[201.56].   Characteristically projecting HCE's lack of sexual interest
onto her own fading charms, Anna feels the need of a corset or girdle
to contain her overflowing riverrun.  She complains of being "wore out"
from "waiting for my old Dane hodder dodderer, my life in death companion, my frugal key of our larder, my much-altered camel's hump . . . to
wake himself out of his winter's doze" [201.8-11].  HCE has degenerated
into a moribund companion to his wife--a dotty old gentleman who resembles a "doddered" tree, shattered and infirm.

   Anna's letter vindicates Humphrey of a sexual crime by protesting
his age and erotic infirmity.  The senility of this "life in death companion" suggests illness and impotence.  HCE's "key" to the larder of
Anna's fecundity is diminished and "frugal," and his "camel's hump" is
"much altered"--a euphemism suggesting that Humphrey's "humping" days
are over.  Anna grieves for the loss of her "maymoon's honey," now reduced to a "Decemberer" fool in this May / December marriage.  Yet she
expresses the hope that he is merely hibernating, and that, like the
dead god of ancient fertility rites, he will be resurrected "out of his
winter's doze" and resume his manly posture with the full force of sexual renewal.

   Bound to onerous maternal and spousal duties, Anna nevertheless
dreams, as does Molly before her, of liberating herself from her snug
domestic nest and leaping away to the careless freedom she once knew as
a "lovely seaside girl."  She clings to fantasies of recapturing the
delights of her promiscuous adolescence and escaping "to the slobs
della Tolka or the plage au Clontarf to feale the gay aire of my salt
troublin bay" [201.18-19].

   How many children had the gadabout Anna, and who were their
fathers?  "How many aleveens had she in tool?" the curious washerwomen
query [201.27].  Popular opinion suggests "a hundred eleven, wan bywan
bywan."  Having bred this gargantuan brood, Anna "can't remember half
of the cradlenames she smacked on them" [201.31-32].  Faced with such
prodigious fecundity, the crones remark smugly: "They did well to re-
christien her Pluhurabelle," the whore of multiple beauties.  The one
hundred and eleven progeny she has borne, "one by one," imply a long
line of fertile progenitors embraced with wild abandon by Anna in her
libertine youth.

   As soon as the prurient washerwomen try to "pin down" Anna's protean history, they wallow in a bog of confusion.  Filled with salacious
curiosity, they follow the endless sequence of Anna's lovers and attempt to trace her fluid meanderings back to the "first, last, only and
alone" [U 731] act of virginal violation, the "original sin" that for-
feited her chastity.  "Waiwhou was the first thurever burst?" [202.12-
13] they ask excitedly, trying to find the mysterious identity of the
male who initially burst the fragile hymen of Anna's seedbed.

   The crones long to discover the name of this primordial suitor:
"That's the thing I'm elwys on edge to esk" [202.15].  But Anna herself
admits to some confusion about her first love affair: "She sid herself
she hardly knows whuon the annals her graveller was" [202.23-24].  Her
first lover proved a "grave-dealer," a "deathsman of the soul" to

Anna's virginity, and left her "gravid" with potential life. Topographically, her despoiler contaminates the purity of her river-water by "gravelling" her soil-bed and polluting the purity of her stream.

Joyce recalls the cradle of civilization and the Garden of Eden, as Anna responds to her seducer "with nymphant shame when he gave her the tigris eye! O happy fault!" [202.33-34]. The story is Joyce's version of the fall of Adam and Eve, the "happy fault" (Felix culpa) that inaugurated both the shame of mortality and the coming of Christ as redeemer. Here the "fault" evokes sheer sensuous delight rather than a promise of future salvation. Man and woman fall together into erotic pleasure to rise again and be redeemed in their offspring. This is the age-old lesson of the Garden of Eden / Erin, Ireland's little "split pea" of a biblical story of Genesis (Guinnesses).

Anna's very first lover was apparently a "holy man," the "local heremite, Michael Arklow" [203.18]--an Irish archangel and hermit / priest dwelling in a Celtic dell somewhere in the heart of the Hibernian hinterlands. Arklow is a spiritualized HCE persona, portrayed in a sanctified, mock-heroic incarnation. The time of their "natural nuptials" is equally equivocal: the union takes place "one venersderg in junojuly" [203.20], a winter's Venus-day ripe for venereal perambulations, when ALP could play Juno and goddess, the ox-eyed woman in search of her man.

Anna emerges as a teasing ingenue with "kindling curves you simply can't stop feeling" and "singimari saffron strumans of hair" that weave a web of feminine charm around her shy but willing lover. The traditional Irish analogue to the tale is the hagiography of St. Kevin of Glendalough, the hermit tempted by a threatening female. In Joyce's mock-heroic version of the narrative, the monk does not cast the temptress Cathleen into the lake; instead, he embraces the lake / river as holy water / lover. Arklow parts the "reignbeau's heavenarches" of Anna's saffron tresses, "deepdark and ample like this red bog at sundown," and immerses himself in her silt-laden streams. Goaded on by her "enamelled eyes," indigo and enticing in their ether-blue beauty, the monk is seduced into "vierge violetian"--a virginal violation that "baptizes" Michael in the amorous waters of Liffey's violet streams [203.28-29].

Characteristically, the pious hermit protests his innocence and projects his desire onto the woman he lusts after. The lapsed celibate claims he was seduced by the lascivious Anna: "He cuddle not help himself, thurso that hot on him, he had to forget the monk in the man" [203.32-34]. As he showers the beautiful maiden with kisses, Arklow warns her "never to" give in to his erotic titillations. With "niver to, niver to nevar" [203.36] on his lips, the monk fondles his lover, "rubbing her up and smoothing her down," plying her with "kiss akiss after kisokushk" [203.35] until the "vierge" to be violated is vertiginously aroused.

The preamble to this "holy communion" between Michael and Anna is described in tantalizing, lubricious prose. But the parting and mingling of Anna's "hindmoist" waters is an act that occurs almost entirely offstage. The reader can only imagine the mad monk Michael plunging with salacious delight into the "majik wavus" of Anna's "elfun . . . meshes" [203.31]. We are told, opaquely, that "Simba the Slayer of his Oga is slewd," as he lewdly relinquishes his religiously prurient vows of celibacy.(11) Losing male reason and logocentric control, he kisses Anna's "freckled forehead" and immerses himself in the life-giving waters of her mortal stream.

Anna, for her part, "hielt her souff" (held her breath, panted in ecstacy) in an act of delight rather than capitulation.(12) Yielding her virginity to this bold priest's entreaties, she revels in the sex-

ual initiation that inaugurates her river / womanhood:  "She ruz two
feet hire in her aisne aestumation. And steppes on stilts ever since"
[204.2-3].  The ecstacy of lovemaking elevates Anna's ingenuous self-
image; she emerges from the erotic moment whole, hearty, and transcendent.  The virginal "sacrifice" proves an act of psychic healing that
gives her a sense of personal integration.  If the rent (or hole)
caused by sexual congress was experienced as a physical wound, her monk
/ priest / lover provided verbal balm and healing kisses:  "That was
kissuahealing with bantur for balm!  O, wasn't he the bold priest?  And
wasn't she the naughty Livvy?" [204.3-5].  No longer a maid, Anna delights in her newly acquired status of womanhood and is filled with
pride at her feminine consummation.  Her estuaries have risen, and her
sense of self is bright and untarnished.  She has emerged from the
stream of her youth into the full flower of maturity as woman and
river, Anna Livia / Anna Liffey.
     The sobriety of this "sacramental" rite of passage is immediately
undercut by the voyeuristic gossip of the washerwomen, who continue to
excoriate the "naughty Livvy" for the imputed sins of her youth.  The
hermit Arklow, violating a vestal virgin with all the guilt and excitement of sacred sin, believed that he was Anna's first lover.  Rumor has
it, however, that the precocious Anna had already been tainted by earlier erotic experiences.  According to popular opinion, "two lads in
scoutsch breeches went through her before that, Barefoot Burn and Wal-
lowme Wade, . . . before she had a hint of a hair at her fanny to hide
or a bossom to tempt a birch canoedler" [204.5-9].  These lascivious
scouts defiled her long before she had pubic hair or the nub of a bosom
and snatched the unripe fruit of her budding adolescence before it had
a chance to blossom.
     Even before that, in an incident that mimics the mythic rape of
Leda by Zeus in the form of a swan, the innocent Anna "all unraidy, too
faint to buoy the fairiest rider, too frail to flirt with a cygnet's
plume, . . . was licked by a hound, Chirripa-Chirruta, while poing her
pee, pure and simple" [204.10-12].  The young girl was helpless and
vulnerable even while urinating.  And in her youthful naivete, she was
violated by a dog that caught her with her knickers down during "shear-
ingtime."  Thus was the ingenue laid ("leada / laida") against her will
by a rapacious hound in a scene that suggests a conflation of rape and
oral sex.  And further back in her infatile past, at the dawn of proto-
history, "first of all, worst of all, the wiggly livvly, she side-
slipped out by a gap in the Devil's glen while Sally her nurse was
sound asleep in a sloot and, feefee fiefie, fell over a spillway before
she found her stride" [204.13-16].  In her early sexual researches, the
wiggly, elusive child experienced a primordial fall:  the rivulet lost
her innocence to "stagnant black pools" and lay and laughed amid blushing hawthorns.(13)
     Ultimately, of course, Anna's sexual "fall" into womenhood is
shrouded in ambiguity and mystery.  Joyce acknowledges, like Freud before him, the erotic delights of a "polymorphous perversity" that characterizes infantile sexual researches.  Anna, he tells us, lost her
girlish innocence when she escaped the surveillance of her nurse and
fell over a spillway.  The exact nature of her "sin" remains obscure.
Is the infant ingenue innocent and free ("innocefree") as her laughter,
and Joyce's Yeatsian pun, would suggest?  Or is she, in fact, guilty of
a mysterious autoerotic transgression?  We do not know.  And neither
Joyce nor the washerwoman will tell us.  Anna's "virginal violation" by
a godly monk, two boy scouts, a hound, and viscous black pools of rain-
water comprises a sexual mystery woven into the tapestry of the Wake.
It becomes part of that unfathomable persona of Joyce's "eternal geo-

mater" that Shem and Shaun will try, unsuccessfully, to penetrate and unravel.

The fluid river-woman is a female Proteus, and we are warned to "saise her quirk for the bicker she lives the slicker she grows. Save us and tagus!" [208.1-2]. As she matures, the mysterious Anna becomes all the more elusive and incomprehensible. Losing the narcissistic focus of adolescent self-centeredness, she slips into the thousand protean shapes demanded by nurturance and sympathetic projection. As the boundaries of the ego gradually dissolve, this mother-woman begins to assume the multiple personalities of those in the realm of her care.

As fertile mother and womb of the world, Anna hides in her "nabsack" (womb, wordsack, female genitalia) all the "plurabilities" that she bestows on her progeny. "Anna high life" impartially distributes a hoard of presents, both good and evil, to "her furzeborn sons and dribblederry daughters, a thousand and one of them, and wickerpotluck for each" [210.4-6].(14)    In the riotous catalogue that follows, Joyce introduces his own authorial signature in the person of "Sunny Twimjim," the boy from Clongowes Wood College--an institution now demoted to a kind of savage outpost of Christian myth and ritual. Through Anna's beneficence, the author receives "a Congoswood cross on the back" [211. 5], to be borne on the new Via Dolorosa of aesthetic martyrdom. Shem / Seamus, Sunny's shade or fictional alter ego, sports the traditional "crown" of laurel that gives him the illusion of feeling big--though, in fact, the poetic crown of momentary glory is interchangeable with the artistic crown of thorns decorating the exiled Twimjim.

After a catalogue of Anna's maternal gifts to her children, the Dublin washerwomen reassert the central paradigm of Finnegans Wake: "Every telling has a taling and that's the he and the she of it" [213. 12]. Every tale is both history and "herstory," reflecting the binomial bifurcation of male / female conflict polarized around kinetic patterns of amorous desire. Man and woman clash, fall, and sexually collide to give birth to a new breed / brood of daughter / sons that will reenact age-old sagas of marital/martial conquest. The male rises to phallic grandeur only to fall into the womb of his hindmoist mother / wife. His seed is cast on the waters of humanity, to be brought to fruition in endless cycles of racial renewal.

Every story has a "taling"--a tell-tale narrative base rooted in irrational forces of conflict and creativity. More often than not, public myth and legend are constructed around a private hermenuetic code obscuring a "seminal" story of unresolved sexual conflict. Impelled by erotic desire, man and woman love, clash, fight, and "do the coupler's will." The thrill of Eros drives them to pursue, resist, and eventually capitulate to the consummation of natural law. From sexual congress will come children who must learn both the laws of nature and the secrets of the universe, from grandaddy's martial arts to the more semiotic, anarchic elements of "grandma's grammar."

All taling has a tail or end in an eschatology that climaxes in the dissolution of that final distinction between self and other, between subjective personality and objective impotence. Subject loses its will and reason and is reabsorbed into the larger, impersonal cosmic cycles that "begin again" the endless drama of human existence. "It saon is late. 'Tis endless now . . . Wharnow are alle her childer, say? In kingdome gone or power to come or gloria be to them farther? Allalivial, allalluvial!" [213.15, 30-32].

Out of universal suffering, we turn as a tribe to the patriarchal leader, "the great Finnleader himself in his joakimono on his statue riding the high horse there forehengist" [214.12]. The author Giacomo Joyce writes himself into this Möbius strip of a narrative when he puts the Finnleader "in his joakimono" and makes a lexical joke of male

authority and patriarchal pretension.  The hero is little more than an
anachronistic clown, sprung fully blown from the head of a facetious
Giacomo.  Though riding a "high horse," this stupefied authority figure
is moribund and frozen, confined to a stone pedestal that immobilizes
him in haughty but impotent pride.

The Dublin washerwomen implicitly reject an omnipotent Lord and
patriarchal divinity by directing their prayers to a more earthly and
compassionate goddess, the holy "Maria, full of grease" [214.18].  This
new proletarian protector is both divine intercessor and female drudge,
bearing the "load" of earthy toil in her spiritual dealings with the
deity.  The crones call on female saints to mitigate the wrath of an
angry god, and, in a more atavistic invocation, importune "Icis," the
Egyptian Isis who resurrected her god-husband Osiris from death by re-
storing his castrated manhood.  In a burst of Catholic devotion, the
women pray to "marthared mary allacook" (Margaret Mary Alacoque from
"Eveline"), the self-martyred saint who now appears as both cook and
"kook" in a new proletarian dispensation.(15)  Uttering semi-religious
orisons, the washerwomen remind us that the promise of paradise comes
each evening with sunset and urge us to "Wait till the honeying of the
lune, love!  Die eve, little eve, die!" [215.3-4].  As the "little eve"
reminiscent of our first mother fades into sunset, a new life of moonlight, dream, romance, and fantasy will be born again.  "Anna Livia,
trinkettoes" emerges as boon companion and twinkling star, drinking and
twinkling at eventide, "the queer old skeowsha anyhow."  She embraces
and revitalizes her "quare old" mate, "Dear Dirty Dumpling, foosther-
father of fingalls and dotthergills" [215. 13-14].  In the incarnation
of Finn MacCool, HCE is father of an atavistic race of preternatural
progeny—son / daughters with fins and gills who comprise a male-female
androgynous species.  The hermaphroditic Humphrey inaugurates a primordial polis of social organization:  "Hircus Civis Eblanensis!"  Celebrated as the legendary "goat" founder of Dublin, he functions as mythic progenitor of the Irish race:  "He had buckgoat paps on him, soft
ones for orphans.  Ho, Lord!  Twins of his bosom.  Lord save us!" [215.
27-29].  Nurturing twin antagonists, he fosters the sons who will eventually defy, castrate, and supersede their impotent father.

RICORSO

As Anna Livia, at the end of Finnegans Wake, flows into the sea of
death, she confesses to years of "soffran" from the loss of children
and lovers.  With some confusion, she wonders if it is she who is being
transformed by the shadow of mortality, or if her loved ones are drawing away from her.  "But you're changing, acoolsha, you're changing
from me, I can feel.  Or is it me is?  I'm getting mixed" [626.35-36].
She takes comfort from "Tobecontinued's tale" and the knowledge that
"there'll still be sealskers" [626.19] (Danish elske, to love), both
self-lovers and true romantic lovers, long after her departure.

The sweetness and innocence of her daughter Issy reminds Anna of
her own traumatic separation from the great sweet mother protecting her
in the secure "blue bedroom" of the sky.  Why did she ever abandon the
peace and silence of that ethereal sanctuary?  "I could have stayed up
there for always only.  It's something fails us.  First we feel.  Then
we fall" [627.10-11].  In true Plotinian fashion, Joyce describes the
initial stirrings of sexual desire that lead the individual toward
change and maturation—the need, absence, or gap in experience that
draws one forward into conjugal union.  "Feeling" the impetus of both
desire and sympathy, the self abandons the splendid isolation of prepubescent wholeness and "falls" into the painful perturbations of Eros.

Knowing that "something fails us," we fall into sin and into language, into a restless desire for personal communication that leaves us

forever unsatisfied by the lack—the astonishing gap and failure of articulation—that always separates us from another's subjectivity. The self is isolated in a hostile universe, where communication is faulty and understanding rare. "A hundred cares, a tithe of troubles and is there one who understands me?" [627.14-15]. As Anna recuperates the freedom and innocence of her childhood, she finds her loved ones becoming loathsome in her sight. "How small it's all!" she exclaims. [627.20] In her girlish loyalty, the child / bride Anna romantically exaggerated her husband's mythic stature: "I thought you were all glittering with the noblest of carriage. You're only a bumpkin. I thought you the great in all things, in guilt and in glory. You're but a puny" [627.21-23]. And so she now turns "home" to her wild, primitive ancestors, a Celtic race of Lesbian sisters, seahags who celebrate life through wild dances and ecstatic din. Already, she envisions herself transformed, raising with her sister-waters "the clash of our cries till we spring to be free" [627.31-32].

Although Anna has served as an archetypal figure of the altruistic, nurturant mother and lover, her final thoughts before death cast off the emotional ties, as well as the stereotypical female roles, that have shackled and defined her. Love and loathing are fused, and both are lost in the "bitter ending" of death. As Anna flows toward the impersonal source of life that extinguishes the self, she affirms, ineluctably, the primordial isolation of consciousness. Womb flows into tomb, bearing on her tumultuous river-waters a solitary leaf "a way a lone a last a loved a long the" riverrun of cosmic life. [628.15-16]

## NOTES

1. Philippe Sollers, "Political Perpsectives on Joyce's Work," in Joyce and Paris, ed. Jacques Aubert and Maria Jolas (Paris: Editions du CNRS, 1979), 107; "Joyce and Co.," in In the Wake of the "Wake," ed. David Hayman and Elliott Anderson (Madison: University of Wisconsin Press, 1978), 120.

2. Judith Johnston, "Teaching Finnegans Wake from a Feminist Perspective" (Paper was delivered at the Centenary Conference "James Joyce: A Portrait of the Artist," State University of New York at Purchase, 15-18, February 1982.

3. Julia Kristeva, Polylogue (Paris: Editions du Seuil, 1977), 16. Translation mine.

4. Colin MacCabe, James Joyce and the Revolution of the Word (London: Macmillan, 1979), 146.

5. Ibid., 150.

6. Ibid., 145.

7. Ibid., 151.

8. Paul Ricoeur, The Philosophy of Paul Ricoeur, ed. Charles E. Reagan and David Stewart (Boston: Beacon Press, 1978), 133.

9. Bernard Benstock, Joyce-Again's Wake: An Analysis of "Finnegans Wake" (Seattle: University of Washington Press, 1965), 160.

10. Ibid., 157.

11.    See Roland McHugh, Annotations to "Finnegans Wake" (Baltimore:  The Johns Hopkins University Press, 1980), 203.  McHugh tells us that "Simba" in Kiswahili is "lion" and that "oga" means "to bathe." "Siva the Slayer," furthermore, is a Hindu god of destruction, and "oga" is the Old English word for "fear."  Joyce's syntax in this passage suggests a double negative—perhaps implying that the lion-slayer of Michael's fear is both "lewd" and "slain" and that, as a result, his erotic passions undergo a phoenix-like resurrection.

12.    The French verb souffler means "to blow, breathe, utter, or pant."  The noun secheresse implies drought, dryness, harshness, or a lack of feeling.  A possible exegesis of this passage, then, would suggest that "while you would parch your dryness" (slake your thirst?), she "held her breath," or alternatively, "held herself panting."

13.    Roland McHugh reminds us that the word "Dublin" originally meant "black pool" (Annotations, 204).

14.    See Adaline Glasheen, Third Census of "Finnegans Wake" (Berkeley and Los Angeles:  University of California Press, 1977), pp. xlv-xlvi.  I disagree, however, with Glasheen's analogy between Anna Livia's gift-giving and the release of evils from Pandora's box. Anna's gifts appear to be both beneficent and punitive, according to the "potluck" of their recipients.

15.    Roland McHugh confirms the rather idiosyncratic nature of this saint's hagiography when he notes that St. Margaret Mary Alacoque distinguished herself as a "visionary who preferred drinking water in which laundry had been washed" (Annotations, 214n).

# Part II
# The Rhetoric of Joyce's World

# 6

# Joyce and Popular Literature:
# The Case of Corelli

## *R. B. Kershner, Jr.*

We sometimes forget that Ulysses belongs to the genre of historical
novel, that 1922 was virtually contemporary times by comparison to
1904, the year for which Joyce compiled his immense sottisier. Things
were different from 1922, and from today: hats, shawls, cigar stands,
cabs (which were still horse-drawn), and brothels (which had mandatory
chandeliers, at least if they catered to the middle class). Most of us
forget this while reading Ulysses, despite Joyce's efforts to re-create
a milieu; Bloom unthinkingly accepts the objects about him, and we follow suit. But styles and fashions are only one aspect of Joyce's mas-
sive historical portrait. Just as the historian Louis Chevalier gleans
from atmospheric passages in great nineteenth-century novels a picture
of the quotidian life of ordinary French citizens, we can read Joyce
for a picture of the time of his young manhood. But we can do more,
for Joyce directed his attention to one specific area of popular culture, the one which seems to him most indicative and most formative of
the popular consciousness of that time. This was popular literature.
    The year 1904 was crucial in the development of popular litera-
ture. The following year, according to the N.E.D., the word best-sel-
ler entered the language, pejoratively, in an article in the Atheneum.
The best--known novelist of the time was Marie Corelli; the best-known
poet, after Browning and Tennyson, was probably Stephen Phillips, auth-
or of the verse drama Ulysses.(1) But popular novels, perhaps the most
influential form of popular literature until the turn of the century,
had been alarming people since Wordsworth. Matthew Arnold in 1869 had
warned against people who "will try to give the masses . . . an intellectual food prepared and adapted in the way they think proper for the
actual condition of the masses."(2) This, he stressed, was not what he
meant by culture. The "masses," however, weren't listening. In the
mid-nineteenth century, Dickens and Thackeray had been "literature"--at
least if you were modern in your sensibilities--and Dickens and Thackeray had also been what everybody read.
    "Everybody," of course, was a term pretty much confined to the
middle classes, who were responsible for the novel in any case. Nobody
much knew or cared what the charwoman read, and chances were that she
couldn't read. The Education Acts after 1870 changed that. In Ireland, for example, about 41 percent of the populace was literate in
1861; in 1901, the figure was 79 percent and higher in the cities.(3)
This unfortunately did not mean that everybody, including the charwoman, read the same books. In fact, everybody read different books, and
different kinds of books. By the turn of the century, literature had

clearly stratified into "highbrow," "middlebrow," and the growing category of "lowbrow." Artists for "art's sake" were heatedly writing for
the ghost of Flaubert, while popular novelists were turning out books
which ranged from the aesthetically acceptable to the shoddiest hack
work.

"Popular" novels fell into numerous subgenres: air-raising adventures, "scare" stories about the invasion of England or about a Jewish
plot to discredit Christ and thus wreck Western civilization, humdrum
domestic novels, the remnants of the spate of "silver fork," "society"
novels which Bulwer-Lytton had inaugurated, and several varieties of
religious or mystical novels.(4)  Religion, which perhaps reached its
popular apotheosis in Lew Wallace's Ben Hur, was still selling well,
particularly if it was mixed with Robert Hichen's scarcely subdued sexuality. Perhaps most pervasive were what Nathaniel Hawthorne, in a fit
of bad temper, referred to as "that damned mob of scribbling women."
Writers like Mrs. Henry Wood, Charlotte Yonge, and Maria Cummins wrote
domestic romances, laced with melodrama and spiked with sentiment,
which were still going strong at the turn of the century. The detective story, sprung from the loins of Edgar Allan Poe and Arthur Conan
Doyle, was awaiting the imminent arrival of Father Brown. But the important point about each of these popular forms is that they had become
codified, formalized; often they were produced by a specialist publishing house, using its own stable of writers, for a faithful and clearly
delineated audience. Mass culture was arriving.

Perhaps just as significant as the novels were the magazines.
Particularly for women, they were usurping the place of the hardcover
novel. A bewildering variety of periodicals flourished, with an amaz-
ing show of reserve strength in some areas. In 1904 a homemaker could
choose from among Home, Home Chat, Home Circle, Home Companion, Home
Fashions, Home Friend, Home Life, Home Links, Home Messenger, Home
Notes, Home Stories, and Home Words; if her interests were less domestic, she might prefer the Ladies' Review, Lady of the House, Lady's
Companion, Lady's Home Herald, Lady's Home Magazine, Lady's Magazine,
Lady's-Own Novelette, Lady's Realm, or Lady's World. A different sort
of audience might receive the Woman at Home, Woman's World, Woman's
Life, Woman's Work, or Womanhood. Such magazines had a variety of
biases and special audiences, but in general one could expect a sampl-
ing of news, stories, advice, essays, and a generally high moral tone.
This last characteristic was soon to change.

A far smaller group of magazines enjoyed a rage in the British
Isles around 1904. These were what might be termed "conundrum" magazines, offering a potpourri of faintly spicy stories for gentlemen,
quizzes, puzzles, games, jokes, oddities and curiosities and, above
all, contests. The leaders in the field were Tit-Bits (still extant)
and Answers. Answers, significantly, was founded by Alfred Harmsworth,
Lord Northcliffe, who is said to have invented modern journalism,
bought out the Times and the Observer, and died of megalomania. Answers and Tit-Bits were among the first periodicals to take full advantage of the notoriously short attention span of a mass readership. No
single "bit" required more than five minutes to read in its entirety,
and no effort was made to provide continuity between separate "bits."
These were also the first magazines to strive for a total involvement
in the reader's life. Weekly prizes were awarded for solutions and
stories sent in, correspondence was all but mandatory for subscribers
and, in a rather grisly sales effort, automatic insurance was offered
to anyone who died in London with a copy of Answers in his possession.

Other entries into the field included the remnants of the great
Victorian literature of self-improvement, which by now had undergone a
sea change into various "How To" series, including Ernest Sandow's ad-

vice to the physically unfit, of whom Bloom is one; erotica, which was
mainly submerged but becoming prevalent in dilute forms such as the
"racy" novels of the Frenchman Paul de Kock (whose name Molly enjoys);
and of course the daily and weekly newspapers, which in 1904 were a
chaotic mixture of news, commentaries, essays, and stories. There were
general magazines, society magazines, and specialty magazines galore.
And everywhere were advertisements, indistinguishable from the news in
newspapers, indistinguishable from advice in the women's magazines. A
remarkable exception, the great selling point of Pearson's Weekly, was
that its advertisements were set off on pages facing the regular matter.

All of these Joyce researched, writing to friends from Paris and
asking them to send him back numbers of Tit-Bits or the ladies' journals [L I 144].(5)  There are over one hundred specific allusions to
newspapers, magazines, and ephemeral books in Ulysses, without counting
formal allusion—"Cyclops," with interspersed newspaper-style headings,
or "Nausikaa," with its "namby-pamby-jammy-marmaladey-drawersey" voice.
Numerous passages parody society journals and sporting journals, while
SacherMasoch's pornographic novel Venus in Furs provides the basis for
the book's major erotic fantasy [JJI, 380-81].  "Ithaca"'s question-
and-answer form clearly suggests both the conundrum magazines and the
"improving" historical texts such as Mangnall's Questions,(6) whose authors anticipated the techique of Dr. David Reuben by realizing that
any information is more palatable when given in response to a question,
no matter how absurd.  Stephen Dedalus is a highbrow writer who the editor of the Evening Telegraph makes a misguided attempt to draft for
the pressgang; Leopold Bloom is an advertising canvasser whose driving
ambition is to become a Tit-Bits prize author with an autobiographical
bit like "The Mystery Man on the Beach" or "My Experiences in a Cab-
man's Shelter."

What is the point of all this?  I would argue that Joyce believed,
quite literally, that literature in any form tends to structure consciousness, to affect one's assumptions, expectations, and perceptions.
That great literature does this on an individual basis was no news in
1922, but Joyce was probably the first major writer to appreciate the
fact that popular literature does so as well, more insidiously, and on
a grander scale.  Joyce was by no means all Stephen Dedalus, the disen-
gaged esthete; he had watched his father, who was a canvasser for the
Freeman's Journal, relax at home by puzzling for hours over the pic-
ture-puzzles of Tit-Bits and Answers [JJI 39](7), certain that here at
last form would succeed chaos, solutions could be found, and life would
offer up the prize it had always withheld.  As a child Joyce had attempted a "prize" story of his own, and as a struggling young writer he
published an article on hoof-and mouth disease in the Freeman's Journal.  He knew the newspaper men there, friends of his father, and about
this time—still dogged by cattle—he even published stories from Dubliners in the agrarian magazine The Irish Homestead.

Soon after his arrival in Pola, Joyce began to immerse himself in
current novels in English, perhaps as an attempt to fight linguistic
homesickness.  On February 28, 1905, he wrote to his brother:

> I have read the Sorrows of Satan [by Marie Corelli], A
> Difficult Matter (Mrs. Lovett Cameron) The Sea Wolves
> (Max Pemberton) Resurrection and Tales (Tolstoy) Good
> Mrs. Hypocrite (Rita) Tragedy of Koroshko (Conan Doyle)
> and Ziska. [(also) by Corelli].  I feel that I should be
> a man of letters but damn it I haven't had the occasion
> yet (. . . .) If I had a phonograph or a clever steno

grapher I could <u>certainly</u> write any of the novels I have
read lately in seven or eight hours. [<u>L</u> II 82-83]

Frustrated by his long, slow work on <u>Portrait</u>, Joyce here, like Bloom
later, fantasizes about a popular literary success.  In fact, Corelli's
<u>Sorrows of Satan</u> had at publication the highest initial sales of any
novel up to its time.(8)  Clearly, the book had a horrible fascination
for Joyce.  Years later, he described Marcel Proust arriving at a party
in Paris in a heavy fur coat, "like the hero of <u>The Sorrows of Sa-</u>
<u>tan</u>."(9)  By the time he was drafting the "Scylla and Charybdis" sec-
tion of <u>Ulysses</u>, Joyce had John Eglinton refer to a project of
Stephen's:

> --Have you found those six brave medicals, John Eglinton
> asked with elder's gall, to write <u>Paradise Lost</u> at your
> dictation?  <u>The Sorrows of Satan</u>, he calls it.

Stephen, after smiling "Cranly's smile," merely recites mentally a
bawdy Mulliganesque rhyme about a "jolly old medical" who (ambiguously)
"passed the female catheter" [<u>U</u> 184].
  Whether the six medical students are a variant of the infinite
number of monkeys with typewriters, upon whom Stephen will rely to du-
plicate Milton's effort, or whether they are to be the amanuenses for a
wholly new <u>Paradise Lost</u> directed toward a modern sensibility, is unclear.  But we do have Corelli's work, a book with a contemporary turn-
of-the-century setting, which does reinterpret the fall of Satan.
Rather than a <u>Paradise Lost, The Sorrows of Satan</u> is a Faust variant;
it involves the experience of Geoffrey Tempest, an aspiring author,
with his close friend Lucio Rimañez, a thinly disguised Lucifer.  For a
modern reader, the novel resembles the work of a blundering and very
British d'Annunzio.  Nevertheless, it still retains a curious sort of
obsessive power.  More interesting for our purposes, it has a number of
elements that Joyce adapts to the form and substance of <u>Ulysses</u>.
  As with Joyce's works, the author's life looms behind <u>The Sorrows</u>
<u>of Satan</u>.  Corelli was a fascinating figure, notorious in the popular
press at the time when Joyce read her work.  Her half-innocent taste
for making inflammatory accusations earned her the mocking title, "The
Life-Boat of Journalism."  Corelli's first book, <u>A Romance of Two</u>
<u>Worlds</u>, struck a chord with the public.  Her personal mysticism, which
she dubbed "Electric Christianity," was at base a conventional-enough
Protestantism laced with elements of popular Eastern religions, theos-
ophy, reincarnation, vague talk about "science," and spiritualism.
From childhood, Corelli dramatized herself; by her death in 1924 she
had so obscured her past that it only gradually emerged that she was
the natural child of Charles Mackay, a failed man-of-letters and journalist, who married her mother after his wife's death, and who adopted
his own daughter Minnie.
  Minnie Mackay, in Rebecca West's words, "had a mind like any milliner's apprentice; but she was something much more than a milliner's
apprentice."  After a failed attempt at a career as a piano <u>improvisa-</u>
<u>trice</u> and singer, Corelli took to writing to support her indigent and
neurotic father and half brother Eric, both of whom she worshipped, and
both of whom specialized in treacly sentimental domestic verse that
generally failed to capture the public's fancy.  From the first,
though, Corelli's novels did.  <u>Romance of Two Worlds</u> sold surprisingly
well, <u>Vendetta</u>, a straight melodrama, sold even better, and <u>Thelma</u> combined the spiritualistic and melodramatic elements in what was to be
her most successful formula, which she repeated happily until the First
World War.  Neither Lew Wallace's earlier <u>Ben-Hur</u> nor the Christian no-

vels of her rival Hall Caine could attract her devoted readership; nor
had Ouida, a predecessor she admired, been able to capture so large a
share of the public with her more sophisticated social romances.    In
part, Corelli's success was due to her sincerity.    Rimañez, in The Sorrows of Satan, observes, "Not one author in many centuries writes from
his own heart or as he truly feels--when he does, he becomes well-nigh
immortal."(10)  Not only did Corelli write from the heart, she publicly
admitted that she considered herself the handmaiden of God, writing the
outline of the true religion from inspiration.

Indeed, The Sorrows of Satan was hailed on its publication by a
number of influential churchmen.  This and the public adulation lav-
ished on her Corelli enjoyed as her due.  She was shocked by the mali-
cious press rumors that she was working on a sequel to be entitled The
Sins of Christ, and by the rumors--probably unfounded--that she was engaging in Byronic incest with her beloved half brother.  But what first
wounded, then frustrated, and finally enraged her were the damning
press notices she received in nearly all the literary journals.    Her
revealed religion was labeled "pure bosh."  One anonymous wit claimed
that the secret of her popularity was that she wrote in "impeccably bad
taste."    In Reading Gaol, Oscar Wilde was asked by a friendly jailer
whether he considered Corelli a great writer and replied, "Now don't
think I've anything against her moral character, but from the way she
writes--she ought to be here."(11)  Honestly baffled as to why so many
reviewers she had never injured could fail to see her genius, Corelli
launched a counterattack on the press.  The members of the press, will-
ingly or not, were in league with Satan, she decided, and the fashionable "new" novels in the wake of Ibsen and Zola, her two bêtes noires,
were in fact responsible for the moral decay of England.  Joyce in his
epistolary and poetic diatribes could muster no more bitterness against
the publishing establishment than did Corelli.

This is the burden of The Sorrows of Satan, which anticipates
Joyce's criticism of popular literature but ironically cheapens its
significance.  Although Corelli felt that the mass readership was corrupted by realism in literature, especially the popular novels of high
society that exploited the loose morals of the rich for popular titil-
lation, she would throw into the same category Grant Allen's The Woman
Who Did--a serious, indeed "spiritual" exploration of love without mar-
riage--and Ibsen's social dramas.  Had she read it, she would no doubt
have been equally appalled by Dubliners.    Joyce, as Ulysses makes
clear, saw the problem differently.  When Lenehan spots Bloom pawing
through used books and suggests that he is purchasing Leopoldo or The
Bloom is on the Rye [U 233], he is making Joyce's point:  we buy ourselves from the huckster's cart.  Gerty MacDowell, raised on Maria Cummins's The Lamplighter and other sentimental, cheaply romantic novels,
has been made spiritually lame by their unconscious hypocrisies and
contradictions.

But Corelli's book does not really belong to the genre of sentimental domestic romance, for rather than enlightening Gerty or Molly
for us, it bears particular ironic significance for Stephen.  Virtually
devoid of plot, the book concerns an aspiring author, Geoffrey Tempest,
whose devout writings have been blasted in the press.  Like Joyce and
Stephen, Tempest fantasizes about literary revenge:

> I smiled as I thought of the vengeance I would take on
> all those who had scorned and slighted me in my labour--
> how they should cower before me!--how they should fawn
> at my feet like whipt curs and whine their fulsome adu-
> lation! [18]

Suddenly Tempest is rescued by an inheritance of several million pounds from a mysterious relative.  As he learns of this bequest, he is visited by the enigmatic Prince Lucio Rimañez, a wealthy and well-traveled exile who offers to conduct Tempest into society.  Tempest agrees with a handshake, thunder booms, and the lights go out.  In the remainder of the book, Tempest is guided through gambling hells and horse races by the dark prince.  He acquires and marries the noble-born Lady Sibyl, who reveals herself as irrevocably corrupted by reading fashionable novels.  She attempts to seduce Rimañez, who sadistically rejects her as Tempest looks on, and finally dies horribly by her own hand.  The heavy-handed morality play offers no real suspense or surprise of its own, serving mainly as a scaffold for a running commentary on contemporary mores, the corrupting influence of wealth, and the degeneracy of the popular and literary press.

Ostensibly, the book's suspense involves the identification of the mysterious Rimañez, but in fact it is clear from the first pages that Rimañez is Ahrimanes, a Zoroastrian name for Satan.  Nevertheless, Corelli plays out the melodramatic mechanisms of suspense, including the death of one of Satan's victims just as he is about to reveal Rimañez's real nature.  For Corelli, literary gesture overrides context and content.  The novel is really a series of tableaux interspersed with social commentary by the narrator, Tempest, or the principal speaker, Rimañez.  Indeed, tableaux vivants arranged by Rimañez figure heavily in the novel.  A related metaphor for the book's un-novelistic structure would be grand opera:  at crucial points Rimañez bursts into song.  We are constantly submerged in the melodramatic tradition of moral and sentimental tableaux which Joyce parodies in "The Dead" as he shows Gabriel entitling his wife's pose "Distant Music."

But Corelli's didacticism is responsible for a series of technical ironies which, although the result of incompetence, must have intrigued Joyce.  First, Tempest, having been established as a noble artist, one of the "saved," is completely corrupted by his money and then saved again when, at the book's end, he sees the error of his ways.  The narration is retrospective.  Thus Tempest fluctuates between his role as satirical butt and his earlier--and later--roles as Corelli's spokesman.  Further, Rimañez, the diabolic figure, is made immensely attractive--handsome, dark, powerful, a brilliant raconteur, scientist, pianist, and singer.  He is also, Corelli explains, very much a fallen angel, playing out a diabolic role.  Although he must tempt Tempest, he wants Tempest to spurn him because he can return to heaven only when all mankind can turn toward God.  "Pray for me then," Rimañez begs, "as one who has fallen from his higher and better self, —who strives, but who may not attain--who labours under heavy punishment, —who would fain reach Heaven, but who by the cursed will of man, and man alone, is kept in Hell" [339].

Thus Rimañez, no less than Tempest, alternates between devil's advocate and Corelli's advocate, until we have a series of overlapping ironies which recalls the situation of Stephen in Portrait and Ulysses.  For of course Stephen plays out his own diabolic role, from casual blasphemy to his ultimate non serviam, at one minute destroying the universe and crying, "I'll bring you all to heel!", at another cowering at the crack of thunder.  A performer throughout, Stephen disavows even his most complete work of art in the book, his Shakespeare soliloquy in "Scylla and Charybdis," claiming not to believe in his own theory.  As Rimañez observes when questioned about whether he believes what he has just said, "I think I was born to be an actor . . . I speak to suit the humour of the hour, and without meaning a single word I say!" [64].  Passionate and violent, dégagé and sophisticated, he is an amalgam of Heathcliff and Wilde.  Like Stephen, he is the relentless enemy of mat erialism; like Stephen, he suffers the Agenbite of Inwit, or, as he puts it, "A very strange illness . . . Remorse!"; like Stephen, he fears and scorns women.

All women, that is, except the angelic Mavis Clare, a popular author of surpassing spirituality, adored by millions of readers but attacked, out of sheer jealousy, by the critics.  Clare, who like Corelli lives in a cottage with her two cute dogs, surrounded by framed quotations from Shelley and Byron, plays no part in the novel's plot; she is simply there, charming, lovelier than anyone would expect, the confidante of princes and men of real genius, for Rimanez and, eventually, Tempest also to worship.  Everywhere Joyce looked in Corelli, he must have found a distorting mirror.  If Dedalus is a triumph of ambiguous self-portrayal, Mavis Clare is a horrible warning against the novelist's autobiographical impulse.  By the time she wrote The Sorrows of Satan Corelli was already a victim of authorial megalomania, an obsession which Joyce was able to distance into great art.  If Corelli's fascinated identification with Shakespeare led her to move to Stratford-on-Avon and hint mysteriously at literary reincarnation, Joyce's gave way to Stephen's brilliant attempt to prove "by algebra" that Shakespeare was really Joyce.

Corelli and Joyce stand at the start of our century, both convinced from youth of their own genius, both busy writing and acting out the myth of themselves.  Each was bitter against the publishing establishment and sought literary revenge for slights, each was obsessed by betrayal, each was fascinated by the Byronic pose.  Both authors, irresistibly drawn to self-portrayal, were convinced of the ultimate, religious importance of art, and the crucial significance of its cheapening for a mass readership.  All that finally separated them was art itself.(12)

## NOTES

1.   See R. B. Kershner, Jr., "Joyce and Stephen Phillips' Ulysses," James Joyce Quarterly 13, no. 2 (Winter 1976), 194-201.

2.   In Culture and Anarchy, which was published in 1869, but first appeared in Cornhill, July 1867, January, February, June, July, and August 1868.  A second edition was issued in 1875.

3.   Encyclopaedia Britannica, 11th ed., s.v. "Ireland."

4.   Good characterizations of the popular literature of the time can be found in Claude Cockburn, Bestseller:  The Books Everybody Read, 1900-1939 (London:  Sidgwick and Jackson, 1972); Amy Cruse, After the Victorians (London:  Allen and Unwin, 1938); and Margaret Dalziel, Popular Fiction 100 Years Ago (London:  Cohen and West, 1957).

5.   Joyce asks for such material in most of the letters he wrote to Frank Budgen.

6.   See R. A. Copland and C. W. Turner, "The Nature of James Joyce's Parody in Ithaca," Modern Language Review 64, no. 19, 759-63. Although Joyce specifically mentions Mangall's Questions in another context, it is likely that his reference in parody includes an entire genre of juvenile histories, such as A Sketch of Irish History, compiled by way of Question and Answer, for Use of Schools (Cork, 1815).

7.    Eugene Sheehy, quoted in Robert Scholes and Richard M. Kain, The Workshop of Daedalus (Evanston, Ill.:    Northwestern University Press, 1965), 175.

8.    Eileen Bigland, Marie Corelli:    The Woman and the Legend (London:    Jarrolds, 1953), 156.  I am indebted to Bigland for most of the details regarding Corelli's career.

9.    Padraic and Mary Colum, Our Friend James Joyce (Garden City, N.Y.:  Doubleday, 1958), 151.

10. The Sorrows of Satan (New York:    American News Co., 1899), 77. Further references to this work will appear in the text.

11.    Bigland, Marie Corelli, 164.

12.    Marvin Magalaner in "James Joyce and Marie Corelli," in Modern Irish Literature, Raymond J. Porter and James D. Brophy, (New York: Twayne, 1972), 185-93, covers some of the background information and points to the parallels between Stephen and Tempest.

## 7

# "After the Lessions of Experience I Speak from Inspiration": The Sermon in *Finnegans Wake* III, ii

*Cheryl Herr*

The text for this paper is section III, ii of Finnegans Wake.(1) Because it is generally agreed that this section is one of the most linguistically accessible in the Wake, there is no need to rehearse the events of the chapter, but it is worth mentioning that--possibly because of its relative simplicity--this chapter has received little critical discussion. However, the sermon (gotten out in bits) that Shaun-Jaun delivers, the most consistently satiric of the sermons which show up in Joyce's works, is a complex statement of the intersection of Roman Catholic doctrine and economics. Wakean parody and dream-distortion alike do not mask the fact that Jaun's sermon goes beyond mere reflection of twentieth-century Irish popular theology (although it does reflect that theology quite accurately); rather, chapter 14 offers a critique of the usually unspoken messages to which popular theology kept itself reasonably blind. The economic message that Joyce detected in the sermons of his era has been made explicit in the Wake, the sermon form being allowed to speak its own content in Joyce's appropriation of that form for subversive uses. At the very least, Jaun's sermon demonstrates on the level of metaphor the compatibility of his brand of moral absolutism and a system of economic exchange that seeks to encompass all phenomena in its own value system.

Three topics in the Wake sermon that were regularly discussed by popular preachers were: sex and marriage, bad books, and the general corruption of the modern era. Joyce's treatment of these topics in Jaun's sermon is part of the Wake's larger attack on contemporary morality and on the concepts of good and evil themselves.

The chapter opens with Jaun's encountering twenty-nine convent girls, one of whom is his sister Issy. Against her Jaun directs an oration--at times a philippic--about sexual virtue. Jaun advises the girls to obey as many precepts of the Church "as probable" [FW 432.26], and he specifies a few of these rules: "First thou shalt not smile. Twice thou shalt not love. Lust, thou shalt not commix idolatry" [433. 22-23]. A partly clear, partly suppressed message, like all ideological statements, the sermon maintains that to commix and commingle in adultery is equivalent to committing idolatry. (Of course, "commix" also suggests the comic side of any institution's attempt to control human sexuality.) In fact, Jaun avers that to enjoy oneself in idle courtship without the goal of marriage or simply to answer spontaneously to any of the various calls of nature and pleasure is to violate a religious, a universal, law. In more personal terms, the implied emphasis of Jaun's sermon is twofold: as Issy's brother, he wants no one

in bed with her but himself; as priestly father, he wants the girls to
avoid sex until they trade hymens for husbands.  If Stephen Dedalus is
a sexually adept young man in whom the "cursed jesuit strain" is "injected the wrong way" [U 8], then Jaun is a priest in whom the sexuality is injected the wrong way--at least given the norms of his temporary
vocation.

Jaun's clerical viewpoint was shared by preachers contemporary
with Joyce, for whom not only did sex have its dangers, but marriage
itself also was in danger.  The late nineteenth and early twentieth
centuries saw the Church, threatened by the advance of civil divorce in
England and America, mounting a propaganda offensive to bolster belief
in the sanctity of the Christian marriage bond.  Bernard Vaughan, an
advocate of marriage so pious in his declamations that, his country of
origin aside, he was more than once referred to or claimed as an Irish
priest, preached on the subject in his famous Mayfair sermons of 1906,
published as The Sins of Society.  Later, Vaughan's collection What of
To-Day? (1914) discussed divorce and a projected decline in the birthrate in terms of "race suicide."  Vaughan argued against what even Jaun
might have found innocent enough:  "Such aids to marriage as moonlight
strolls (or) . . . dreamy music . . . ought to play no part in a man's
final choice [of a wife]."(2)   And Vaughan's denunciation of modern
laxity in these matters echoes Father Thomas Burke's rather untheologi-
cal argument that the greatest of the sacraments is marriage.  Such
works as the Reverend Charles J. Callan's Illustration for Sermons and
Instructions (1916) and The Vademecum ("by Two Missionaries," 1921),
typical of the sermon handbooks of the era, treat the topic of marriage
in such a standardized fashion as to indicate that in the pulpit devia-
tion from such doctrine was unthinkable.

Having mapped out for Issy and her friends their ideal futures as
wives, Jaun turns to denounce "Secret satieties and onanymous letters"
[435.31].  We recall Stephen Dedalus's anguish over his own "secret
satieties," including the scandalous letters that he left about for
girls to discover, but we think also of the hard line adopted by Pope
Leo XIII against secret societies such as the Freemasons and the Fen-
ians.  The popular theology of the era inevitably reflected Pope Leo's
dictates, especially once they were codified in his 1897 revision of
the Index prohibitorum librorum.

That work concentrated primarily on bad books and harmful periodicals, which the popular mind conceived of as sweeping in waves from
France up to England and over to Ireland to contaminate the minds and
hearts of schoolboys and convent girls.(3)  Jaun's sermon contains several pointed references to this major propaganda issue.  Mentioning
"Autist Algy" Swinburne, Jaun says that the poet had been "stated by
the vice crusaders to be well known to all the dallytaunties in and
near the ciudad of Buellas Arias" [434.36-435.2].  As in most of the
sermon, the language undergoes only minor distortions from ordinary
English in order to emphasize the transparency of the Church's ideological messages.  Just as for Issy there is no masking of the principle
message of the address (which is to control not her morality but her
sexuality), so too for the reader there is no question that Jaun's
transformation of Swinburne into both a lower form of life ("Algy" /
algae) and a victim of exaggerated subjectivity (the artist as "Autist") parodies the Church's popular mistrust of art and artists.  If
the girls were to accept Jaun's jaundiced view of art as autism, as a
production of discourse characterized by an almost masturbatory self-
engrossment and disconnection from the world, they would quite natural-
ly reject the alternate views of reality which art has always provided.
Perhaps the Pre-Raphaelite vision of Swinburne and associates of his
such as D. G. Rossetti and William Morris would be particularly

disquieting to a Church intent on holding onto its always-already lost monopoly on a vision of paradise and right conduct.

And Jaun's charge against Swinburne, of course, is characteristically evasive: he was known to the "dallytaunties" (dilettantes, certainly, but also dalliers—no doubt in sexual activities—and those who would deride and mock Jaun's lessons ("taunt" him). That Swinburne is known to such folks is bad enough, but that they live in "Buellas Arias" suggests a double condemnation. It has been argued that Eveline, in Dubliners, might have faced substantial danger had she gone with Frank to Buenos Aires; there she might easily have been sold into the white slave trade. Further, "bellas arias," though presumably more acceptable to an early twentieth-century Irish audience than, say, music-hall songs, are nonetheless part of the world of art from which Jaun wants to distract his audience.(4) In sum, dalliance, mockery, and a life of sin are some of the possibly soul-damaging results of reading bad books that the "vice crusaders" of Joyce's day fought against. And Jaun specifically asserts in a typically illiberal moment, "I'd burn the books that grieve you" [439.34].

He then proceeds to cite those works of "pious fiction" which, having been "licensed and censered by our most picturesque prelates" [440:8, 11], are acceptable reading, all of them written by what seem to be members of the Wakean Church establishment: Carnival Cullen, S. J. Finn, and the Curer of Wars. Here the text implies that to censor and to cense (offer incense, possibly with the suggestion of consecrating or blessing) are equivalent and related functions. The comic names of the priests are enhanced by calling them "picturesque," no doubt Joyce's allusion to figures like Vaughan or Burke, media priests whose every activity, every word were reported by the press, even down to the clerical dress they wore to deliver important sermons and lectures.

Jaun goes on to advise: "Strike up a nodding acquaintance for our doctrine with the works of old Mrs. Trot, senior, and Manoel Canter, junior, and Loper de Figas, nates maximum. . . . Egg Laid by Former Cock and With Flageolettes in Send Fanciesland. Chiefly Girls." He notes that he "used to follow Mary Liddlelambe's flitsy tales, especially with the scentaminted sauce" [440.15-21]. That these works demand only a "nodding acquaintance" is perhaps indictment enough of their spiritual or intellectual worth, but Jaun's lack of interest even in this material is easily betrayed ("I used to follow"). Typically, he is more interested in food than in doctrine or art; it is the "scentaminted sauce" and lamb that occupy his language, as well as the "sacramental tea" (though possibly the same sort of tea that Mother Grogan is so handy with) that the "saucer-dotes" serve up [440.21,22].

What we cannot help noticing is the comic irony of some of Jaun's choices of supposedly worthwhile books. Mrs. Trot's name alone gives us pause, betraying as it does her status as old crone and suggesting the slang meaning of "trot"—diarrhea. No doubt a good friend of Mrs. Grundy, Mrs. Trot seems to have a verbal disease that places her in the ranks of Hawthorne's sentimental "scribbling women," which Mary Liddlelambe also occupies. This latter name is puzzling because it suggests not only the fable world of Mother Goose and the looking-glass world of Alice Liddell but also the linguistic expertise of Henry George Liddell, the nineteenth-century Greek lexicographer.(5) Perhaps the sophisticated use of language in these worlds of fancy and fantasy is enough to yoke them together here and to explain why they failed to keep Jaun's attention; indeed, he regards them as "flitsy tales." Perhaps the flightiness of these fairy tales is less on Jaun's mind than the slang sense of "flit," homosexual. Certainly, a sexual undercurrent runs through this passage. Even Lope de Vega's name has become "de Figas," obviously suggesting the obscene gesture of making a fig;

it is an appropriate transformation of name considering his appended
title of "nates maximum" or "biggest buttocks."(6)

Similarly, Egg Laid by Former Cock sounds like a fairy-tale version of a yellow-press headline, the story of a transsexual who performs badly (lays an egg)(7) or who discovers in himself procreative
powers beyond the normal.  With Flageolettes in Send Fanciesland, the
title of a story supposedly designed for schoolgirls, implies that
every work of literature—even a fairy tale—carries sexual content.
"Send Fanciesland" is, no doubt, Assisi (St. Francis's land), but it is
also the place of fancy, the world of the fairy tale.  In the word
flageolettes, self-scourgers (flagellants) blend uneasily with the
French flageolet (wind instrument, species of bean) and the French
flageoler (to tremble, shake).  The world of Catholic charity associated with St. Francis is here mingled with the darker side of Catholic
sainthood, its trembling mortification of the flesh.  Given the "Sirens" episode, where Bloom's "little wee" "piped eeee" [U 288], a reader
may be tempted to see the wind instrument allusion as scatological,
while the bean reference reinforces the several allusions in this passage to legumes:  Lentil Lore [440.9] and Pease in Plenty [440.10], two
books recommended by Jaun on the basis of their being authored by religious figures, and "Their Graces of Linzen and Petitbois" [440.11, 12],
the "picturesque prelates" mentioned above.

As many readers have noticed, in Finnegans Wake we can often assume a surrogate relationship between sexuality and eating.(8)  Both
food and sex, like sermons, are destined for consumption.  And on the
most innocent level, beans, tea, lamb, mint sauce, and figs all provide
more evidence that Jaun's mind is not totally occupied with religious
"instructual primers" [440.23].  To cap off the general absurdity of
Jaun's recommendations, we can note that "Trot," "Canter," and "Loper"
show Joyce's fondness for conventional verbal patterns.  Obviously an
important part of the rhythm and delight of his prose comes from the
trot, canter, and lope of such sequences, but these devices also contribute significantly to the comedy of the sermon, to undermining any
pretense to logical soundness in Jaun's counsel.

To return to the Dublin of Joyce's day, we might note that during
that period the indictment of bad books—often almost as badly argued
as Jaun's—turned up constantly in sermons and Catholic periodicals.
One example will suffice to give us the flavor of such writings:  Canon
P. A. Sheehan, himself a famous and much-translated novelist, published
a sermon in which he claimed that "corrupt literature" "is the most
powerful enemy of God, and the most powerful ally of His enemy."  He
adds, "You may pass from end to end of France, and you will not find a
single book in a single bookstall that you can touch without fear of
committing a mortal sin."(9)

Such denunciations of bad books and of flirting and courtship
coalesced in popular theology into the pulpit's oft-repeated denunciation of the Modern Age.  In this period, it was argued, yielding to one
of the era's typical pleasures inevitably led to indulgence in others.
Hence, again in his sermon on bad books, Canon Sheehan observes that
"novel-reading" can be compared to opium-eating, since readers become
unfit "for the real practical business of life" and inclined to sin:
"They fancy, feed upon their fancies, live by fancy and the consequence
is they become dissatisfied with their condition in life, they perform
their duties mechanically, they acquire a love of dress and
finery."(10)

An implicit wholesale denunciation of the age is a topos so common
at the end of the nineteenth century that Father Thomas Burke began a
lecture in Cork on "The Catholic Church and the Age We Live In" with
these words:

> There may, perhaps, be some amongst you who imagine from
> the title of this lecture that I am come here to praise
> the Catholic Church and to denounce the age we live in.
> I am going to do one and not to do the other. One of
> the common errors of our day is that a Catholic priest,
> as such, must make it his especial business to denounce
> this age of ours. I myself received a curious illustra-
> tion of this when I asked a poor man in the west of Ire-
> land some time ago what he thought was the proper busi-
> ness of a Catholic priest. He scratched his head,
> thought for a few moments, and then: "I suppose, your
> reverence," said he, "the proper business of a Catholic
> priest is to tell us all we are going to the devil."(11)

While Burke went on to praise the late nineteenth century as an era of
accomplishment, he found the "moral spirit of the age" in disarray.(12)
Jaun's sermon makes clear his reflection of this assessment: "O," he
says, "the frecklessness of the giddies nouveautays!" [435.11-12].
"Frecklessness" incorporates "recklessness," "fecklessness," and perhaps "fickleness" (with the Middle English meaning of false or treacherous?)--all of which Jaun denounces along with the giddiness of the
kiddies in a "nowadays" that is composed of novelty and change, dictionary descriptions of the French word nouveauté.
    To this indictment, Jaun adds a comment on modern sex and society:
"All blah! Viper's vapid vilest!" [435.16]. At the center of satanic
viper and moral vileness we have not absolute evil but only vapidity;
as always, such flatness characterized much of the popular culture, including the religious popular culture, of the era. Hence it is important that Jaun locates his sermon in the liturgical calendar as taking
place "Several sindays after whatsintime" [432.33]. Not long after
Whitsuntide (or Pentecost) and therefore outside of any festal period
in the Church,(13) Jaun's oration refers only to a lethargic "lithurgy"
[432.32] befitting his sense of an age both _in_ time and in _sintime_
("whatsintime"). Later mentioning the "slack march of civilisation"
[438.25], Jaun worries over the effect, especially on Issy, of what the
frame narrator for chapter 14 calls, using an obvious political pun,
the oncoming "devil era" [473.8]--with its bad books, empty flirta-
tions, too-willing seductions, and general carryings-on.
    Yet no one would argue, despite the correlation of Jaun's sermon
topics and those typical of the time, that _Finnegans Wake_ in any way
supports the Church's assessment of modern society and its mores. Nor,
as is often assumed by readers, is Joyce simply criticizing Church doctrine as out of touch with the needs of contemporary Dubliners.
Rather, the satire, punning, irony, and wordplay of this sermon-parody
suggests that what we tend to see as moral absolutes are not only culturally but also economically conditioned. Hence, it is not enough for
us to note that Jaun's ideas derive from popular theology. We need also to recognize that the _Wake_ posits a compatibility of theological
doctrine and the capitalist frame of mind.
    There are explanations for this congruence of religious and eco-
nomic design. The Church's attempt to repress premarital, nonprocrea-
tive sex (an attempt that is the focus of Joyce's parody in the _Wake_
sermon) by upholding the institution of marriage instigated the kind of
procreative sexuality which would lead more or less inevitably--and
within, ideally, a stable and productive home environment--to the birth
of many more children than would be true in casual, nonmarital relationships. The effect of this population growth would be of strategic
benefit to the Church, by maintaining and extending the Church's social

hegemony. But to accomplish this growth in power, the Church had to support the social status quo. The sermons in Joyce's day that denounced the modern era did so largely because the changes threatened the Church's place in its society as well as the foundations of that society itself. While trying to be separate from the world, the Church actually fought for active control of secular culture. This competition for mastery is obliquely targeted in Jaun's sermon, which is far from otherworldly in its local and large-scale intentions. In fact, the Wake sermon tends to demystify the Church's assumption of authority and possession of absolute truth by emphasizing the presence of economic interests within its religious dictates.

Of course, the Catholic Church of the era actively forestalled criticism to this effect by announcing that the social order and the family unit were direct reflections of divine law. Burke, in his address "The Church and Civil Government," states unequivocally, "Civil government is the ordinance of Almighty God, coming as the reflection of His glorious and greatest authority."(14)    More specifically, Stanley B. James, writing in the 1930 Irish Ecclesiastical Record--one of the major organs of Catholic opinion in Ireland at the turn of the century--argues that the Church works actively against the "essentially bourgeois," standard culture present in the United States, a culture termed "tyrannical" in its assumption that its values are as authoritative and "universal as that of Christian morality."(15)    James cites the popular argument that the various Protestant "sects" grew during the Reformation in response to and as a support for class mobility, yet he maintains that the Church "stands above all classes."(16)    Citing Pope Leo XIII's Encyclical on the Condition of the Working Class, which insists that class division is natural, James says that the church resists threats to this natural order as it does to the family itself. Popular preaching of the time agreed that preserving both aspects of society conforms to divine law. It is not hard to see either the defensive posture of the Church in such assertions or the way that the Wake undermines any notion that modern European family life and social organization are anything but mundane, conventional, and pragmatic.

That the Church encouraged marriage--and thereby a higher birthrate--in Ireland, where late marriages and a declining birthrate were the norm, may be attributed, without disrespect, to its assessment of social needs as much as to its spiritual mission. This compatibility of theological doctrine and economic orientation is suggested repeatedly throughout Jaun's discourse. In fact, the sermon presents all relationships in terms of economic exchange. When Jaun cautions the girls, "Collide with man, collude with money" [433.32-33], his statement may seem ironic or even bitter, yet such a tonal imposition is out of place in his sermon, which straightforwardly argues that Issy and her friends should have the ring in hand before they hand over their own precious jewels: "Never lose your heart away till you win his diamond back" [433.14-15]. Further, Jaun advises, "Ere you sail foreget my prize" [433.33], with the emphasis on fore-getting (getting beforehand) as well as on simply not remembering that the basis of the marital agreement is an economic arrangement.

Such cynical "look before you leak" [433.34] attitudes are enjoined by Jaun as a supplement to the moral system which, according to Church propaganda and public opinion, normally determines religious counsel. For Jaun, even the trinity of essential virtues is associated with an economic matrix: "Keep cool faith in the firm, have warm hoep(17) in the house and begin from athome to be chary of charity" [434.2-3]. No longer does faith have anything to do with man's relationship to the deity; faith is placed in the corporate "firm." Displacing God, Jaun loses authority for his statements except insofar as he relies on the system of economic exchange to ground and guarantee the soundness of his advice. And the notion that charity begins at home undergoes significant revision: "begin from athome to be chary of charity." The suggestion of the German fremd (foreign, unknown) counters the conventional association of home and divinely ordained familial bliss; being "athome" thus seems to be a less congenial state than being "at home." Joyce's arguments cuts doubly—against the Church's doctrine of the family's spiritual sanctity, a doctrine tending to conceal its economic origin, and against the likelihood of any family's conforming to the roles prescribed by religious theory (any family in Finnegans Wake at least).

Jaun's "brokerly advice" [439.27] continues unabated throughout the sermon. If the girls forget themselves, he says, they will "pay for each bally sorraday night every billing sumday morning" [436.26-27],(18) a statement which connects their sorrow not to spiritual contrition but to the pain of having to pay a debt. This replacement of divine retribution with a kind of one-for-one accounting system is not unique in Joyce's works. When in "Grace" Father Purdon relies on an accounting metaphor to "explain" and thereby substitute for the concept of theological grace, and when in Portrait Stephen Dedalus sees his acts of virtue as going directly into a divine cash register to keep his account well in the black, both situations reflect Joyce's larger assessment of the Church as an economic institution.

Joyce's presentation of the Church's capitalist-inspired attitudes obviously works to undermine that institution's spiritual authority as codifier of modern morality. Because Jaun delivers his opinions as moral dictates, they are subject to the Wake's general subversion of an absolutist moral system, especially in the novel's recasting of the Garden of Eden myth. Speaking of the sacredness of virginity, Jaun comments: "A coil of cord, a colleen coy, a blush on a bush turned first man's laughter into wailful moither. O foolish cuppled! Ah, dice's error!" [433.28-30]. Joyce's handling of the Adam and Eve exemplum suggests that our moral system is not so much a result of disobedience (error is not "willful" but only "wailful") as it is a result of misfortune, sheer chance; Dies Irae, or day of judgment, becomes "dice's error."(19) The coil (presumably a stand-in for the snake), the colleen, and the blushing fruit simply coincide. Certainly sex is at fault here: "felix culpa" is now "foolish cuppled." But egotism is equally to blame; we have not murder but moither. Finally, the pressure of a kind of conventional inevitability also shares responsibility for man's sin. In the Wake, Satan is not only tempter but also a theatrical "prompter" [435.20](20) for what must be taken as an already scripted fall. Instead of an immortal tragedy, Adam and Eve can be said to have enacted a melodrama in which an absolute system of good and evil is not so much proven as assumed.

And such a comparison is appropriate in this case, for Jaun tells Issy as he begins his sermon that he is only retelling to her the "gross proceeds" of her own teachings, which seem to have been heavily informed by melodramatic literature. That is, Jaun describes the way that Issy, when they were children, used to tell the two brothers, Shem and Shaun, bedtime stories, which he calls her "oldworld tales of homespinning and derringdo and dieobscure and daddyho" [431.31-32]. The provisional truths that Issy has shared with her brothers are no more than the moral imperatives of popular culture. She speaks to them of the family ("homespinning"), of the father ("daddyho"), of good and brave deeds ("derringdo"), and of the proletariat's fate ("dieobscure"). As sister-mother, Issy narrates the tales that popularly propagate the Western world's version of right conduct. And Jaun decides to recapitulate these tales in his own form, telling Issy, in his authoritative role of priest, what she already knows.  The priestly Jaun's taking possession of these folk stories suggests a patriarchal appropriation of cultural topoi as Truth, topoi which developed as much in response to economic conditions as to putatively higher ones.

The Wake's demystification of religious doctrine is supported by the fact that Jaun has no more elevated sources of information than Issy for the moral message he delivers.  His only other source of information is the disgruntled parish priest, Father Mike, who is preoccupied with money matters and whose advice he claims to pass on to the twenty-nine girls.  Armed with Issy's stories and "mikeadvice" [432: 18], Jaun nonetheless asserts that his ideas are "from above" [432:19]. Yet he slips to let us know that his particular "inspiration" has grown out of what he calls the "lessions of experience" [436.20-21].

In sum, the Wake targets the source of popular religious doctrine—not revelation but economic utility and the resulting cultural conventions.  Of course, the preachers of Joyce's day were disconcerted by these phenomena Jaun denounces—loose behavior, bad books, the change in tenor of the age—as threats to what they saw as the divinely established social order and the moral system which supported it, but Jaun's send-up of a sermon would have us agree that the denunciatory posture of the Church as institution had a lot more to do with maintaining its social hegemony than with anything approximating inspiration.  The "lessions of experience" on which Jaun bases his message to the rainbow girls are thus not only lessons but also lesions, pathological points in the cultural surface which reveal the perhaps not diseased but certainly diseased intertwining of dogma and economics, of spirituality and the social order.

## NOTES

1.    Much of the research for this paper (which is part of a book entitled Joyce's Anatomy of Culture (Urbana:   University of Illinois Press, 1986) was completed in Dublin under the auspices of an American Philosophical Society (APS) grant; I am indebted to the APS for its generous support of my work.

2.    Father Bernard Vaughan, S. J., What of To-Day? (London:   Cassell, 1914), 238.

3.    For instance, the editor of the Catholic Bulletin, in writing about a new monthly magazine published by the Christian Brothers and entitled Our Boys, mentions "the torrent of impure cross-channel literature daily pouring in upon" Irish youth.  Catholic Bulletin (Dublin), 4 (1914), 663.

4.    It might also be argued that the phrase bellas arias refers to the beauty of the so-called higher and purer arts which Juan is simply too dense to appreciate.  Along this line, note also that dilettante means not only a dabbler, but also, though rarely, a connoisseur, which one might argue Swinburne might have been but Jaun is not.

5.    Brendan O Hehir and John M. Dillon, A Classical Lexican for Finnegans Wake (Berkeley and Los Angeles:   University of California Press, 1977), 384, 610-11.

6.    Roland McHugh, Annotations to "Finnegans Wake" (Baltimore: Johns Hopkins University Press, 1980), 440.

7.    The Dictionary of American Slang, 2d ed., ed. Harold Wentworth and Stuart Berg Flexner (New York:  Crowell, 1975) cites this term as in popular use in the 1920s, especially in reference to failure in a stage performance.

8.    For example, see Fritz Senn, "Every Klitty of a scolderymeid: Sexual-Political Analogies," in A Wake Digest, ed. Clive Hart and Fritz Senn (Sydney:  Sydney University Press for Australian Humanities Research Council, 1968), 30.  Senn discusses the "replacement of sex by food" in FW 239.16-22 and in relation to Freud's Interpretation of Dreams.

9.    Canon P. A. Sheehan, "Bad Books," in Sermons, ed. M. J. Phelan, S. J. (Dublin:  Maunsel, 1920), 267, 268.

10.    Ibid., 273.

11.    Thomas Nicolas Burke, Lectures on Faith and Fatherland (Glasgow:  Washbourne, [191-]), 234.

12.    Ibid., 246.

13.    The New Catholic Encyclopedia, (v.11, 1967, p. 110) states, "The two great liturgical cycles of Easter, from Septuagesima to Pentecost, and of Christmas, from Advent to Epiphany, have developed into a continuity of from 6 to 7 months, leaving from 5 to 6 months with no special festal character."

14.    Burke, Lectures, 224.

15.    Stanley B. James, "The Church and the Class War," Irish Ecclesiastical Record, 5th ser., 36 (August 1930):  167.

16.    Ibid., 170.

17.    Not only is "hope" scrambled here into "hoep," suggesting at the very least a distortion or confusion of that virtue in Jaun's world, but the Dutch hoep (barrel hoop or petticoat hoop) calls to mind the replacement of hope with liquor (often kept in barrels) or with sex (to be found inside petticoats).

18.    Compare FW 5.10-12:  "Comeday morm and, O, you're vine! Sendday's eve and, ah, you're vinegar!  Hahahaha, Mister Funn, you're going to be fined again!  Fun always leads to fines on the Church's day of reckoning"—"sumday" / "Sendday".

19.    McHugh, Annotations, 433.

20.    See FW 435.19-20, "Stick  icks in your earshells when you hear the prompter's voice."

# 8

# The Sow That Eats Her Farrow: Gender and Politics

## Jeanne A. Flood

In a famous passage of A Portrait of the Artist as a Young Man, the child Stephen Dedalus, sick and lonely, while trying to study his geography lesson locates himself safely inside a widening series of social structures: "Stephen Dedalus, Class of Elements, Clongowes Wood College, Sallins, County Kildare, Ireland, Europe, The World, The Universe" [P 15]. He is troubled when he thinks of what lies beyond the outermost edge of the ultimate structure: "What was after the universe? Nothing. But was there anything round the universe to show where it stopped and the nothing place began? It could not be a wall but there could be a thin thin line there all round everything" [P 16]. Stephen's thoughts lead him into mystery and bafflement; he thinks first of God and then of politics. "It pained him that he did not know well what politics meant and that he did not know where the universe ended" [P 17].

The linking here of a concern with boundaries and boundlessness to religion and to politics is an example of a central configuration of these elements in Joyce's mind. In this same section of Portrait one more element in the configuration appears, that of deep hatred between the sexes. Young Stephen has noted that there are two sides in politics: "Dante was on one side and his father and Mr. Casey were on the other side" [P 16]. The mutual loathing of Dante and her male adversaries is to frighten Stephen in a few months as he listens to the two sides that are politics assault each other in spitting rage. The argument ends as Dante, faithful to the Church and the clergy, revels triumphantly in the death of Parnell: "'We won! We crushed him to death!'" [P 39]. Stephen sees the men in tears and is, the narrator tells us, terror-stricken.

The pious and nationalistic, Irish woman, exulting in the death of a male, is an important figure to Joyce. Dante is only one of her embodiments. In the brutal formulation of Stephen Dedalus, she is Ireland, the sow that eats her farrow. She is the mother who claims as her right the sacrificial death of her son. This terrible woman haunts the consciousness of Stephen Dedalus in Ulysses as the pitiable ghost of his mother who wants from him a submission which he defines as death. In her comic form she is Old Gummy Granny, who wants Stephen to kill a British soldier and suffer his own execution. "'Remove him, acushla. At 8:35 a.m. you will be in heaven and Ireland will be free'" [U 600]. As I will later suggest, this murderous woman is also an aspect of the most appealing of Joyce heroines, Gretta Conroy of "The Dead."

    This woman, though Joyce's obsession, is not his creation.  She is
Yeats's Kathleen ni Houlihan, who lures young Michael Gillane away from
his wedding to his death in the Rising of 1798.  She is Synge's Maurya,
who accepts with marvellous equanimity the death of every male connected with her.  She is everywhere in the plays, poems, and stories of
Pádraic Pearse.  In a notable moment in his play "The Singer" she
blesses her son, who is about to lead fifteen unarmed men against an
army of four thousand, and with joy advises the female relations of the
fifteen to weave winding sheets, "for there will be many a noble corpse
to be waked before the new moon!"(1)
    This woman has more than a literary existence.  She appears in
historical reality at a moment of crisis in Irish life, a crisis centered on the question of boundaries, specifically the boundary between
Ireland and England.  Since the Act of Union (1801), the repeated as-
sertion of national autonomy by Ireland was repressed by England on the
insistence that no boundary existed between Ireland and England, Ireland being simply a part of Great Britain.  In essence the Irish nationalist tradition in both its revolutionary and parliamentary forms
has always insisted that there is a boundary.  In the summer of 1921,
however, the existence of a boundary between Ireland and England became
a negotiable issue.  England reached this decision after almost two
years of guerrilla fighting between the army of the illegal Irish government and the combined constabulary and military forces of Great
Britain.  A truce went into effect on July 11, 1921.  Negotiations for
a treaty began on October 11, and one was signed in London on December
4.  By the terms of the Treaty, Ireland was to have Dominion status
within the Empire.  The relation of Ireland, to be called the Irish
Free State, and Great Britain was to be based on the Canadian model.  A
Governor-General, appointed by the Crown and approved by the Irish Government, was therefore to serve as a figurehead of Crown authority in
Ireland.  As in Canada, the members of the Irish Parliament were to
take an oath of allegiance.  While Canadians took this oath to the
King, however, the Irish were to take it primarily to the Free State
Constitution and secondarily to the King.  The Treaty also provided for
what was envisaged as a temporary partition of Ireland, since it allowed Northern Ireland to refuse to accept the jurisdiction of the Free
State.(2)
    Although the Treaty was received enthusiastically by the majority
of the Irish people, it was opposed from the start by a vigorous minority of doctrinaire Republicans.  The main focus of their attack was
the oath; however, they were also opposed to partition.  After the
Treaty was signed, the Irish delegation headed by Arthur Griffith and
Michael Collins presented it for ratification to Dáil Éireann.  The
motion to accept it was made by Arthur Griffith at a meeting of the
Dáil on December 19.  The Treaty was accepted by a vote of 64 to 57 on
January 7, 1922.  In the interim, through eight long public sessions,
the Dáil debated it.  This debate, in which pro-Treaty speaker was fol-
lowed by anti-Treaty speaker in a seemingly endless succession, was
remarkable for its bitterness.  Profound antagonisms between people who
had long worked together were revealed in venomous personal attacks.
Former comrades accused each other of corruption, treason, betrayal.
At the end of the debate, although the Treaty was ratified, the tragic
division between those who voted for it and those who voted against it
was not healed.  Within five months, the battle in Dáil Éireann became
a Civil War.
    The need for members of the Dáil to articulate a position on the
Treaty, as one of them remarked, was overwhelming.(3)  The record of
what they said in the debates encapsulates a central moment in Irish
national life.  A large number of Irish men and women, elected as re-

presentatives of the people and actively engaged in Irish political and social life, expressed passionately held and violently opposed ideas at a time that was recognized by all as critical. For the pro-Treaty forces, the association with England established by the Treaty was acceptable because, in exchange for it, the British presence would disappear from most of Ireland. Further, they thought that an Ireland with control over its own educational system, its own economy, and its own army would quickly be in a position to achieve complete independence. For the anti-Treaty forces, compromise was impossible. They saw the Treaty as the final betrayal of the separatist ideal of a free and united Irish nation, and insisted that "the absolutely rigid line of the isolated Irish Republic" [31] was to be defended, even though its defense demanded the extermination of the last Irishman.

These debates are particularly interesting for the way in which their central issue, whether Ireland could be associated with England or had to be completely autonomous, attracted to itself themes that can be found repeatedly in the work of Irish writers, specifically in the work of Joyce, and more specifically in "The Dead." Two themes reappear: the first can be called the reproach of the dead men, the second, the reproach of the bereaved women.

The dead who died for Ireland were constant presences in the debate. On its second day, Count Plunkett, whose son Joseph had been executed after the Rising of 1916, rose to speak against the Treaty. "I am faithful to the dead," he announced. "I am faithful to my own boys, one of whom died for Ireland with his back to the wall and the other two who were sentenced to death" [29]. Plunkett's speech shows the two ways in which the heroic dead were to be used by the anti-Treaty forces throughout the debate. First, his own refusal to accept less than full independence for Ireland constituted fidelity to the dead, just as acceptance of the Treaty would constitute their betrayal. Second, the dead men, though they seemed to have failed since they did not win their battle and since they were dead, did not in fact fail, but most gloriously triumphed: "The men of 1916 went out and fought the whole power of the British Empire. Did they lose? They went down, but they went down as victors" [29]. The patriotic dead win victories by dying. Their deaths are not failure but success. It was not simply the men who had died in the recent past, however, who were presented as being betrayed by the signing of the Treaty, but all the men who had ever died in the cause of Ireland. Sean Ectingham, an ardent opponent of the Treaty, remarked: "I say here that the men who fought and had the Fenian tradition, the men who are in their graves, it is unfair to their memory, a defamation of their memory, ever to say that they died for Colonial Home Rule, that they died to have us march with our heads up into the British Empire" [54].

Though generations of dead men from the revolutionary separatist past were presented as being opposed to the Treaty, the opinions of the executed heroes of 1916 on the Treaty written five years after their deaths were confidently presented by their friends or their relatives in the debate. All, it was asserted, would have belonged to the anti-Treaty party. On the pro-Treaty side, however, a sort of living dead man, a man condemned but not executed, had seconded Griffith's motion to accept the Treaty. Sean MacKeon was an elected representative to Dáil Éireann and a commandant in the Irish Republican Army (IRA) as well. MacKeon had led an ambush against British forces in County Longford in November of 1920. In January of 1921, he killed a police officer leading a party attempting to arrest him. A month later he was captured and badly wounded. When he recovered sufficiently, he was tried and condemned to execution. During the truce in the summer of 1921, the British released all imprisoned members of Dáil Éireann with

the exception of MacKeon.  When the Irish threatened to terminate the
truce and to cease to consider the proposals for peace negotiations if
MacKeon were not set free, he was released.(4)   Sean O'Ceallaigh pointed out that MacKeon's status as a condemned man speaking in favor of
the Treaty in that assembly made necessary the incessant attention paid
by the anti-Treaty forces to the heroic dead:  "I am far from desiring
to 'indecently rattle the bones of the dead,' but I say here now that
the rattling of the bones of the dead was rendered inevitable by those
who put Commandant MacKeon in the false position of seconding this motion" [134].
     The formidable Mary MacSwiney, sister of the Terence MacSwiney who
had died on hunger strike in Brixton Prison during the guerrilla war,
informed MacKeon and the assembly that it would have been more honor-
able for him if the sentence had been carried out:   "Commandant Sean
MacKeon seconded that abominable document, I am sorry to say.  I know
that he would fight to the death for the Republic of Ireland still, but
he does not realise what he is giving away.  I am glad that he is here
alive today to fight for the Republic again, but if he were my brother,
I would rather he were with Kevin Barry" [122].   There are two interesting things about this remark.  First, MacKeon is simultaneously presented as a living man dishonored by his support of the Treaty and as a
potential dead man—he will die for the Republic yet.   Second, Mary
MacSwiney mourns MacKeon's indecent survival by juxtaposing him with
both the executed Dublin student Kevin Barry and her own self-starved
brother.
     Sean O'Ceallaigh followed his attack on MacKeon by insisting that
acceptance of the Treaty with its oath of fidelity to an alien King was
"an outrage on the memory of our martyred comrades . . . and an open
insult to the heroic relatives they have left behind" [134].   For
O'Ceallaigh the significant dead man was Terence MacSwiney.  O'Ceallaigh would rather, he said, cut off his hand and tongue than swear the
Treaty oath:

            Am I so soon to forget the outstanding martyr of the hu-
            man race, who, to restore us our freedom, suffered his
            young life to ebb away gasp by gasp, for twenty, thirty,
            forty, fifty, sixty, seventy, aye, seventy-four weary,
            dreary days of unending agony—to the eternal disgrace
            of England and the undying honour of the race he has ex-
            alted for ever- and whose last articulate gasp was a re-
            quest that he be buried in the uniform of a soldier of
            the Irish Republic? [135].

To MacSwiney, O'Ceallaigh appropriates the powerful trappings of martyr
and saviour.   The pure passivity of MacSwiney's death is notable.
O'Ceallaigh remarks it when he states that MacSwiney died of breathing.
England killed him not by any direct action, but simply by insisting
that it had legal and political authority over him because he was a
British subject.
     For the anti-Treaty forces, MacKeon was disgraced, because in ex-
pressing support for the Treaty he was perceived as preferring his own
life to Republican principle.  In so doing, he failed in his obligation
to the dead, which was to become a dead man.  Not only MacKeon but all
the men, especially the young men, who supported the Treaty were accused of this betrayal.  The most vicious attacks were aimed at Michael
Collins, who at the time of these debates was thirty-one years old.  He
was a major and romantic figure in the guerrilla war, not only as the
Finance Minister of the Dáil, but also as a military strategist and as
the Director of Intelligence for the IRA.   In this latter capacity,

Collins penetrated and destroyed the intelligence system operating through Dublin Castle, a thing no other Irish revolutionary had ever done. Collins was young, handsome, courageous. His impeccable Republican credentials made the Treaty he helped to negotiate acceptable to many. But to the anti-Treaty party, Collins had lost those credentials by negotiating and then supporting the Treaty. Like MacKeon, he had chosen life for himself over faith to the principle of Irish autonomy for which the dead had died.

The voting figures show that while the majority of the men in the Dáil supported the Treaty, many others opposed it. All six of the women delegates, however, were united in their opposition. Four of these women were in the Dáil because of their relationship to dead men: Mrs. O'Callaghan of Cork, the widow of a Republican who had been murdered in March of 1921 by the Black and Tans; Mrs. Clarke, the widow of the 1916 leader Tom Clarke; Mrs. Pearse, the mother of the leader of the Rising, Pádraic Pearse, and his brother Willy, both of whom were executed; and Mary MacSwiney, the sister of Terence. Each derived her authority to oppose the Treaty not simply from husband, son, or brother, but from her own suffering at the time of the deaths. As Mrs. O'Callaghan asserted quite directly, "lest anybody should afterwards question my right to stand here and criticise and condemn this Treaty, I want it to be understood here and now that I have the clearest right in the world. I paid a big price for that Treaty and for my right to stand here." [59] Mrs. Pearse, too, insisted that "no matter what anyone says, I feel that I and others here have a right to speak in the name of their dead" [223]. Mary MacSwiney held that she could speak, as she in fact did for two hours and forty minutes, because of her experience of her brother's death: "I consider the fact that what I went through for seventy-four days at Brixton gives me a right to speak for the honour of my nation now" [166].

Having won the right to speak by suffering the pains of bereavement, these women insisted that they and indeed all Irish women could claim the deaths of young Irish men in the service of the Republican ideal. "What has been the agony and the sorrow for?" cried Mrs. O'Callaghan.

> Why was my husband murdered? Why am I a widow? Was it that I should come here and give my vote for a Treaty that puts Ireland within the British Empire? . . . I do feel bitter now that the thing [my husband] and I cared about and worked for, the thing I lost my happiness for, should be voted away by young men, the young soldiers in whom we had such hope. [60]

Mrs. Clarke, after telling of her visit to her husband just before his execution, expressed her belief that the young men who had fought with him in the Republican cause would come back to it, and in turn face their own deaths:

> And though sorrow was in my heart, I gloried in him, and I have gloried in the men who have carried on the fight since; every one of them. I believe that even if they take a wrong turn now they will be brave enough to turn back when they discover it. I have sorrow in my heart now, but I don't despair, I never shall. I still believe in them. [141]

Mrs. Pearse asserted, by virtue of her sorrow, that the women of Ireland were against the Treaty, and by implication in favor of the continued killing of the men:   "I know the hearts and sorrows of the wives of Ireland.  I have studied them; no one studied them more, and let no one here say that these women from their hearts could say they accept that Treaty" [222].

Though Mrs. Pearse had seniority in affliction, it was Mary Mac-Swiney who was the most notable and vociferous advocate for the right of the bereaved women to the lives of the men, not only in her major speech, but in her many interventions and interruptions.  She attacked by name and to their faces three of the most distinguished men in the assembly, Arthur Griffith, Michael Collins, and Eoin MacNeill, for treachery and for cowardice.  She was mesmerized by a vision of the extermination of an Ireland intransigently faithful to the ideal of the Republic:

> (England) has the military.  I know that, but she cannot
> win this battle, for if she exterminates the men, the
> women will take their places, and, if she exterminates
> the women, the children are rising fast; and if she ex-
> terminates the men, women, and children of this genera-
> tion, the blades of grass, dyed with their blood, will
> rise, like the dragon's teeth of old, into armed men and
> the fight will begin in the next generation. [118]

MacSwiney saw in Ireland's hopeless military position if the war with England were to resume the proof of Ireland's moral superiority:

> This fight of ours has been essentially a spiritual
> fight; it has been a fight of right against wrong, a
> fight of a small people struggling for a spiritual ideal
> against a mighty rapacious and material Empire. . . .
> It is those who stand for the spiritual and the ideal
> that stand true and unflinching, and it is those who
> will win--not those who can inflict the most but those
> who can endure the most will conquer. [118]

Maddened by the prospect of the men turning to what she saw as a poli-tics of compromise, she insisted that the women and children of Ireland would choose national annihilation rather than national surrender of the Republican ideal:  "[The Republic] is not dead while there is a wo-man or child in Ireland.  It is not dead if every man in Ireland turned his back on it" [125].  She envisaged and accepted war to extermina-tion:

> You have told us it is between acceptance of that docu-
> ment and war.  If it were, with every sense of deep
> responsibility, I say then let us take war.  I am not
> speaking as a young ardent enthusiast.  I am speaking as
> a woman who has thought and studied much, who realises,
> as only a woman can, the evils of war and the sufferings
> of war. . . . Ireland must choose extermination before
> dishonour. [118-19]

What is most interesting in Mary MacSwiney's position is that it con-dones extreme violence while using the rhetoric of passive resistance and heroically accepted suffering.  The victims of that violence who are most present to her imagination are Irish men, who at the will of the women of Ireland will march to certain destruction in the pursuit of an ideal of righteous Republicanism, that is, of total separation from England.

It is a truism of the criticism of Joyce's "The Dead" to note in the story the mortality of the living and the vitality of the dead. The connection between the political material just considered and Joyce's story centers on that point. The Irish past as Joyce presents it is not the Irish past as it was presented in the Treaty debates. In "The Dead," the past is the time in which those who are not living now once lived and died: Gabriel's mother, the forgotten tenor Parkinson, the Morkan grandfather, and Michael Furey. The past in the story is the past of personal memory, of the private experience of loss, change, bereavement. In the Treaty debates, the past is a communal memory of political events. For Mary MacSwiney, it is "seven centuries of torture and brief intervals of repose" [125]. Even Michael Collins, who wanted to demystify and to escape it, also defined the past in historical and political terms: "I am the representative of an Irish stock; I am the representative equally with any other member of the same stock of people who have suffered through the terror of the past. Our grandfathers have suffered from war, and our fathers or some of our ancestors have died of famine" [35].

The grandfather in "The Dead" did not die for his political beliefs or from famine. Nevertheless, his life is presented in a social and political framework that suggests the historic repression of the Irish in Ireland. His starch mill or glue boiler was powered by his one horse, the horse he drove out to watch a military display with the quality, that is, a display of British power within Ireland. The Morkan horse circled the statue of the ultimate conqueror of Ireland, William III, King Billy. The Irish grandfather in "The Dead" died as a pitiably pretentious citizen in an oppressed country; the Irish grandfathers in the debates died as political martyrs or as victims of political decisions, such as that which permitted the great famine. But both kinds of grandfather lived and died in humiliation and failure conditioned by the historical position of Ireland in relation to England.

Both the Treaty debates and "The Dead" suggest the cost of those deaths. The offspring of the Irish dead are obliged, if they are men, to die also. The one reparation they can make to the living and bereaved women is to die. In the Treaty debates, none of the women suggested that the men who would die if hostilities with England were resumed would win Republican status for Ireland, because no one believed that they had the remotest chance. But the women insisted that the young men owed the dead the gesture of their own extinction.

In the story, as Lily remarks, "'the men that is now'" [D 178] are inferior to the men that once were. The dead tenors are greater than the living ones, the dead Michael Furey is loved more deeply than the living Gabriel Conroy. Because of Michael Furey's death, because of Gretta's bereavement, Gabriel must begin to die at the end of the story. Though Michael Furey died neither in insurrection nor in famine, his death is placed in the context of separatist politics by the conversation between Gabriel and Miss Ivors. Miss Ivors is interested in the West of Ireland because she is an Irish nationalist; she wants the separation of Ireland from Great Britain. That is why she is involved in the Irish language movement, and that is why she taunts Gabriel for writing book reviews for a Unionist newspaper. She insults Gabriel by noting that he is not a separatist, and it is genuinely an insult when she calls him "West Briton" [D 188]. Through Miss Ivors, the West of Ireland is associated with the Gaelic language and the Gaelic past, with what in Ireland has been left untouched by the seven-century association with Great Britain. Michael Furey's name, and his passionately offered death in the West of Ireland, associate his dying with that of the dead haunting the Treaty debates who died in insurrection and famine.  Because he is an Irish man, and not a West Briton, Gabriel must follow Michael Furey into death.

Stephen Dedalus associated politics and boundlessness and saw them as opposed to the ordered universe controlled by God.  It is fitting that his meditation took place in the exclusively masculine context of Clongowes.  "The Dead" is set in a feminine world, that of the Miss Morkans' home.  The feminine for Joyce is what lies outside the formed and bounded structure created by the male.  It is the disintegrating, the chaotic, the deathly.  Dante rejoices that Parnell has fallen into it:  "'We won!  We crushed him to death!'" [P 39].  In "The Dead" age, death, and the sexual deprivations of women suffuse the Morkan home. In that place, a woman tries to lure Gabriel into politics, into the West.  He resists her, but he is overcome with desire for his wife; he goes with her into darkness and snow, and then, in the shadows of the hotel room, it is revealed to him that one man has died for her already and that he must join that man in Gretta's world of flesh and death. Like Stephen witnessing the defeat of his father and Mr. Casey by Dante, Gabriel alone with his wife is overcome by terror:  "At that hour when he had hoped to triumph, some impalpable and vindictive being was coming against him, gathering forces against him in its vague world" [D 220].  The vague and the impalpable are the formless and the feminine.  Gabriel, like Parnell, succumbs to them as he falls into sleep and into the terrifying unformed that lies outside the line bounding the universe and giving structure to the human world.  "His soul swooned slowly as he heard the snow falling faintly through the universe and faintly falling, like the descent of their last end, upon all the living and the dead" [D 224].

Ultimately, I would suggest, terror of the female is central to Joyce's work and to his achievement.  That terror is related to a powerful theme in Irish nationalist life—the call of women for the death of men.  Joyce does what the great novelist always does; he deeply understands the "race, country, and life" which produced him, and builds complex and beautiful structures with what he has understood.

NOTES

1.   Pádraic H. Pearse, Plays, Stories, Poems (Dublin:   Phoenix Publishing Co., 1917), 42.

2.   See Dorothy Macardle, The Irish Republic (London:   Gollancz, 1937), 953-58.

3.   Official Report:  Debate on the Treaty Between Great Britain and Ireland, Dáil Éireann Session December 1921–January 1922 (Dublin: Talbot Press, 1922), 205.  All references in the text to speeches in the Treaty debates are taken from this volume.

4.   Piaras Béasli, Michael Collins and the Making of a New Ireland, vol. 2 (Dublin:  Phoenix Publishing Co., 1926), 66-67, 185, 215, 263.

# 9

# Hanna and Francis Sheehy-Skeffington: Reformers in the Company of Joyce

*Bonnie Kime Scott*

The centenary commemoration of James Joyce's birth was used to remind scholars not only of Joyce, but also his period in Irish and, indeed, modern culture. Seamus Deane, for example, noted that in the birth year of 1882 Nietzsche announced the death of God, Mikhail Bakunin published God and State, and Matthew Arnold offered his more traditional Irish Essays.(1) An understanding of Joyce's rejection of traditional social theory and his engagement with progressive ideas can be enhanced by turning to a pair of his Irish contemporaries. Born four years before Joyce, Hanna Sheehy and Francis Skeffington married in 1903 as the Sheehy-Skeffingtons. Their approach to reform was practical rather than literary, though they both had literary connections, Francis as an editor and prize-winning college essayist and Hanna as a teacher of literature. Their work took the forms of journalism, oratory, and direct protest. The Sheehy-Skeffingtons shared the educational and cultural milieu of the youthful Joyce and were his friends, but the relationship was not without interesting personal differences and tensions. Joyce transformed the facts of their lives into fiction laden with social and political significance.

In Stephen Hero and A Portrait of the Artist as a Young Man, Joyce vividly characterizes Francis as MacCann,(2) the student advocate of international peace and votes for women. Hanna is present less directly; she was one of his models for the young, Catholic, middle-class women of his early works. Miss Ivors ("The Dead"), like Hanna, went from the Royal University to a teaching career. Several of Joyce's early epiphanies are set at her parents' home (2 Belvedere Place), and the Daniels' daughters (Stephen Hero) are usually identified as Sheehys. McCann is suitably provided with a Daniels as a fiancée. It is also possible to encounter the Sheehy-Skeffingtons in Joyce's letters and in his brother Stanislaus's memoirs. These nonfictional Sheehy-Skeffington representations, though closer to fact, have their own biases and artistic purposes. A third view of the couple emerges from their own writings and speeches. Francis wrote Michael Davitt: Revolutionary Agitator and Labour Leader, coedited the feminist journal Irish Citizen, and edited the National Democrat. Hanna left scattered articles, lecture notes, and a reputation as a powerful public speaker. The Sheehy-Skeffingtons may be best revealed in their less public writings--the typescripts, diaries, and notes collected in the National Library of Ireland.

There are remarkable differences between the Francis in Sheehy-Skeffingtons sources and the MacCann of Joyce's Portrait. Francis has probably been dismissed unfairly by Joycean critics with the fictional model in mind. Dominic Manganiello, for example, finds that Sheehy-Skeffington's "heterodoxy" --defined as "the attempt to embrace all" --leads to "a patent absurdity."(3) Any assessment of MacCann is further complicated by the ironic view taken of his primary critic, Stephen Dedalus. Stephen and MacCann represent different aspects of a larger effort to challenge the conventions of their day, a project that withstands the ironic reading Joyce encourages for both of his immature fictional characters.

Joyce jested to his brother that Francis was "endowed with an enthusiasm that responded mechanically to all the more obvious appeals to justice, reason and humanity."(4) Many of his interests can be trivialized if one is so disposed. He advocated vegetarianism and temperance, he opposed innoculation and vivisection, and he insisted on freedom of dress (adopting the knickerbockers commemorated in Portrait). He repeatedly affirmed principles of progress and rationalism. Joyce's description of MacCann's brisk movements and insistent solicitations comes close to this spirit, as does the precise ticking of a clock, which reminds Stephen of MacCann [P 177]. In a typescript called "My Philosophy," Sheehy-Skeffington supports his position on innoculation with Darwinian reasoning: "Disease is the test of the race, the true instrument of survival of the fittest. And my death, declining to be innoculated, would be of more value to the race than my cowardly self-preservation by such a hideous means." He plans to improve his body with Sandow's exercises (a system embraced by Joyce's Leopold Bloom in Ulysses), and lays out a complete system of education for his young son. But Sheehy-Skeffington has critical perspective, admitting his philosophy is "personal and somewhat arbitrary." He also senses a drift from his essential rationalism toward "mystical ideas and theories."(5) Thus, he was more than the inflexible, precise, ticking machine laughed at by Stephen.

Joyce makes no direct remarks about Hanna's interests and attitudes, but his brother Stanislaus, who seems to have found her attractive, comments on her repeatedly in his diary. He remarks, however, that she was a "practical animal" and did not "understand those disattached personalities, the world's poets and artists and cranks," a group that presumably included James. He underestimates her interest in his brother.(6) In a radio interview, Hanna recalled that Joyce and Francis engaged in a common effort when they "defied together the College censorship" in jointly publishing Two Essays. She also had a lively appreciation of Joyce at Belvedere Place: "Joyce was then gay and boyish, flinging himself into topical charades. He loved to 'dress up' and produce plays and parodies and to sing old folk ballads in his sweet tenor."(7) Indeed, Joyce and Francis were treated together as eccentrics in their college's periodical, St. Stephen's. In fact, Francis's response to the epithet "Crank" was to say, "A crank is a small instrument that makes revolutions."(8)

In their own way, the Sheehy-Skeffingtons were as impractical about life as Joyce. All three sacrificed economic security to moral purpose. Francis resigned as Registrar of the Royal University rather than renounce his agitation for women's admission to University College. Hanna lost her teaching job at Alexandra College because she had been imprisoned for militant feminist agitations. Later, her connection with the Republicans during the Irish Civil War cost her a post at Rathmines Technical School. Francis's efforts to prevent looting during the Easter Rising cost him his life. Joyce repeatedly risked poverty rather than compromise his critical opinions of the Irish Literary Revival or University College [JJII 120, 140]. The motivations of activists and artist did seem to differ. The Sheehy-Skeffingtons

concentrated on ideal, collective objectives, and their inconveniences
and losses fit their ethic as a form of sacrifice. Joyce's decisions
may seem more egotistical, and he admitted to his brother that he was
"morally intrepid," but not physically brave [LII 108]. His impracti-
cality often took the forms of irresponsibility and self-indulgence,
qualities that met with the reproof of his responsible, activist
friends.

The cause of Irish nationalism was greeted with ambivalence by
both James Joyce and Francis Sheehy-Skeffington.(9)  Hanna was the radical, more traditional nationalist, ready to run errands during the
Rising and to side with the Republicans.  She described intrepid, active nationalism as a family tradition; details survive with the Dan-
ielses of Stephen Hero.

> Both my parents were Fenians.  My uncle, Father Eugene
> Sheehy, the "Land League Priest," was one of the "Sus-
> pects" in the Kilmainham Jail with Parnell, Dillon and
> Davitt.  My Great-Grandmother in her youth knew Lord
> Edward Fitzgerald . . . Grandfather Sheehy was a native
> Irish speaker who was beaten at the "National" school
> for every Irish word he spoke.(10)

One interest that tempered Hanna's nationalism was feminism.    She
charged Parnell with "cautious opportunism" that sacrificed the gains
made by the Ladies Land League and his sisters, Anna and Fanny, on the
bargaining table, and was wary of women's future in Sinn Fein.(11)   The
Sheehy-Skeffingtons worked for a time to shape the Young Ireland branch
of the United Irish League along progressive and feminist lines.   Francis shared Joyce's skepticism about nationalist cooperation with the
Catholic clergy and their enthusiasm for a material culture of Irish
Ireland.  Hanna was one of a group of young women who paid admissions
fees before organizers thought to ban women in their constitution.  But
the Sheehy-Skeffingtons parted company with home-rule nationalists in
1912, when the party sacrificed a pro-suffrage policy in order to pla-
cate the British in Home Rule negotiations.  Francis found Hanna's imprisonment for feminist window-breaking at Dublin Castle in keeping
with Irish nationalist traditions:

> There is stronger and purer nationalism in Mountjoy
> Prison at this moment than any of Mr. Redmond's follow-
> ers can claim.  There was a time when the Irish Party
> used to go to prison in pursuance of their ideals.
> Those were the days when the spirit of true Nationalism
> blazed in their blood, when the Party and its leaders
> were worthy of respect.(12)

Joyce and his persona, Stephen Dedalus, cultivated deafness to such
romantic nationalist nostalgia.   There is a similar ring to Simon
Dedalus's rhetoric when he regrets that nationalists of the past such
as Flood and Grattan "wouldn't be seen dead in a ten acre field with
the noble men we have now" [P 97].

Readers of Portrait will recall that Stephen is offered two nationalist heroes by his first tutor, Dante, who tells him that her two
brushes stand for Parnerll and Davitt.  Predictably, Parnell made the
more permanent impression on Joyce and Davitt, on Francis Sheehy-Skeffington.  Joyce's father (as reflected in Simon Dedalus) idolized Parnell, and Joyce felt an early attraction to Parnell's aloof, aristo-
cratic version of political heroism.  Parnell enjoyed the adulation of
the masses until his sexual scandal toppled him from public grace—a

judgment abetted by the Catholic church.   Even Parnell's downfall
served Joyce's favored plot of the fall, as well as his expression of
the modernist concern with sexuality.   Sheehy-Skeffington preferred
Davitt's unassuming manner, his nonconformity, and his restless commitment to change through socialism.(13)   Unlike Parnell, Davitt survived
through Joyce's and Sheehy-Skeffington's youth.   He was a present, active mentor for Francis, not the lost, romantic hero Parnell was for
young Joyce.  A further contrast is that Francis maintained an attitude
of serious admiration for Davitt, while the irreverent Joyce turned the
trivia of Parnell's disgrace into the stuff of human comedy.

Feminism was a cause embraced by both Sheehy-Skeffingtons, and
Joyce acknowledged it as significant to his age [JF 47-48].   Marriage
reform was one of the turn-of-the-century ideas Joyce took up in Stephen Hero, Exiles, and Ulysses.   In life, Joyce avoided the legal ceremony until the 1930s.   The Sheehy-Skeffingtons adapted marriage to
their strong characters, agreeing to have their own lives.   Their
joined surnames brought their ideal of equality to language itself.
The nature of their sexual passion was the subject of Joycean curiosity.   In Stephen Hero, Emma Clery's amusement that MacCann should think
of matrimony with one of the Daniels daughters suggests that outside
observers found it difficult to believe in their physical affection.
Hanna concealed her emotions, according to her daughter-in-law,(14) but
Francis's unguarded feelings can be found in his papers.   Love poems
written around 1903 display a rare mixture of physical and intellectual
admiration for a woman--a combination Joyce never displays.   One poem
shows measured ardor, idealizing Hanna's voice, both as the tool of an
effective orator, and as an instrument of love:

> I've loved the tones that voiced Love's vow
> Aye Sweetheart! —though I never said it
>
> Or ringing angry-clear for right
>     Or softly, whispering word-caresses,
> Or rippling into laughter bright
>     Your voice delights whom it addresses
>
> And if a high-pitched word I blame,
>     Forgive, O dear the reason this is
> That mere monopoly's my aim
>     I'd share no more your voice than kisses!(15)

The poem contains notable self-satire; Francis's progressive ideals on
labor would hardly permit "monopoly."   In another poem, he admires the
extraordinary physical traits of his beloved, but proclaims as her tru-
est beauties "refined thought, acute perception, heart pure, sympathetic, void of all disguise/Sweet gentleness."(16)

The Sheehy-Skeffingtons' public feminism focused on two issues,
equal education and the vote.   In publishing Two Essays with Skeffington, Joyce underwrote a feminist publication on education, Francis's
contribution being "A Forgotten Aspect of the University Question,"
which argued for coeducation in Catholic universities.   Its statistics
on women's achievements in national examinations remain interesting,
both as an argumentative strategy and as a resource on Irish women.
Hanna took up the campaign for coeducation in the New Ireland Review.(17)   The couple's quest of votes for women was based in the Irish
Women's Franchise League, founded by Hanna with Margaret Cousins in
1908, and publicized in the Irish Citizen.

Socialism was another cause of the Sheehy-Skeffingtons in which
Joyce also took an interest.   Although Francis, in particular, was

active in Irish labor groups, he probably was more concerned with workers on an international scale--an interest he shared with Davitt, and commemorated in the biography. This internationalism helps explain Francis's promotion of the Russian Tsar's Peace Rescript, an episode recorded in Stephen Hero and Portrait. Francis founded the National Democrat in the hope of advancing a humanized socialist party which, true to the style of Davitt, would concentrate its immediate efforts on "practical reforms instead of upon propagation of a creed."(18)   Although a less visible socialist than her husband, Hanna Sheehy-Skeffington had among her correspondents Emma Goldman. Joyce's explorations of international socialism while living in Trieste and Rome may owe something to the Sheehy-Skeffingtons' example; his suspicion of creeds was certainly comparable.

Though they shared a reputation for eccentricity at University College, it seems likely that Francis and James were rivals for the attention of conventional students. Joyce signed neither the Peace Manifesto nor the petition Francis circulated for coeducation at University, though undoubtedly he was challenged to so. Francis gave him a more personal challenge just before Joyce departed from Dublin with Nora Barnacle in 1904. Francis wrote a letter turning down Joyce's request for a loan and ended with an expression of concern about Nora's future with his unsettled friend [JJII 179].(19)  Joyce's subsequent actions and correspondence seem preoccupied with this brief letter. He adopts Francis's term for Nora, "the companion," and refers to Sheehy-Skeffington as "hairy Jaysus" --an epithet he retains in Stephen Hero. Once, when bewildered by Nora's behavior, he mockingly recommends that Stanislaus consult with "hairy Jaysus." Joyce made sure that reports of his son's birth reached Sheehy-Skeffington and he considered--perhaps mockingly--making him the godfather [L II 81]. During his 1909 visit to Dublin, Joyce failed to accept an invitation to the Sheehy-Skeffingtons' home, but reported without mockery that "Skeffington has a son two months old" [L II 230]. Also remarkable in the report is Joyce's failure to use the hyphenated, feminist name Francis adopted after marriage. Joyce read Francis Sheehy-Skeffington's journalism, which he had sent to him in Trieste, labeling one column "three pages of puff" [L II 153]. He had difficulty believing in the altruism Francis claimed for his socialism: "There cannot be any substitute for the individual passion as the motive power of everything" [L II 157]. Joyce's name calling, "stupid mountebank" and "the bloodiest impostor I have ever met" [L II 157], probably betrays considerable competitive emotion.

Joyce's letters spar with an absent opponent for a sympathetic audience (Stanislaus). The competitors are present in Stephen Hero and to a lesser degree in Portrait, both of which feature dialogues on the subjects we have been considering: nationalism, feminism, pacifism, and socialism. In a scene in Stephen Hero used to poke fun at McCann's many causes, Joyce's search for an adequate style is also evident. Stephen and McCann walk from the library toward the latter's lodgings. Joyce establishes time and place and supplies a summary of McCann's "theories," introducing a suggestion of free indirect discourse that biases the report: "Stephen delighted to riddle these theories with agile bullets" [SH 49]. "Agile" seems to be Stephen's assessment, "delighted" shows access to his feelings, and "bullets" betray a militant attitude. There follow three seldom-interrupted pages of dialogue. The stark, unrelieved alternation of statement and rebuttal emphasizes verbal conflict itself, as the identity of the speakers becomes unclear; this deliberate narrative confusion would be cultivated to greater effect in Finnegans Wake. The Stephen Hero passage is overdone, repetitive in its report of both theories and reactions. On the

rare occasions when the narrator interrupts, the explanation continues
to favor Stephen's probable report: "Whenever the conversation reached
this point, McCann refused to follow it further" [SH 50]. It allows us
to see not only Stephen's assessment of McCann's ideas, but also Stephen's biases.

The exposition announces two of McCann's subjects, "feminism and
rational life." The feminist material is taken almost directly from
Sheehy-Skeffington's contribution to Two Essays:

> He believed that the sexes should be educated together
> in order to accustom them early to each other's influ-
> ences and he believed that women should be afforded the
> same opportunities as were afforded to the so-called
> superior sex and he believed that women had the right to
> compete with men in every branch of social and intellec-
> tual activity. [SH 49]

Joyce does not use the original statistical arguments, and ignores basic issues of equal education and the androgyny implied in Sheehy-Skeffington's blending of male and female influences. Stephen artfully
sets up McCann by taking aim at issues of applied feminism: problems
of the woman soldier, police officer, or fire fighter; woman as doctor,
lawyer, or "confessor." McCann can foresee women doctors and lawyers,
but is more conservative about "certain social duties for which women
are physically unfitted." Stephen replies sardonically, "I believe
you," diverting "physically" toward the sexual nature of woman, and
concentrates for the moment on the priestly role. McCann's response,
to call Stephen "flippant," acquieses to Church authority; in effect
McCann curtails this aspect of discussion. Sheehy-Skeffington might
not have supported Catholic doctrine in this way (some years after
Joyce, he, too, relinquished Catholicism), any more than he would have
promoted soldiers of either gender, being a pacifist.(20) McCann's ac-
cusation of flippancy, as much an attack on style as ideas, becomes an
authoritarian gesture. This first phase of the dialogue sets up McCann
as the less revolutionary reformer.

The second phase begins lightly with a funny reference to McCann's
tone-deafness. But it reaches another impasse over a discussion of
human needs in which Stephen again injects the sexual, the need for
"women . . . at times." McCann responds: "Never!" uttering it "with
a moral snap of the jaws and in such a business-like tone of voice that
Stephen burst out into a fit of laughter." Significantly, Stephen is
"annoyed and stung" by "McCann's insistence on a righteous life and his
condemnation of license as a sin against the future." He is annoyed
"because it savored so strongly of paterfamilias" and stung "because it
seemed to judge him incapable of that part" [SH 52]. Sheehy-Skeffington probably played authority figure more to Joyce than he did to
Hanna, judging at least by their vows to lead individual lives. Yet,
by detecting the ambiguities of male relation to social power in both
young men, Joyce introduces a serious aspect of the problems of feminist reform. With his laughter, Stephen performs what Mikhail Bakhtin
would call a countercultural function, while McCann represents rejected
traditional norms.(21)

Sexual purity was an important aspect of many of the revolutionary
philosophies of Joyce's day, including the form of feminism espoused by
the Pankhursts. McCann's identification of "self-repression" with the
"teaching" of Ibsen in Ghosts gets deserved objections from Stephen
late in the debate: "Bah! You regard a play as a scientific document"
[SH 52]. In his letters, though, Joyce condemned both Ibsen and Sheehy-Skeffington for their doctrine of purity [L II 191-92]. One of

Stephen's major revolutionary arguments with Lynch and Emma Clery, as
well as with McCann, is that sexuality is natural, but the restraint
advocated by Victorians, Puritans, and Catholics is unnatural.  It is
an issue that divides social reformers who otherwise have much in common.

In Portrait, the deliberately staged peace rescript scene recalls
one of Francis Sheehy-Skeffington's favorite methods, the petition.  It
is written with greater assurance than the earlier passage in Stephen
Hero.   The preliminary description of MacCann's "brisk" movements,
rapid talk, and solicitation of signatures seems to be taken from life.
Stephen is aloof at first, consulting with Cranly over "icons," the
photographs flanking the petition.  Throughout the scene, other characters constantly intervene.  This supporting cast lets Joyce locate
the harshest remarks apart from his two major protagonists.  Thus Mac-
Cann's numerous causes are mocked by the "stage-Irishman" Moynihan.
Sheehy-Skeffington's Ulster accent is shifted to MacAlister, who delivers the parting blow to Stephen as artist:  "Intellectual crankery is
better out of this movement than in it" [P 199].  Despite diversions,
there are still two central characters.  It seems an acknowledgment of
Joyce's self-serving tribute that Sheehy-Skeffington was "the most intelligent man in St. Stephen's College after myself."(22)

When MacCann and Dedalus meet, there is a "ring of listeners" who
clearly expect a "war of wits," an ironic metaphor, considering that
the issue is international peace.  MacCann opens with masked flattery
of the progressive ideal they share:  "Late as usual. Can you not combine the progressive tendency with a respect for punctuality?"  Instead
of the lengthy expositions of Stephen Hero, we receive a summary of Mc-
Cann's arguments in favor of the peace rescript, a new humanity, and
the advocacies of British journalist William Stead.(23)  While Stephen
had taken the initiative in the dialogue of Stephen Hero, here MacCann
urges Stephen into politics, the more usual pattern with Joyce and his
friend.(24)   MacCann aims what Stephen terms his "wooden sword" at
Stephen as artist and condemns "metaphors," challenging him to "come to
facts!"  This juxtaposition of metaphor with fact offers a paradigm of
the differing discourses of artist and activist.  In his most "hostile"
moment, MacCann declares, "Minor poets, I suppose, are above such triv-
ial questions as the question of universal peace" [P 197].  MacCann is
realistic about Stephen's progress as an artist, and may challenge him
to seek the foundations of serious artistic achievement.  Stephen then
advances what has troubled him from the start--the icon of the Csar.
Stephen is wary that in overthrowing old objects of veneration, reformers will offer only inferior replacements.  He may be questioning
the very process of accepting icons.

Stephen does offer a conciliatory closing, "My signature is of no
account, he said politely.  You are right to go your way.  Leave me to
go mine."  MacCann's concession retains a critical, authoritarian tone:
"I believe you're a good fellow, but you have yet to learn the dignity
of altruism and the responsibility of the human individual" [P 199].
The call for altruism gets back to a basic difference between the living men, suggested earlier--collective responsibility against individual passion.  By the end of Portrait, Stephen attempts to combine the
two in a reforming mission:  "I go to encounter for the millionth time
the reality of experience and to forge in the smithy of my soul the uncreated conscience of my race" [P 252-53].  This implies that no one,
Stephen's critics included, yet understands the nature of moral action
in Ireland.  Stephen is allowed to stand as the ultimate revolutionary
of Portrait, though his success is quickly denied in Ulysses, and the
reader alert to irony must agree with MacCann's charges of irresponsibility.  MacCann, too, is ironically made to reveal flaws in his au-

thoritarian denial of sexual passion and endorsement of male priest-
hood.  Whatever the motivation, both characters are richly endowed with
a male penchant for verbal display.  But they move beyond their country's passion for nationalism in favor of social progress.  Both move
confrontation from the field of battle to the forum of debate, though
their militant metaphors invite criticism on a deeper level.  In the
final analysis, there can be little doubt that Joyce, like the Sheehy-
Skeffingtons, was a pacifist.

    MacCann probably does not mark the end of Francis Sheehy-Skeffing-
ton's presence in Joyce's works.  In Leopold Bloom we encounter his
rational projects for social improvement and his vision of the androgynous potential of men and women living under each other's influences.
Protest demonstrations like those that sent the Sheehy-Skeffingtons to
jail enliven the "Circe" episode of Ulysses and the pages of Finnegans
Wake.  Although he mocked them at first, Joyce also employed propaganda
and journalism like that of the Irish Citizen in the popular discourse
of his late works.  In another centennial presentation, Hugh Kenner
identified Francis as one possible model for HCE in Finnegans Wake,
where he is a man executed in a strange happening that made no
sense.(25)  Hanna Sheehy visited Joyce in Paris in the 1930s and reported receiving a last postcard from him in 1939.  Though we have no
details of the visit, and the card seems lost, it appears that the
Joyce-Sheehy-Skeffington relationship was never abandoned.


NOTES

    1.    Seamus Deane, "Joyce and Nationalism," in James Joyce:  New
Perspectives, ed. Colin MacCabe (Bloomington:    Indiana University
Press, 1982), 168-83.


    2.    The spelling varies: MacCann (Portrait), McCann (Stephen
Hero).

    3.    Dominic Manganiello, Joyce's Politics (London:  Routledge and
Kegan Paul, 1980), 36.

    4.    Stanislaus Joyce, My Brother's Keeper (New York:  Viking,
1958), 145.

    5.    Francis Sheehy-Skeffington, "My Philosophy," MS. 22,256ii,
National Library of Ireland, Dublin.

    6.    Stanislaus Joyce, The Complete Dublin Diary of Stanislaus
Joyce, ed. George H. Healey (Ithaca, NY:    Cornell University Press,
1971), 23.

    7.    Hanna Sheehy-Skeffington, "Hanna Sheehy-Skeffington's Radio
Interview with Dr. Charles Dixon," MS. 24,164, National Library of Ireland, Dublin, 4-5.

    8.    Owen Sheehy-Skeffington, "Francis Sheehy-Skeffington," in
1916:  The Easter Rising, ed. O. Dudley Edwards and F. Pyle (London:
1968), 137.

    9.    Francis's eulogy in the Irish Citizen listed "Women, Ireland,
Labour and Peace" as his four great causes.    Irish Citizen 4, no. 38
(July 1916):  219.

10.    Hanna Sheehy-Skeffington, radio interview, 2.

11.    See Bonnie Kime Scott, Joyce and Feminism (Bloomington:  Indiana University Press, 1984), 17-26.  Cited hereafter in the text with
the abbreviation JF.  The writing of this essay preceded publication of
the book.

12.    Francis Sheehy-Skeffington, "Home Rule and Votes for Women,"
Irish Citizen 1, no. 2 (July 1912):  58.

13.    See F. S. L. Lyons, Introduction to Michael Davitt:  Revolutionary Agitator and Labour Leader, by Francis Sheehy-Skeffington
(1908; reprint London:  MacGibbon and  Kee, 1967), for a fine comparison of Davitt and Sheehy-Skeffington.

14.    Andree Sheehy-Skeffington, interview with author, June 1977.

15.    Francis Sheehy-Skeffington, "To Hanna," handwritten manuscript, MS. 22,256ii, National Library of Ireland.

16.    Francis    Sheehy-Skeffington,    handwritten    fragment,    MS.
27,256ii, National Library of Ireland.

17.    Alice Oldham had touched off a series of articles in the New
Ireland Review.  One group favored separate women's colleges to spe-
cialize in "feminine arts"; Hanna looked forward to wider professional
opportunities for women and cited the success of coeducation in the
United States.  Mary Hayden and Hanna Sheehy-Skeffington, "Women in Universities:  A Reply," typescript, MS. 22,262, National Library of Ireland.

18.    Francis Sheehy-Skeffington, "Michael Davitt's Ideals," National Democrat 1, no. 1 (February 1907):  10.

19.    See Leah Levenson, With Wooden Sword (Boston:   Northeastern
University Press, 1983), 41.

20.    For Sheehy-Skeffington's changing views of religion, as expressed in his diaries, see Levenson, With Wooden Sword, 23-24.  Levenson examines these same scenes, though not from a literary standpoint,
on pages 23-27.

21.    Mikhail Bakhtin, Rabelais and His World, trans. Helen Iwolsky
(Cambridge, Mass.:  MIT Press, 1965), 73ff.

22.    Stanislaus Joyce, My Brother's Keeper, 145.

23.    Sheehy-Skeffington corresponded with Stead, who accepted one
of his articles on women's education for the Westminster Review in
1903.

24.    Eugene Sheehy, May It Please the Court (Dublin:   J. C. Fal-
lon, 1951), 35.

25.    Hugh Kenner, "Signs on a White Field" (Paper presented at the
International James Joyce Symposium, Dublin, June 1982).

# Part III

## Joyce's Connections to the Writers of His Time

# 10

# Through a Cracked Looking Glass:
## *The Picture of Dorian Gray* and
## *A Portrait of the Artist as a Young Man*

### *Dominic Manganiello*

"Poor Wilde was Irish and so am I!"(1) With these words James Joyce articulated his view of Oscar Wilde as a type of his race: a dishonored exile and a Celtic scapegoat at the hands of the puritanical English who threw stones at him. These elements of Joyce's portrait of Wilde as betrayed artist, even the imitation of his compatriot's pseudonym of exile, Sebastian Melmoth, in the name Stephen Dedalus, are well-known.(2) But the figure of Wilde cast its shadow over Joyce's imagination in other ways.

Wilde had died only a few years before the first draft of Portrait was begun, and by the time the revised version was underway, Joyce made a point of reading The Picture of Dorian Gray. He considered Wilde's self-portrait not candid enough: "Wilde seems to have had some good intentions in writing it--some wish to put himself before the world--but the book is rather crowded with lies and epigrams. If he had the courage to develop the allusions in the book it might have been better!" [L II 150]. Joyce made no mention of the inner tensions of the work which re-create, at least in part, those which Wilde was describing as interior to himself; that is, Lord Henry, Basil, and Dorian all reveal some aspect of Wilde's own psyche.(3) Joyce, it seems, failed to recognize this three-dimensional quality of Wilde's portrait of the artist. The result shows us that, in forging the identity of his own hero, Joyce was, as usual, highly selective in what he borrowed. When we juxtapose the two works we find that Dorian and Stephen do not, in fact, lead parallel lives; however, their stories intersect at a number of crucial points before they diverge, and it is this partial convergence that I want to examine here.

Wilde provides the background for his enterprise in his wily essay, "The Critic as Artist," in which he plots a course for fiction in the future:

> He who would stir us now by fiction must either give us
> an entirely new background, or reveal to us the soul of
> man in its innermost workings. People sometimes say
> that fiction is getting too morbid. As far as psycho-
> logy is concerned, it has never been morbid enough. We
> have merely touched the surface of the soul, that is
> all.

The desire to put the self in a book may be proof that, in literature at least, "indiscretion is the better part of valour."(4) Wilde was probably thinking of his own novel, but it was left to Joyce to extend some of its psychological implications. He began the first draft version of <u>Portrait</u>, for instance, by enunciating the theory that the features of infancy hold as much importance as the features of adolescence in tracing the growth of a soul. This introspective narrative, which analyzes the currents of thought and feeling of a nameless hero in a particular ambiance, suggested rather than described, resembles one of Walter Pater's "imaginary portraits."(5)   In the final version Joyce continues this strategy by winnowing many details of person and of place that would detract from Stephen's mental life. In this attempt at interior portraiture, at narrating, in Wilde's phrase, "The Story of a Soul," the two works under consideration share common ground.

Dorian and Stephen can be seen as modern pilgrims whose progress is made possible only by contravention of the moral law. They both follow the lead of Pater's epicurean Marius, who weighs "the claims of that eager, concentrated, impassioned realization of experience, against those of the received morality."(6)   Wilde formulates this struggle to transcend the categories of good and evil in "The Critic as Artist":

> What is termed Sin is an essential element of progress.
> Without it the world would stagnate, or grow old, or
> become colourless.  By its curiosity Sin increases the
> experience of the race.  Through its intensified asser-
> tion of individualism it saves us from monotony of type.
> In its rejection of the current notions about morality,
> it is one with the higher ethics.(7)

This transvaluation of words recalls the policy of Milton's Satan, who is also a model for Stephen:  "Evil be thou my good."  Sin no longer ravishes the beauty of the soul, as in the traditional view, but rather helps it to flourish.  Stephen concurs with these notions:   "He came to the knowledge of innocence through sin . . . He hoped that by sinning whole-heartedly his race might come in him to the knowledge of herself."(8)   Stephen reverses the movement of Bunyan's pilgrim from the self-directedness and snares of this world towards a spiritual destination:  "He was destined to learn his own wisdom apart from others or to learn the wisdom of others himself wandering among the snares of the world.  The snares of the world were its ways of sin" [P 162].  His adventures read like the confessions of a self-justifying sinner who contemplates "his own soul going forth to experience, unfolding itself sin by sin" [P 103].  Stephen's eventual substitution of "error" for "truth" recalls the philosophy that Lord Henry instills in Dorian: "Experience was of no ethical value.  It was merely the name men gave to their mistakes."(9)   Like Pater, both heroes celebrate the experience as an end in itself and enjoy the intensely lived moment of beauty regardless of morality.

Wilde ultimately insists that aesthetics are higher than ethics since only through art can "we attain to that perfection of which the saints have dreamed, the perfection of those to whom sin is impossible, not because they make the renunciation of the ascetic, but because they can do everything they wish without hurt to the soul, and can wish for nothing that can do the soul harm."(10)   We are confronted here with the double irony of an individual who, while maintaining that sin doesn't exist, desires to sin and yet at the same time is said to be incapable of sinning.  In adopting this sensationalist philosophy of curing the soul by means of the senses and the senses by means of the soul [DG 37], Lord Henry exhibits the circular and contradictory logic of an asceticism achieved by self-titillation rather than by self-

denial, by wakening rather than deadening the senses.  As a result,
Lord Henry, like Wilde, acknowledges the existence of sin in the very
act of denying it.   In essence "sin" is, as Joyce pointed out, "the
pulse of Wilde's art" [CW 204].

It is the pulse of Joyce's art, too.  Stephen follows Lord Henry
most closely when he is cast in the role of pilgrim amorist, ecstati-
cally languishing.  Joyce describes Stephen's visit to a prostitute as
"the holy encounter . . . at which weakness and timidity and inexperi-
ence were to fall from him."  Later, we witness the "holy silence" of
Stephen's ecstasy at the moment he divines his vocation in the form of
a wet-dream vision of a birdlike girl.  Stephen's soul is "all dewy
wet" in the act of composing the villanelle sequence for his temptress:
"While his soul had passed from ecstasy to langour where had she been?
Might it be, in the mysterious ways of spiritual life, that her soul at
those same moments had been conscious of his homage?" [P 99, 172, 217,
223].  Stephen's homage is autoerotic; like Pygmalion, he is aroused by
the work of his own hands.(11)

That brute body and refined soul could interpenetrate, that the
senses contain spiritual mysteries, restates a conviction of Giordano
Bruno's in Gli Eroici Furori, a conviction Lord Henry adumbrates to
explain the whole man thinking and feeling:

> Soul and body, body and soul--how mysterious they were!
> There was animalism in the soul, and the body had its
> moments of spirituality.  The senses could refine, and
> the intellect could degrade.  Who could say where the
> fleshly impulse ceased, or the psychical impulse began?
> . . . Was the soul a shadow seated in the house of sin?
> Or was the body really in the soul, as Giordano Bruno
> thought?  The separation of spirit from matter was a
> mystery, and the union of spirit with matter was a mys-
> tery also. [DG 73]

Lord Henry's musings reflect the revival of interest in Bruno by the
late Victorians, signalled in an article Pater published in 1889.(12)
Bruno's heroicrenzies as interpreted by Pater serve as a primer for
Stephen, too.  Pater, for instance, notes that Bruno conceded, long
after he had withdrawn himself from it, that "the monastic life pro-
motes the freedom of the intellect by its silence and self-concentra-
tion."(13)  Similarly, after Stephen rejects the "chill and order" of
the priestly life, he paradoxically retires into the "cloister of [his]
mind," which is adorned in "the vesture of a doubting monk."  It is in
terms of his "monkish learning" that he strives to forge an aesthetic
philosophy [P 161, 192, 176, 180].  Stephen exhibits the monastic temper that characterizes his intellectual kinsman in another, related
way.  Pater highlights how Bruno parallels the workings of the soul of
the artist with those of the world soul and how in this mystical experience the soul is greatly expanded.(14)  Stephen's soul, once it has
flown by these nets attempting to hold it back, will expand into the
world soul, which carries the conscience of the Irish race.

The process of transformation that the individual conscience undergoes in Portrait and in Dorian Gray provides a fascinating key to
both novels.  The strange case of Dorian has been described in terms of
Matthew Arnold's division of life into Hebraism and Hellenism, attitudes for which Lord Henry is chief spokesman.(15)  He is all for the
Hellenic ideal, which sponsors what Arnold calls "the spontaneity of
consciousness," as opposed to the Hebraic ideal of "strictness of conscience," which inculcates a sense of sin or what Lord Henry calls "all

the maladies of medievalism."  Wilde's own sympathies come into play
here, and account for Lord Henry's attraction.  "But he [Wilde] is honest," as Isobel Murray puts it, "in examining the consequences of these
doctrines."(16)  Dorian at first adopts Lord Henry's perspective but
soon finds it to be limited.  Selling one's soul to art necessarily
implies the existence of a moral order or the Hebraic impulse which
cannot, finally, be so easily dismissed.  Dorian's picture becomes "the
visible emblem of conscience" and "a symbol of the degradation of sin"
as it looks out at its subject from the canvas and calls him to judgment.  Dorian's cold-blooded murder of Basil, the voice of conscience,
and its symbolic reenactment in his stabbing of the portrait, represent
the individual's ultimate rebellion against ethics and the moral dimen-
sion of art.  Wilde does not sidle here.  Conscience is an interior law
written in the heart; transcribed as such, it cannot be effaced or destroyed.  Nor can the "objective reality" under which it operates.(17)

In Portrait art also catches the conscience of the individual, but
in an altogether different manner.  In "The Soul of Man Under Socialism" Wilde himself had urged a "new Hellenism" or a new libertarian in-
dividualism, a political remark Joyce transferred to the national level
when he spoke in his early critical writing of Ireland's becoming "the
Hellas of the north" [CW 172].  The importance of this concept in Ulysses can make us overlook the seeds of its workings in Portrait.  Stephen's inner struggle to follow the dictates of conscience can be
equally illuminated by Hebraism and Hellenism.  The name Stephen Dedalus itself, drawn from both traditions, reflects this double tension.
In the early part of the book Stephen feels "the ache of conscience"
(or the "agenbite of inwit" of Ulysses) prompting him to repent of his
sins.  It is clear that the Catholic sensibility predominates at this
point; conscience acts as the voice of truth in accordance with an external, objective authority, God's revelation to man.  Stephen eventually repudiates the existence of objective truth, however, and sets up
his own conscience as a subjective but nonetheless unimpeachable guide.
He refuses to accept anything on authority, and relies instead on his
"best self."  This autonomous sensibility allows the individual to become his own priest and king, the self-acknowledged legislator of Ireland.  As constituted, the Dedalian conscience functions as a tribunal
before which the artist pronounces his "J'accuse" and those guilty of
Irish paralysis are summoned and tried.  Joyce translates Dorian's selling his soul to art into a heroic and, paradoxically, a Messianic act.
Dorian attains freedom from coercion but not from blame, whereas Stephen, sanctioned by his attempt to discover a mode of life or art
whereby he could express himself in unfettered freedom, emerges as the
prime specimen of the new individual, himself the standard by which to
hit the old conscience of the race, and by which to forge the new.

This ability of the artist to remake a whole nation and particularly the individual in his own image and likeness has its counterpoint
in Dorian Gray.  Wilde is constantly preoccupied with creation and re-
creation, and with art as a mirror of false and true images of the
self.  A modern-day Narcissus, Dorian exchanges his "original self" or
soul for the reflection of which he grows increasingly enamoured, becoming, in Blake's phrase, "idolatrous to his own shadow."(18)  Wilde
revamps the Faust legend to blend it with the "curious artistic idolatry" of which Basil speaks.  Basil refuses to unveil his portrait of
Dorian Gray for public scrutiny for fear he has put too much of himself
in it or, in effect, for fear he has bartered his own soul away [DG
28-29].  Lord Henry, in turn, can also consider Dorian his own "creation" because, as he says, "to influence a person is to give him one's
soul" [DG 72, 34].

Wilde compounds his book with three versions of the Faustian pact to make a telling point about the relation between art and life.  In his last meeting with Dorian, Basil recognizes that his folly imitates Pygmalion's--that he has fallen in love with his own painting come to life, and that he worships the work of his own hands.  He then offers Dorian the possibility of a counter-transformation through the mercy of the divine Artist in whose image his soul was originally fashioned [DG 170].  Lord Henry, on the other hand, to the end exalts rather than renounces his idolatry.  He believes Dorian remains unscarred by the pursuit of sensation for its own sake.  In allowing no possibility for the deterioration or the progression of the soul, or for an art which mirrors this process, Lord Henry challenges the basic premise of Wilde's book, that of transformation.  Or, to put it another way, Lord Henry mistakes, Wilde suggests, the fabricated mask for the original face.  There may be inevitable misconstruing, as Joyce Carol Oates puts it, in a self-referential art in which we encounter "both the puzzling contempt for real worlds and the sentimental hope for a forcible remaking of the universe as if there were not already a universe to be acknowledged."(19)

Joyce's fabulous artificer, however, bases his venture on just such a hope:  he will make a new heaven and a new earth out of the sluggish matter of the old.  Human creativeness, from this vantage point, does not participate in the original creation but repeats it. Joyce elaborates what is only limned in Wilde.  Stephen considers himself not only a Dedalus and a Pygmalion, but also three persons in one godlike artist.  Joyce's hero relates to God the Father by authoring through the alchemy of the word a second creation to rival the first. In transmuting the primal materials the artist aims to usurp Christ's power of transubstantiation while, pari passu, in giving life to inanimate matter he outsoars the Holy Spirit in renewing the face of the earth.(20)

This new trinity of the self, or Sabellian conflation of models, mythical and divine, goes still further.  Stephen conceives of the artist as his own mediatrix who, curiously enough, offers no mediation beyond the self:  "In the virgin womb of the imagination the word was made flesh."  There is no reference point, historical yet transcendent, as in the original Incarnation which Stephen mimics here.  What we are witnessing is how Stephen becomes less concerned with external reality and more concerned with the internal processes of his own psyche.  This increasing self-consciousness is signalled by two stages:  Stephen first cloisters his temptress-muse within the confines of his own being and then pays homage to her as to himself by bowing before the altar of his own imagination.(21)  The narcissism which this self-contained and self-referential process necessarily entails leads to the worship of the man-made sign, the written word, for its own sake, or to what, in Wilde, is called artistic idolatry.

Joyce, it seems, does not fret like Wilde about putting the self too much in the foreground of a work of art.  But Wilde's perspective proves no less relevant for that.  In Dorian Gray narcissism proves fatal because it provides at once an image of the self and all that the self is not; it distorts as it reflects.  Dorian's attempt to annihilate the true image of the self and its visible emblem results in his own annihilation, a cracked mirror of the self.  The portrait remains a mirror nonetheless, something by which we can see, in retrospect, Dorian in his pristine innocence.  It becomes the medium through which we can see ourselves, too.  Everyone, Joyce quotes Wilde as writing, "sees his own sin in Dorian Gray" [CW 204].  Wilde seems to have taken the implications of his novel to heart.  The end of his life reads like a counter-Dorian Gray where author and fictional hero exchange destinies.

As Joyce aptly remarked, Wilde "closed the book of his spirit's rebellion with an act of spiritual dedication" [CW 203].(22)
     Some readers like to imagine Joyce in a similar light.  He is the
author who rejects his hero as a fatal alternative and becomes, in effect, the character in Flann O'Brien's The Dalkey Archive whose side-
line was writing pamphlets for the Catholic Truth Society.(23)  But I
think we can imagine him spending his leisure time, like his hero Stephen, in the company of subversive writers [P 78].(24)  Joyce focuses
his "nicely polished looking glass" [L I 64] on a political angle that
Wilde engages only in his plays and in his critical writing.(25)   In
Dorian Gray the artist or individual who rebels against spiritual real-
ities incurs grave personal consequences.  Joyce's book does not reflect the shortcomings of the artist, but rather those of God and nation when measured against him.  Even Stephen's literary compatriots
fall short of his bold maneuver of mirroring the race's conscience in
his own; contemporary Irish art is, as Joyce has Stephen point out in
Ulysses by extending one of Wilde's metaphors, merely a cracked looking
glass of a servant.  Stephen's own image, as we have seen, must be the
standard of all experience, personal and national.(26)  Whether such a
perspective captures or magnifies the self is a question Wilde poses
but Joyce doesn't; still, it remains a central question for our understanding of Joyce in his self-characterization as artist.


NOTES

     1.   Joyce uttered these words during a performance of The Impor-
tance of Being Earnest in Zurich [JI 439].

     2.   Hugh Kenner, "The Cubist Portrait," in Approaches to Joyce's
Portrait, ed. Thomas F. Staley and Bernard Benstock (Pittsburgh:  University of Pittsburgh Press, 1976), 175-76.

     3.   Wilde explained his own personality in terms of the charac-
ters who peopled his novel:  "Basil Hallward is what I think I am; Lord
Henry is what the world thinks me; Dorian is what I would like to be--
in other ages perhaps."  See The Letters of Oscar Wilde, ed. Rupert
Hart-Davis (New York:  Harcourt, 1962), 352.

     4.   See Complete Works of Oscar Wilde (London:  Collins, 1971),
1054-55, 1010.

     5.   I will refer to a number of parallels between the complete
Portrait and Pater's Marius the Epicurean (1885; reprint, New York:
Modern Library, 1967) in the course of the essay.  For the moment it
seems worthwhile to point out one such parallel with the first draft of
Portrait.  Marius's devotion to language, to "weighing the precise power of every phrase and word, as though it were precious metal" [p. 79]
anticipates Joyce's artist-hero who, "like an alchemist . . . bent upon
his handiwork, bringing together the mysterious elements, separating
the subtle from the gross.  For the artist the rhythms of phrase and
period, the symbols of word and allusion, were paramount things" [P
261].

     6.   Peter, Marius the Epicurean, 123.

     7.   Wilde, Complete Works, 1023-24.

     8.   From The Trieste Notebook; see P 292-93.

9.    The vision of the birdlike girl throws open before Stephen "the gates of all the ways of error and glory," and he exclaims, "To live, to err, to fall, to triumph, to recreate life out of life" [P 172].    The second reference is to The Picture of Dorian Gray (New York:  Signet, 1962), 73.  Further references to this work will appear in the text, identified by DG and page number.

10.    Wilde, "The Critic as Artist," 162.

11.    Stephen's own poetic practice ironically undercuts his aesthetic theory in this respect.  His poem excites what he calls his "kinetic emotions," rather than the "static" or "esthetic" emotion that he considers to be the product of a "proper" art.  According to Stephen's own definition, then, the villanelle stands as an example of "improper" art [P 205, 207-8].

12.    The article later formed a chapter of his posthumous novel, Gaston De Latour.  See W. Schrick, "On Giordano Bruno, Wilde and Yeats," English Studies 45 (1964), 257-264.

13.    Walter Pater, Gaston De Latour, ed. Charles L. Shadwell (London:  Macmillan, 1910; reprint, Oxford:  Blackwell, 1967), 39.

14.    Ibid., 142-43.

15.    See Jan B. Gordon, "'Parody as Initiation':  The Sad Education of "Dorian Gray," Criticism 9 (1967):  367.

16.    Isobel Murray, Introduction to The Picture of Dorian Gray, by Oscar Wilde (Oxford:  Oxford University Press, 1981), xii.

17.    This is Isobel Murray's point [xiv].

18.    William Blake, Jerusalem, plate 43; quoted in Northrop Frye, The Secular Scripture (Cambridge:  Harvard University Press, 1976), 108.

19.    Joyce Carol Oates, "The Picture of Dorian Gray:  Wilde's Parable of the Fall," Critical Inquiry 7 (1980-1981): 427.

20.    In Ulysses Stephen assumes the power of the Holy Spirit, referred to as the Lord and giver of life in the Nicene creed:  "If I call them into life across the waters of Lethe, will not the poor ghosts troop to my call?  Who supposes it?  I, Bous Stephanoumenos, bullockbefriending bard, am lord and giver of their life" [U 415].

21.    Stephen's worship of his temptress-muse takes the form of a 'eucharistic hymn,' his own poem; see P 221-24.

22.    Yeats recorded Joyce's reaction to Wilde's conversion:  "He spoke of a friend of mine [Oscar Wilde] who after a wild life turned Catholic on his deathbed.  He said that he hoped his conversion was not sincere.  He did not like to think that he had been untrue to himself at the end" [JJI 106-7].  A person's interior motives are always difficult, if not impossible, to evaluate.  In the novel, Dorian, much like Wilde himself, is attracted by the aesthetic side of Catholicism.  Unlike Basil, however, Dorian ends by believing in a vindictive rather than in a merciful God:  "Not 'forgive us our sins' but 'Smite us for our iniquities' should be the prayer of a man to a just God" [DG 231].

On his deathbed, if not before, Wilde's change of heart may have been prompted by the Basil in him.   In any event, a possible explanation might be found in "De Profundis" where Wilde calls Christ the supreme artist because he forgives all aberrant behaviour.   See Wilde, Complete Works, 931ff.

23.   This is not to suggest that there is no distancing of the self or irony in Portrait.   Stephen might not be the mature artist, but he is at least a partial portrait of the author as he was in his early promise.   Stephen is not simply the butt of Joyce's irony either. Joyce adopts the attitude towards his hero that he called, paradoxically, "indifferent sympathy" in an early critical essay.   Joyce obviates the possibility of the failure of Stephen's enterprise by making his cry of Icarus and Lucifer, "to err, to fall," a triumphant and heroic one.   Or, as William Empson puts it, "Joyce was an extremely self-centered man, fiercely determined to become a great novelist; he is wildly unlikely to have presented himself, without any warning or explanation, as impossible of becoming one"; see "Joyce's Intentions," Twentieth-Century Studies 4 (1970):   27.   Joyce describes Stephen's feelings at every stage of his development with detailed consideration that forestalls any suggestion of a lack of sympathy.   The other characters in Portrait, according to C. P. Curran, are too little individualized and act as a foil to the only character in which Joyce is really interested; see James Joyce Remembered (London:   Oxford University Press, 1968), 63.   Joyce himself indicated in response to a query by his Spanish translator that the title implies a "self-portrait"; see Jerome Hamilton Buckley, Season of Youth (Cambridge:   Harvard University Press, 1974), 240.   Basil Hallward's point in Dorian Gray might equally apply here too:   "Every portrait that is painted with feeling is a portrait of the artist, not of the sitter" [DG 23].

24.   For fuller documentation on this point see Dominic Manganiello, Joyce's Politics (London:   Routledge and Kegan Paul, 1980).

25.   Joyce used this phrase to describe Dubliners.

26.   In Stephen's view the mind is its own country.   His declaration in Stephen Hero, "My own mind is more interesting to me than the entire country" [248] is matched by the one made in Ulysses, "Ireland must be important because it belongs to me" [645].   Joyce does not allow Stephen to be as direct in Portrait, but the implications of his position are the same.

# James Joyce
# and His
# Contemporaries

**Recent Titles in**
**Contributions to the Study of World Literature**

# 11

## *Candida* and *Exiles:*
## The Shaw-Joyce Connection

### *Rhoda B. Nathan*

There is a Shaw-Joyce connection, in spite of the fact that as late as 1932 James Joyce was to write to William Butler Yeats that he had never met his celebrated countryman and fellow exile from Ireland [JJII 672-73]. That letter was a response to Yeats's announcement that he and Shaw were founding an academy of Irish letters and were inviting Joyce to be its first member. Joyce turned down the invitation. There is a biographical Shaw-Joyce connection as well, arising from the similarities in their backgrounds: their charming, ne'er-do-well, dipsomaniacal fathers, their "downstart" positions in society, and their abandonment of their native land in pursuit of art.(1) Their final connection is a literary one, resting on their plays Candida and Exiles.

The ironies built into the connection are numerous. Candida, Shaw's fourth play, written in 1894, was to become his most successful theater piece. Exiles, Joyce's only completed play, written in 1914, was a disaster in its early performances and has rarely received critical approval since.(2) It has eluded success in staging and performance and remains to this day a species of closet drama, a curiosity which owes its interest to themes that Joyce handled with greater originality and daring elsewhere. Yet both plays deal with the same subject—the popular marital triangle; both owe direct debts to Ibsen and Wagner; both are "well-made" plays in the tradition of the currently popular Scribe and Sardou audience-pleasers; and both examine the plight of the lonely and transcendent artist in his conflict with conventional society.

However, the tameness and timidity with which Joyce handles his "duel" between the antagonists is ironic on two counts: first, because he was to write in a few years the most daring book of the century and turn his back forever on the kinds of veiled allusions to sexuality that mark Exiles; and second, because Shaw, who repeatedly characterized himself as a "Puritan," was able to handle the same theme in Candida so many years earlier with such frankness that an advanced woman such as Beatrice Webb labeled Candida a "prostitute," and the critics reviewing the play alluded to the final "auction" for Candida as spirited bidding in the white slave market. That the Shaw who was a holdover from Victorian gentility should have been able to deal so much more openly with the issue common to both plays is an interesting sidelight to the character of the man who, declaring himself to be too "prudish" to ever write some of the words Joyce had employed in Ulysses, nevertheless offered his full support against the censors who sought to suppress it [JJII 88-89].

One other historical connection should be cited, because it bears, if only tangentially, on the subject of this discussion.  In 1909 Joyce was asked to review Shaw's The Shewing Up of Blanco Posnet for Il Piccolo della Serra, an Italian newspaper.  The play had been banned in England but was produced by the Abbey Theatre.  Joyce disliked the play and dismissed Shaw as a "born preacher" who was incapable of attaining the angular style demanded by the modern theater [JJII 294].  Shaw, in turn, acting as spokeman for the Stage Society in 1919, turned down a performing request for Exiles, claiming it was "obscure."(3)  Shaw, however, is on record as admiring Ulysses--with some reservations-- while Joyce, from the evidence offered by his library, read some Shaw but was unenthusiastic.(4)  In spite of their differences, there remains an uncanny, if unintentional, resemblance between Candida and Exiles.

The central plots are nearly identical.  Each is a romantic and domestic triangle, with an interloper who seeks to displace the incumbent lover, master, and father.  Candida is resolved by an auction in which the lover and the husband bid for the love object.  With fine irony Candida gives herself to the "weaker" of the two, and thereby chooses her husband, the Reverend James Morell, rather than the Shelleyesque eighteen-year-old poet, Eugene Marchbanks, who turns out to be the stronger of the two and capable of surviving alone.  Candida chooses Morell because he needs her and she needs to be wife, lover, mother, and advisor.  She has made a man of Morell and, at the eleventh hour, makes him aware of his debt to her.  Eugene sees that she has no real role in the artist's life other than an idealized one, and he withdraws.  The play ends satisfactorily, but one is always aware that Shaw had a reason for subtitling it "A Mystery" when the younger man leaves the reunited couple, who have no inkling of the "secret in the poet's heart."

Exiles, Joyce's version of the domestic triangle, is more complex and ambiguous.  Whereas in the Shaw version the distinction between the artist and the ordinary man, or the idealist and realist, is made abundantly clear, that distinction is not maintained in the Joyce play.  Both men, Richard Rowan and Robert Hand, are artists and idealists.  The major distinction between the former, a creative writer, and the latter, a journalist, is that one is disillusioned, and the other--held firmly in the grip of unsatisfied longing for love, recognition, position, sexual gratification--is still in pursuit while his rival is in retreat.  Because Richard and Robert are the same age and roughly equal, neither is in the position to bully the other.  Thus, the tension that exists in the curiously transposed relationship between Eugene, the threatening little terrier, and Morell, the overgrown protected baby, is lacking.  Although the rivals for the affection of Bertha in Exiles are fairly evenly matched, and a "duel" is proposed, nothing dramatic comes of it.  The climactic center of Shaw's play is merely a throwaway line in Joyce's.  Bertha elects to remain with her common-law husband, just as Candida chooses to stay with Morell, but the decisive scene is discursive rather than dramatic.

Nevertheless, Exiles resembles Candida in its broad structure, its themes, its indebtedness to the Ibsen "problem" play featuring the "new woman" who has choices, its carefully timed entrances and exits typical of the theater of the late nineteenth century, and its conventional solution to its daring premise.  But whereas Shaw's play is neatly tailored to the Scribean principles of organization, and its conflict resolved through rational debate, Joyce's is as murky and naggingly personal at the end as at its uneasy outset.  Shaw would have considered this an "unpleasant" play in contrast to Candida, which is a patently "pleasant" play.  Exiles is obscure in its motives and confusing in its characterizations because they are too close to Joyce's own bone. His Bertha, too much like his own Nora, is alternately long-suffering and philosophical. She never emerges as the radiant love object and autonomous heroine of Shaw's play.

Although Candida and Bertha are formulated according to different principles of composition—the first is fictional, the second clearly modeled on a real person—the two sets of antagonists in each play are both composite and autobiographical characters. In Candida, Morell and Eugene are pieced together from fragments of Shaw's own character, vocation, and philosophy. Morell and Shaw are Fabian Socialists, platform orators of no mean persuasive power, crowd pleasers and born reformers. But Eugene is also like Shaw—an artist, a genius, incorrigible and unique, a human evolutionary step in the direction of the as yet uncreated superman.

In Exiles, Rowan and Hand are as Joycean as Morell and Marchbanks are Shavian. As creative writer and working journalist, they represent both aspects of Joyce's career. Like his creator, Richard Rowan has been living with a woman inferior to him in birth and education. He has, like Joyce, refused to marry her, although they have a family and he depends on her loyalty. He has been abroad—his child, like Joyce's own son Giorgio, speaks Italian—and although he is still spiritually exiled, he has come home to Ireland. He has not attended his mother on her deathbed; he broods over that estrangement as well as on the cultural alienation he nurses. His rival, Robert Hand, although he was ostensibly modeled on St. John Gogarty, Joyce's principal rival in real life, is as much Joyce as Gogarty. He is the younger Joyce, ardently wooing Bertha with lyrical phrases taken almost verbatim from his own letters to Nora.

As the young Marchbanks and the mature Morell present two halves of Shaw, Richard and Robert fulfill that function for Joyce. Robert is a throwback to the younger Joyce courting his Nora; Richard is the domesticated but still resistant Joyce, somewhat jaundiced but spiritually elusive. Although at least four acquaintances went into the composition of Richard's complex character, Joyce himself contributed the chief component.(5) For instance, Hand's sentiments about Ireland's cultural destiny replicate Thomas Kettle's pronouncement: "If Ireland is to become a new Ireland, she must first become European," a point of view shared by Joyce [JJII 61; E 45]. Hand's wildly romantic apostrophe to Bertha is a barely altered version of Joyce's excessive address to Nora: "My beautiful wildflower of the hedges! My wild sun-drenched flower" [L II 269; E 27]. His exaltation of the sexual side of the woman for whom he is vying counters her husband's praise of his wife's preserved spiritual virginity. Rather than establishing a clear distinction between two diametrically opposed characters, Joyce appears to be dramatizing the alternate sides of his own sexuality, externalizing his inner conflicts through the concrete device of the play.

Candida and Bertha are Ibsenite heroines, emancipated versions of Nora Helmer. Both preserve a spiritual purity even though their sexual experience is taken for granted. In Candida, Titian's Assumption of the Virgin hangs over the mantelpiece in the parsonage. In the original version of the play, Morell's spinster secretary, Proserpine Garnett, declares with some vehemence and not a little jealousy: "One would think [Candida] was the Queen of Heaven herself, he thinking of her half the time when he imagines he is meditating on the virtues of the Blessed Lady."(6) Candida's father is shocked by the "high church" icon in his Christian Socialist son-in-law's home. It is instructive to note that the picture was a gift of the poet Eugene, who is passionately in love with Candida.

In _Exiles_, much is made of Bertha's eternal virginity of soul. Her embittered husband fears that he has killed that virginity and will have to pay for his crime [E 67]. Both women are entirely honest and sexually generous. Because they are free, they enjoy the luxury of truthfulness, whereas Ibsen's Nora survives through prevarication and manipulation. Nora must use her kittenish sexuality to wheedle bonbons and trinkets from her obtuse husband, but Candida and Bertha offer their sexual favors freely and magnanimously. Candida declares openly that she would have given herself to Eugene as she would have given her shawl to a beggar. Bertha, wooed by the amorous Robert Hand, gives him the kiss he begs, offers him her body to caress, and, in the spirit of honesty, tells her husband about the episode because she has never lied to him. Her frankness is reminiscent of Candida's telling Morell about Eugene's courtship and her willingness to gratify his need.

These women are permitted by their authors to offer themselves to men other than their husbands and still retain their "virginity." This works only because they have been presented to the audience as well as to their husbands as models of probity. Candida, always tactful to her self-satisfied husband, nevertheless tells him the truth about his popularity in the pulpit. His congregants, she informs him, are all suffering from "Prossy's Complaint," his smitten secretary's disease. They love not his sermons, but his handsome and charming person. To Eugene she is more brutally honest, because he is intuitive and free of vanity. She holds the mirror up and forces him to see himself as he is: a poet in exile, destined to live on the fringe of society. Joyce's play concludes with a similar affirmation of Bertha's honesty. She reminds her tormented and guilt-ridden husband that he may continue to trust her; she has remained faithful to a degrading relationship out of love and loyalty. The juxtaposition of reality and illusion, in Shavian terms the "quintessence of Ibsenism," is Joyce's homage to Ibsen in _Exiles_ and the most powerful structural force in _Candida_. Bertha and Candida are practical, realistic, and free of illusion. Their maternal natures protect their lovers from the rain and discourage their wasteful fantasies about women's eternal desirability. Bertha, setting aside Robert's gift of red roses, warns him that some day she will be old and he will have to cease idealizing her. Candida, discouraging Eugene, asks him to repeat a formula that will restore his sense of reality: "When I am thirty, she will be forty-five. When I am sixty, she will be seventy-five."(7)

The men, on the other hand, are idealists. Robert brings to his courtship every illusion to nourish his fantasy. To Bertha's straightforward question, "Did you think of me last night?" he rhapsodizes, "I think of you always—as something beautiful and distant--the moon or some deep music" [E 27]. Eugene, horrified at Candida's request for a new scrubbing brush, offers her instead "a tiny shallop to sail away in, far from the world, where the marble floors are washed by rain and dried by the sun" [C 43]. On one occasion, in response to Morell's illusions about his manliness and his marital role as protector of her position, Candida puts him in his place by reminding him that she and she alone, in her multiple role as wife, lover, mother, sister, and housekeeper, has made a man of him. Joyce puts nearly the identical words in the mouth of Bertha, when, deploring her husband's disregard, she informs the audience that she alone has "made a man of him." Of course, prostitute or virgin goddess, Candida is a more convincing Ibsenite heroine than the alternately supine and resentful Bertha, but then, Shaw's debt to Ibsen was of longer duration and more passionate commitment than Joyce's. Nevertheless, in his early work, Joyce was profoundly influenced by Ibsen, wrote homages and letters to the Norwegian master and upheld to his peers the example of Ibsen as the

"greatest of undeceivers."(8)    His insistence on dramatic realism in
the person of Bertha—caught between two men trapped in their illusions
and delusions—is proof of Ibsen's influence on his thinking.    The
critic Francis Fergusson, in his introduction to Exiles, asserts that
Joyce had intended to write a "naturalistic drama" in the manner of Ibsen, and that he had succeeded [E vi].
      Male bonding is yet another feature common to the two plays.    In
each, the male antagonists are reconciled through sharing the love of
the same woman.    They articulate their bonding in nearly identical
terms.    Richard Rowan, Joyce's soured hero, in an emotional moment of
insight, expresses not only sympathy but kinship with his suffering
rival:    "I cannot hate him since his arms have been around you.    You
have drawn us nearer together" [E 75].    The Shavian counterpart is giv-
en voice, not by the triumphant husband, but by the defeated but un-
bowed suitor, Eugene.    Having driven Morell nearly to distraction with
his threats to preempt him in Candida's affection, Eugene suddenly
turns to the bewildered parson and cries:    "I disliked you before . . .
but I saw today when she tortured you—that you love her.    Since then I
have been your friend" [C 62].    Then, at the very end, in magnanimous
withdrawal:    "Parson James:    I give you my happiness with both hands:
I love you because you have filled the heart of the woman I loved" [C
75].    And so the contest in each case is decided through bonding.    The
pivotal female characters have effected a rapprochement between the
contending males.    If, as Fergusson maintains, Exiles explores the same
theme as Ibsen's When We Dead Awaken, the conflict between love and
spiritual freedom, then each antagonist—his future defined by the pivotal female—is in possession of the one or the other.    Bonded through
Candida's realistic interpretation of their natures, Morell is awarded
love, while Eugene flies out into the night towards his freedom.    Rowan
in Exiles, as a type of Ibsen master builder, relinquishes his aspira-
tion to create something higher and remains with Bertha.    If, as he
claims, he is in exile, he will have a bride in exile.    Robert, his
friendship reconfirmed, takes his leave, and like Eugene, remains spiritually free.
      If Ibsen is the starting point for both plays, Wagner provides
their underlying mood, motif, and theme.    Bits and pieces of Wagnerian
opera are scattered throughout.    In Exiles, Robert, setting the tone by
wearing a romantic smoking jacket, plays Tannhauser on the piano in
preparation for the seduction of Bertha.    Joyce makes his intention
clear in his notes to the play:    "Robert's position is like that of
Wotan, who in willing the birth and growth of Siegfried, longs for his
own destruction [E 118-19].    Another note citing a second myth clarifies the title as well as the farewell speech:    "Exiles—also because
at the end either Robert or Richard must go into exile. . . . Robert
will go.    But [Bertha's] thoughts will only follow him into exile as
those of her sister-in-love Isolde will follow Tristan" [E 118, 123].
As Richard Ellmann observes, Joyce was intent on presenting the artist
as "truthful to fundamental laws" as they are "expressed in myths as in
Wagner's operas" [JJII 14].
      The Wagnerian motifs are even more clearly defined in Candida, and
have been traced painstakingly by Raymond Nelson in his introduction to
the Bobbs-Merrill edition of the play.    At crucial points in the play
signals are given to identify the young Marchbanks as a full-blown
Wagnerian hero.    The evidence, planted strategically, suggests that the
playwright's conception of Eugene rests on Wagnerian models.    Although
Eugene, like Rowan, has been likened at times to Ibsen's master builder
Solness, the supernal artist, he is too romantic a figure to be contained within Ibsen's naturalistic framework.    When he is introduced,
Shaw describes him as wearing "an expression of hopeless suffering."(9)

Nelson observes that Eugene, like Parsifal, "instantly presses his hand to his heart as if some pain had shot through it." Again like Parsifal, he becomes the "untouched fool rendered wise through compassion."(10)  In the play's crucial scene, the seduction at the beginning of act 3, Eugene says to Candida, "If I were a hero of old I should have lain my drawn sword between us" [C 63]. Opera-goers will recognize that allusion to the wooing of Brunnhilde in behalf of the absent Gunther in The Twilight of the Gods. Finally, Eugene's dramatic farewell speech, "The night outside grows impatient," is a reworking of Tristan's address to the night just before his flight [C 75].

Considering the emphasis on flight and exile in those portions of the two plays which draw extensively on Wagnerian motifs, it is safe to assume that Shaw and Joyce identified as much with Wagner's own exile after the Revolution of 1858 and his consequent anarchism and heroic suffering as with his operas. They peppered their plots with romantic gleanings from Parsifal, Tannhauser, Tristan, and the Ring cycle as a tribute to Wagner the man as much as to Wagnerian themes.

As theater, Candida remains a triumph for Shaw, but Exiles is an embarrassment, or at least a problem, for the equally gifted Joyce. Candida is a superbly crafted play, tight in structure and effective in performance. Exiles may best be described as a "theatre of ideas which dehumanizes the dramatic presentation to the point where even the actors become abstractions."(11)  The underlying reason for the success of the first and the failure of the second might be simply that Shaw was primarily a playwright and Joyce was not. It might also be that Shaw's treatment of the subject is high-spirited and Joyce's bears the marks of his suffering, at a time when he had unhappily returned from his self-imposed exile. More likely, the success of Shaw's play rests on the character of Candida herself, with her radiant yet aloof personality, which owes no single debt to any one person in Shaw's life, whereas Bertha is too much like Nora and thus carries the burden of Joyce's ambivalent regard for her. Both plays, however, are significant in ways that transcend success or failure. Not least among them is the uncanny resemblance they bear to each other in subject matter, sources, and casts of characters. That the "twin" plays should be the work of two towering Irish geniuses who stood outside and above any "set" or "circle" and had little to do with each other is worthy of note. Although each stood magisterially alone, unique in his art and exempt from comparison with his peers, in this instance each was inspired by the same masters to write parallel if unequal versions of a popular problem play of the time.


NOTES

1.    George Bernard Shaw, Sixteen Self Sketches (London:  Constable and Co., 1949), 22. The term "downstart" is a Shavian coinage appearing in chapter 4, "Shame and Feudal Snobbery," in which Shaw describes himself as "a son of a Protestant merchant-gentleman and feudal downstart."

2.    Among the more prominent negative reviews are Harry Levin's "merely an offshoot of a larger work," in James Joyce: A Critical Introduction, 17, and Herbert Gorman's James Joyce (New York:  Rinehart, 1948), 103, in which he calls Exiles "a somber interlude."

3.    Ellmann misquotes the word as "obscene" [JJII 429], but from the content of the play, "obscure" is probably the correct designation.

4.    The contents of Joyce's library in 1920 contained the following books by Shaw: The Perfect Wagnerite, The Up of Blanco Posnet, Three Unpleasant Plays, and Mrs. Warren's Profession; see Richard Ellmann, The Consciousness of Joyce (New York:  Oxford University Press, 1977), Appendix, 128.

5.    The four were Vincent Cosgrave, who Joyce suspected of having had an affair with Nora, Thomas Kettle, Robert Prezioso, and Gogarty; see John MacNichols, James Joyce's "Exiles":  A Textual Companion (New York:  Garland, 1979), 7.

6.    The British Museum MS. also retains the original description of Candida as a "true Virgin mother," and puts Marchbanks into a state of "beatitude" in her presence.  All three references were later deleted by Shaw in the final text.

7.    George Bernard Shaw, Candida:  A Pleasant Play (Harmondsworth:  Penguin, 1952), 75.  Further references to this work will appear in the text, identified by C and the page number.

8.    Ellmann, Consciousness of Joyce, 3.

9.    Raymond Nelson, Introduction to Candida:  A Mystery, by George Bernard Shaw, (New York: Bobbs-Merrill, 1973), xvii.

10.    Nelson, Introduction to Candida, xvii.

11.    Elliott M. Simon, "Joyce's Exiles and the Edwardian Problem Play," Modern Drama (March 1977): 33.

## 12

# Joyce, O'Casey, and the Genre of Autobiography

*Michael Kenneally*

James Joyce's use of autobiographical experience in A Portrait of the Artist as a Young Man has been at the heart of several recurring critical questions about the character of Stephen Dedalus. Matters of sympathy, irony, and identification with the author ultimately lead to a discussion of genre, the parameters of which, in this instance, are bounded by literary autobiography at one end and autobiographical novel on the other. Invariably, critics who tackle the issue of autobiographical situation do so through a comparative analysis of Portrait and Stephen Hero; significant light also can be shed on the role of biographical data if Portrait is examined alongside another complex autobiographical study by Joyce's fellow Dubliner Sean O'Casey. In his multifaceted, six-volume work O'Casey uses third-person narration and weaves surrealistic fantasies, dream sequences, and blatantly fictional treatment of historical events into his narrative. Yet a close examination reveals a careful attention to the selection and arrangement of materials, an often symbolic patterning of experience, and a variety of stylistic innovations--in short, many of the literary devices usually associated with the writer of fiction. If in Joyce's Portrait, then, we find some thinly-disguised events from the author's life, in O'Casey we encounter a novelistic treatment of biographical materials. This critical dilemma may be expressed in two ways: to what extent can the autobiographer employ novelistic techniques before the work ceases to be autobiography? Or, how much autobiographical baggage can a novel carry before it begins to blur back into the realm of the literary autobiography?

Several facets of the autobiographical process are relevant to the issue. When an autobiographer sits down to write an account of his personal history, he is trapped with the matrix of his present perspective on his life. From that standpoint, he traces a pattern in the evolution of his past selves which he sees culminating in his contemporary identity. Autobiography, then, is primarily a process of self-definition at a given moment in time. The character and shape of the work--selection and arrangement of materials, style and technique in presentation--are simultaneously influenced by, and are reflections of, the author's self-image. However, because the autobiographical impulse can be guided by a desire to understand as well as to portray, the writing of the work can be as much an exploration of self as a presentation of an identity already known and understood. Further nuances of identity are often discovered in the process of peeling away successive layers of the palimpsestic past; such discoveries will also contribute to the shape of the work.

In addition, the nature of the recollective process itself significantly influences the completed autobiography. Memory, which controls access to the past, is faulty and irrational in both its conscious and unconscious modes, emphasizing some experiences while censoring or even repressing others. Inadequacies in recollection are compensated for by imagination and interpretation; the act of remembering may frequently become creative, generating material that has little apparent relationship to the historical truth of the life lived. At the heart of the autobiographical impulse, then, is a tension which manifests itself as a conflict between what Roy Pascal, in his pioneering study of the genre, identifies as "truth" and "design."(1) The precise terms of this dynamic relationship cannot be determined by perceiving design as synonymous with ornamentation, a rhetorical flourish which, while pleasing, must not abrogate the claims of truth.(2) Pascal avoids committing himself on the necessary balance between these two elements, for example, he prefaces a discussion of Joyce's Portrait by stating that "In every case . . . the autobiographer is a bit of a novelist."(3) This begs the question of degree, leaving unresolved the issue at hand.

Two characteristics of O'Casey's autobiography are pertinent to our deliberations. The first of these is the portrayal of the hero as evolving inexorably, from his birth, and notwithstanding apparent digressions, to become the autobiographer. Despite the six-volume length and a compositional time-span of twenty-five years, O'Casey draws particular attention to this feature of his autobiography. In the long, two-and-a-half-page sentence that opens the first volume, O'Casey describes how his mother "pressed and groaned and pressed and pressed a little boy out of her womb into a world."(4) What follows is O'Casey's imaginative reconstruction of the hierarchical world of late Victorian Dublin, where the various social classes are epitomized by the different horse-drawn vehicles on the streets—landau, brougham, tramcar, laden lorry, or jaunting car. Despite the cruelties and inequities that the newborn child must face in this world, he doggedly makes his way through the first years of his life. This first volume ends: "Well, he'd learned poethry and had kissed a girl. If he hadn't gone to school, he'd met scholars; if he hadn't gone into the house, he had knocked at the door" [I, 191].

Having presented the young boy at the door of the house of life, O'Casey continues to use this metaphor in subsequent volumes to suggest his hero's progress. With the final volume, the focus, after much adjusting and readjusting of the lens, is back on O'Casey as he nears the end of his journey through life. The last chapter of the volume, echoing the opening of the first volume, again equates the image of the house of life with his world:

> Soon it will be time to kiss the world good bye. An old man now, who, in the nature of things, might be called out of the house any minute. Little left now but a minute to take a drink at the door—deoch an doruis; a drink at the door of life as it had been with him, and another to whatever life remained before him. Down it goes! Slainte! [VI, 218]

Victorian Dublin's street vehicles are again recalled to reinforce the radical transformation of his childhood world.

> It was a long look-back to the time when he remembered
> wearing the black-and-red plaid petticoat--a little
> rob-roy; and he sitting on the doorstep of a Lower Dor-
> set Street house, watching the antics of the elder and
> braver kids let loose on the more dangerous roadside; in
> his ears the sound of lorry, dray, and side-car, with
> their iron-rimmed wheels, clattering over the stony
> setts of the street; in his nose the itching smell of
> dusty horse-dung. [VI, 218]

Having begun with the birth of its hero, the work moves toward that
moment when, on the final pages, the autobiographical subject merges
with his creator.

The second characteristic of O'Casey's autobiography is the presentation of the distinct stages of the hero's development; these punc-
tuate the forward chronological movement, and are expressly or implicitly connected to the author.  This phenomenon goes beyond the depiction of the autobiographical hero as a former version of the autobiographer's self; it is a contemporary expression of identification with,
and responsibility for, the many precursory roles which have emerged on
the autobiographical page.  This acknowledgment is evident in the voice
of the autobiographer periodically manifesting itself in the thread of
historical materials.  For example, O'Casey, following upon the long
opening sentence of volume I, provides a detailed and vivid description
of his mother's appearance at age forty, three years after his birth.
He then continues:

> And all this was seen, not then, but after many years
> when the dancing charm and pulsing vigour of youthful
> life had passed her by, . . . and vividly again, and
> with an agonized power, when she was calmly listening to
> the last few age-worn beats of her own dying heart. [I,
> 11-12]

The portrait of Mrs. Casside at age forty is based on the memories of
the mature man imaginatively projected back into the past.  And such
memories find confirmation in the autobiographer's present recollection
of her, twenty or so years after her death, thereby acknowledging the
connection linking him to the experiences of the autobiographical hero.
O'Casey the poverty-stricken child of Dublin, the nationalist, the socialist, and the dramatist have all contributed to the identity of
O'Casey the autobiographer.  By acknowledging the substantive relationship between himself and key stages of his hero's development, O'Casey
has established the essential truth that the work seeks to present.

Woven through the chronological structure that establishes these
two features of the work are many novelistic devices that give an overall design, an essential unity characteristic of a literary creation.
Yet, though availing of the freedom of imaginative reconstruction and
literary treatment, O'Casey's primary responsibility remains the cap-
turing of the perceived truth of his life.  Because the thrust of a
literary autobiography is centripetal, the focus always returns to that
core of biographical experience which the autobiographer sees as the
shaping components of his identity.  The ultimate point of reference of
an autobiography lies outside the work, in a preordained end which is
arrived at on the last pages of the book.  Despite an autobiographer's
innovations with form, his hero lives a predetermined existence in
which he is denied the freedom of open-ended growth.

A telling instance of how design can augment personal historical truth and thereby clarify present identity is found in Inishfallen, Fare Thee Well, where O'Casey describes an incident that occurred during a train trip he and Lady Gregory took from Coole Park to Dublin. While waiting for a connecting train at Athenry, he wanders alone through the old, desolate, and windswept town. He is keenly aware of the sterility and decay which pervade the place, the former glory of which gave it the name "Ford of the King." Suddenly, out of a grey, half-sunken house a girl emerges, whose youth and vitality hypnotize O'Casey. Though he sees this girl as an image of beauty, he is unable to bring himself to address her, for "his mind had been too full of the loneliness and the ruin to be so suddenly called upon to reflect with words the wonder in his mind." Up to this point in O'Casey's description, there is little to indicate the autobiographical relevance of the passage. Instead, the wistful, evocative power of the language, together with the cumulative impact of the details, might suggest that its significance has been lost sight of in the process of imaginative recollection. Significantly, O'Casey adjusts the focus of the subsequent passage to a more recognizable autobiographical level. The immediate autobiographical development is that he goes back to Lady Gregory, catches his train, and returns to Dublin. Mentioning the names of Lady Gregory and Yeats, as well as the fact that he himself is a dramatist, identifies the hero with the Dublin literary world which was part of his environment at this time. But beyond this, O'Casey connects the incident with an ongoing pattern of design. To the exiled O'Casey, this girl, this "lone cherry-blossom thrusting itself shyly and impertingly forward through the ragged, withering foliage of an ageing tree," is an archetypal Irish figure of youth and vitality being smothered before it achieves fulfillment.

The fourth volume traces the various forces which, at precisely the moment when O'Casey was realizing his full literary potential, made his exile inevitable. To the retrospective autobiographer this vibrant girl doomed by her environment is emblematic of what may have befallen him had he remained in Ireland. He concludes the passage: "Whenever his mind wandered again to the lonely wretchedness of Athenry, he would see this lovely figure, this bud of womanhood, longing for life, standing, alone and radiant, in the midst of the houses, quietly resolute in sinking to their own decay" [IV, 194]. By reintroducing the metaphor of houses, O'Casey suggests his contemporary view that had he stayed any longer in Ireland, in his Irish house, he too could have found himself sinking into a living death. Acknowledging the bond between the hero and the autobiographer confirms the forward autobiographical thrust of the work but, more important, shows how elements of design can render an autobiographer's perception of the truth of his past.

In an autobiographical novel, on the other hand, selection and use of personal experience are governed by the author's aesthetic priorities and artistic goals. Biographical events can be touchstones of reality, points of imaginative departure; under the exigencies of artistic criteria they are soon left behind or radically transformed. Unlike the literary autobiography, the ultimate thrust of the autobiographical novel is centrifugal: the focus moves away from the author out toward artistic ends. Whereas it is a characteristic of autobiography that its pace becomes slower and its atmosphere less intense as the hero more and more resembles the autobiographer, the autobiographical novel usually builds to some decisive climax in the hero's development. The very meaning of an autobiographical novel coalesces in the events of the closing pages and not beyond them in the person of the author.

As has been observed by many critics, Joyce's difficulties with Stephen Hero stemmed from both his proximity to the events being described and his artistic immaturity.  The Joyce who wrote Stephen Hero in 1906 existed on practically the same temporal plane as did Stephen at the end of the fragment; this would have heightened the difficulty in discerning what data might be artistically relevant or merely historically true.  The result was inclusion of many experiences which, to use Joyce's own terms, were "personalized lumps of matter" whose "individuating rhythm" had not been liberated.  Insufficiently transformed biographical events would tend to blur the line dividing hero and author, as well as to work against the achievement of artistic goals.

More significantly, however, Joyce's editorial intrusions--the movement back and forth between his own views and those of his hero which Joseph Prescott and others have pointed out(5) --would also tend to strengthen the identification of hero with author.  These intrusions were more blatant than the "implied author" or "fictional narrator" that Wayne Booth found in Portrait.  The obvious authorial interventions in the Stephen Hero manuscript were close to being the same as those the literary autobiographer uses to establish the precursory roles of the various personae of his autobiographical hero.  These factors, together with Joyce's unclear perception of how the work would end, must have contributed to his frustration with the work.(6)  If he had no clear understanding where an unmistakable divergence could be made between hero and author, and if the significance of the hero's experiences had to be repeatedly interpreted by authorial intrusions, then the autonomy of the hero was being undermined.  The heart of Joyce's problem was to establish the precise nature of the relationship between himself and his literary character, between historical experiences and their potential as literary subject-matter.

When writing Portrait, Joyce was removed in time by about eight years from the closest episodes being described.  With this distance and the maturing experiences of the intervening years (not the least of which was writing Stephen Hero) Joyce found a perspective that freed him from an overdependence on the details of personal history.  The new objectivity and control resulted in the striking differences noted by many critics:  the concentration of material, the disciplined focus on Stephen's growing consciousness, the symbolic patterning, and the authorial distance.  Though Stephen in Portrait becomes a character similar to a former version of the author, these changes diminish the perception of Stephen as a precursor of the author.  The various stages of Stephen's growing awareness of his artistic calling are presented as being remembered by, and sifted through the consciousness of, the mature Stephen.  By employing this fictional narrator Joyce establishes a buffer between himself and the events of his personal history, thereby severing the links between the two.  Stephen's experiences at significant turning points in his maturation create the self-perceived artist figure who is ready to leave Ireland at the end of the novel.  By building the novel toward this climactic moment in Stephen's life, Joyce makes the thrust of the work centrifugal, out to the fictional narrator and away from Joyce the author.

Joyce's use of personal data for artistic ends is dramatically evident when Stephen encounters the seabird girl and dedicates himself to his artistic vocation.  In its essentials--the hero beholding a girl whose beauty momentarily hypnotizes him--the passage is not dissimilar to O'Casey's account of his meeting with the girl in Athenry, but the roles both incidents play and the overall functions they perform are indicative of the essential distinctions between the two works.  Stephen, momentarily mesmerized by the girl's beauty, responds with an outburst from his soul as he turns and goes.  But the significance of the encounter is immediately apparent from its contextual shadings. The girl is the catalyst who has unfolded a vision of life's artistic potential for him.  In a moment of transcendent insight he becomes aware of, and commits himself to, the values of a higher reality: "To live, to err, to fall, to triumph, to recreate life out of life!" [P 172].  Because this incident is the climactic embodiment of Stephen's perception of himself as an artist, it is essential to the achievement of Joyce's aesthetic goals.  The fact that Joyce himself had some such encounter with a girl on Sandymount strand is not relevant; indeed, that Joyce detachedly evaluated historical experiences such as this for their literary potential is confirmed by his further transformation of it in Ulysses, when Bloom reaches orgasm while observing Gerty McDowell on the beach.

In O'Casey's autobiography, the sight of the girl at Athenry has little bearing on the development of the hero; it is presented as a fleeting experience of the kind that is common in quotidian life.  Its significance is much more related to the contemporary autobiographer than to the man who beheld her.  His use of the incident to point to the wisdom of going into exile strengthens the relationship between autobiographical experience and contemporary identity, confirming the genre's centripetal mode of operation.  On the other hand, by freeing Stephen from the inevitability of autobiographical destiny, by disallowing the reader's a priori assumptions about his ongoing relationship with his environment, Joyce can depict Stephen with a potentiality unavailable to the predetermined role that O'Casey's hero must play. Seeing the Stephen of the Portrait as a dramatic character who can freely respond to the nuances of his world lends him an ambiguity, an openendedness toward life which contrasts with the ultimate determinism always hovering over the hero of an autobiography.

## NOTES

1.  Roy Pascal, Design and Truth in Autobiography (London:  Routledge and Kegan Paul, 1960).

2.  In an article on Stephen Hero Patricia Tobin writes that the reader of autobiography "knows life as chaotic, and when he beholds it beautifully ordered, he suspects some foul play with the truth," leading her to conclude that "the assets of the novel become outright liabilities in any system of personal accounting"; see "A Portrait of the Artist as Autobiographer:  Joyce's Stephen Hero," Genre 6 (1973): 193.

3.  Roy Pascal, "The Autobiographical Novel and the Autobiography," Essays in Criticism, 9, no. 2 (1959): 134.

4.  Sean O'Casey, I Knock at the Door (London:  Pan Books, 1980), 9.  All subsequent references to the six-volume autobiography are to this edition, and will be indicated in the text by volume number and page.

5.  Joseph Prescott, "James Joyce's Stephen Hero," in Joyce's Portrait:  Criticisms and Critiques, ed. Thomas E. Connolly (New York: Appleton-Century-Crofts, 1962), 80 passim.

6.  Richard Ellmann notes that Joyce had not yet seen the climactic end of the work in his departure for the Continent in 1902, and before long had carried it beyond that date [JJI 154].

# Part IV

## Joyce and Modern Irish Writers

# 13

# Flann O'Brien:
## *Post* Joyce or *Propter* Joyce?

### Joseph Browne

Woody Allen, that renowned metaphysician and jazz clarinetist, once observed that his one regret in life was that he was not someone else. Brian O'Nolan not only was half a dozen other people, he also arranged for his own spurious death on April Fool's Day, 1966, and then went right on living as at least half a dozen additional people. Prior to his April Fool's Day canard he had existed as Brother Barnabus, the O'Blather, Myles na gCopaleen, and Flann O'Brien. Since then he has become, quite detectably, the Marshall McLoonahan who wrote The Medium is Only Part of the Message, or, A Reader's Guide to At Swim-Two-Birds. O'Nolan's next manifestation was as the philosopher and critic William Gass, who penned such revealing treatises as "From Some Ashes No Bird Arises," "The Case of the Obliging Stranger," and "Cock-a-doodle-doo"; as Gass he also coined the term metafiction and used it to describe Flann O'Brien's novels.(1) A short time later, Gass begat Robert Scholes who began diligently tracking down "fabulators" and "The Orgastic Pattern of Fiction" while simultaneously establishing the range and limits of Gass's theories of metafiction.(2) Wasting little time, he next appeared as Robert Alter and wrote Partial Magic: The Novel as a Self-Conscious Genre, in which he self-consciously but unashamedly referred to O'Nolan's work as "flaunted artifice."(3) Alter was then altered into Steven G. Kellman to beget The Self-Begetting Novel, which proclaims O'Brien as a part of the Proust progeny and presents him as a direct descendant of that "paradigmatic figure in creating . . . illusion."(4) Most recently O'Nolan has blossomed forth at Yale University as Harold O'Bloom (Leopold and Molly's second cousin thrice removed), who has just published The Breaking of the Vessels and is assiduously completing a deconstructionist appraisal of The Third Policeman and The Poor Mouth, the latter being quite slow going because of its composition in Early Middle Irish. Nevertheless, he hoped to complete the text in time for its scheduled publication on April 1, 1984, the eighteenth anniversary of his metadeath.

Whoever or whatever he has been, however, Brian O'Nolan most assuredly was never Robert Martin Adams, who categorically proclaimed in his book After Joyce: Studies in Fiction After Ulysses that Flann O'Brien is "a post-Joyce if not wholly propter-Joyce writer." Adams concludes the less than three pages he devotes to O'Brien with the declaration that in At Swim-Two-Birds, "the evidence of influence is too strong to need further emphasis."(5) Probably every Irish writer since the twenties has been unfairly evaluated or compared, in one way or the other, in terms of Joyce. Of course Joyce was an influence on Flann

O'Brien, and Adams's text was not meant to deal solely with O'Brien, but it is this kind of sweeping and often unquestioning pronouncement that infuriated O'Brien during his career and that has negatively influenced readers and critics to the present day. Like one of O'Brien's own characters in At Swim-Two-Birds, "I prefer the question to the answer," not only because "it serves men like us as a bottomless pretext for scholarly dialectic,"(6) but also because O'Brien deserves to be viewed in a more distinct and equitable context than that of being "wholly propter-Joyce."

Actually, in view of what has been stated about Brian O'Nolan and his personae, this could all be a colossal flim-Flann by Adams since we know, as proven irrefutably in The Dalkey Archive, that James Joyce is alive but only semi-well, writing pamphlets for the Catholic Truth Society of Ireland and aspiring to become a Jesuit. Thus, the question can, indeed must, be asked, is James Joyce really and wholly propter-O'Brien?

Unlike one of O'Brien's best-known characters, John Furriskey, who was born fully grown and matured at the age of twenty-six as a result of the author's literary invention of "aesthoautogamy," Flann O'Brien was born as the infant Brian O'Nolan in Strabane, Co. Tyrone, on October 5, 1911, the third of what would become twelve children. After several moves to accommodate the father's career as an officer in the customs and excise service, the family settled in Dublin in 1923. Although he was almost twelve at the time, the move also initiated Brian's formal education in the Christian Brothers' Synge Street School. Fluent in both Irish and English, he had no academic difficulties but resented the all too frequently applied corporal punishment. Thirty years later O'Nolan explained that he could "read contemporary literature in five languages thanks to the Christian Brothers and an odd hiding now and then."(7)

From 1927 to 1929 he attended Blackrock College and from 1929 until 1935, with the exception of approximately six months spent at the University of Cologne on a scholarship, he matriculated at University College Dublin, from which he received a B.A. with honors in German, Irish, and English. In 1935 he received an M.A. for which he had written a thesis on "Nature in Modern Irish Poetry." In addition to his accomplishments in language and literature, O'Nolan also distinguished himself as a gifted and acerbic member of the Literary and Historical Debating Society and the college magazine, Comhthrom Feinne, in which he first appeared in May 1930 under the pen name Brother Barnabus.

An example of the Brother's work is a stinging lampoon of William Butler Yeats in which he gelds the Willie by portraying him as Lionel Prune, an effeminate, vacuous, versifying dilettante. In August 1934 he began a comic magazine called Blather which he not only edited and illustrated, but also wrote most of the material for under the pen names "The O'Blather" and his cretin son, "Blazes O'Blather." The debating society and especially the magazine were replete with satire and parody, primarily of James Joyce who, as Niall Sheridan, a fellow student of O'Nolan's, explained, "was in the very air we breathed."(8) Blather, which has been described as an "anti-magazine" in the sense that At Swim-Two-Birds is an antinovel, expired in January 1935, after only five issues. A short time later, Sheridan reported in an article in Comhthrom Feinne that O'Nolan was working on a novel.

This abridged biographical statement is meant to establish the literary and linguistic orientation from which O'Nolan took cognizance of and responded to James Joyce. Of course, he is not "propter-Joyce"; if anything, he became increasingly, often erroneously and gratuitously, anti-Joyce in his novels, although he retained an appreciation of Joyce's verbal pyrotechnics, his "capacity for humour," and the manner in which "he palliates the sense of doom that is the heritage of the Irish Catholic."(9)    Mick Shaughnessy, O'Brien's semi-persona in The Dalkey Archive, gives the following "spontaneous appraisal" and "unpremeditated pronouncement" of Joyce's literary work.    It clearly echoes O'Brien's sentiments.

> I think I have read all his works, though I admit I did not properly persevere with his play-writing.    I consider his poetry meretricious and mannered.    But I have an admiration for all his other work, for his dexterity and resource in handling language, for his precision, for his subtlety in conveying the image of Dublin and her people, for his accuracy in setting down speech authentically, and for his enormous humour.(10)

In a later conversation with Joyce, Mick exudes, "You are a most remarkable writer, an innovator, Dublin's incomparable archivist" [DA 144].    Joyce's linguistic finesse, subtle imagery, authentic speech, and "enormous humour" were unquestionably conditions of O'Brien's art; they were certainly not the cause.

Upon first meeting O'Nolan, Sheridan described him oxymoronically as "the incarnation of a satanic cherub," behind whose "penetrating gaze lay the saeva indignatio of a Swift."(11)    These features, together with the parodic style and satiric tone which O'Nolan was cultivating at University College, combined with several influential authors to whom he alludes in his first novel, At Swim-Two-Birds, to create a demonstrable etiology for his art.    In the novel's opening pages Aldous Huxley is referred to by the narrator as that "eminent English writer" who was "generally recognized as indispensable to all who aspire to an appreciation of the nature of contemporary literature" [ASTB 12].

Turning to what may be Huxley's most ambitious novel, certainly in terms of its aesthetic theorizing, Point Counter Point, we find numerous passages which obviously impressed the aspiring novelist Flann O'Brien and which functioned as inspirations for his art.    In the novel's opening pages it is explained that "one shouldn't take art too literally" because art may be "unadulterated with all the irrelevancies of real life."(12)    A short time later, another Huxley spokesperson declares that a "great artist . . . is a man who synthesizes all experience."(13)    These remarks, together with the following, seem veritable guidelines for the creation of At Swim-Two-Birds and, to a somewhat lesser degree, The Third Policeman.

> Put a novelist into the novel.    He justifies aesthetic generalizations, which may be interesting—at least to me.    He also justifies experiment.    Specimens of his work may illustrate other possible or impossible ways of telling a story.    And if you have him telling parts of the same story as you are, you can make a variation on the theme.    But why draw the line at one novelist inside your novel?    Why not a second inside his?    And a third inside the novel of the second?    And so on to infinity, like those advertisements of Quaker Oats where there's a Quaker holding a box of oats, on which is a picture of another Quaker holding another box of oats, on which etc. etc.    At about the tenth remove you might have a novelist telling your story in algebraic symbols or in terms of variations in blood pressure, pulse, secretion of ductless glands, and reaction times.(14)

The Quaker Oats box is similar to MacCruiskeen's chest in The Third Policeman, "perfect in its proportions and without fault in workmanship"; it had "the dignity and the satisfying quality of true art,"(15) and is really a chest within a chest within a chest, and so on, until the final chest can't even be seen with the naked eye. In At Swim-Two-Birds, which is a novel within a novel within a novel within another novel if O'Brien as novelist is included, the narrator states in the opening paragraph that "one beginning and one ending for a book was a thing I did not agree with." Twenty-four pages later he explains that

> a satisfactory novel should be a self-evident sham to which the reader could regulate at will the degree of his credulity. It was undemocratic to compel characters to be uniformly good or bad or poor or rich. Each should be allowed a private life, self-determination and a decent standard of living. This would make for self-respect, contentment and better service. It would be incorrect to say that it would lead to chaos. Characters should be interchangeable as between one book and another. The entire corpus of existing literature should be regarded as a limbo from which discerning authors could draw their characters as required, creating only when they failed to find a suitable existing puppet. The modern novel should be largely a work of reference. Most authors spend their time saying what has been said before usually said much better. A wealth of references to existing works would acquaint the reader instantaneously with the nature of each character, would obviate tiresome explanations and would effectively preclude mountebanks, upstarts, thimbleriggers and persons of inferior education from an understanding of contemporary literature. [ASTB 33]

The narrator/novelist in At Swim-Two-Birds illustrates his theory of the novel by including, as dutifully discerned and compiled by Anne Clissman, "some thirty-six different styles and forty-two extracts."(16) These styles and extracts encompass everything from Irish mythology, folklore, and fairy tales to American Western novels, melodrama, romanticism, and moralistic literature. Each style and extract is thoroughly demonstrated and then parodied with equal thoroughness. Huxley's theories on "the musicalization of Fiction"(17) are also illustrated in the novel and extolled by "The Pooka MacPhellimey" who delights in the "fugal and contrapuntal character of Bach's work" and in the "admirable" four figures of the orthodox fugue [ASTB 156]. As four novels in one, At Swim-Two-Birds is a prose parallel to the orthodox fugue.

If Huxley provided O'Brien with motif and impetus, Heinrich Heine's Die Harzreise provided the paradigm. The narrator in At Swim-Two-Birds cadges money from his uncle to buy Die Harzreise, supposedly a required text for a college course; the money goes for booze instead of the book and thus it remains unpurchased and unread. O'Brien, however, obviously did read it and was sufficiently impressed to emulate many of its features. Heine's witty, hyperbolic pastiche of puns, conundrums, fantasy, romance, fact, and fiction satirizes religion, politics, art, and the middle class, with special emphasis on the "Students, Professors, Philistines and Cattle" of the city of Gottingen, Germany.(18) If transported to Dublin, this could very well be a precis of At Swim-Two-Birds, right down to the cattle. Other formative influences are James Cabell's The Cream of the Jest, Lawrence Sterne's Tristram Shandy, and the novels of James Stephens.

Given the time, place, and circumstances of Dublin in the thirties and the emerging O'Brien metier, it would have been impossible for him not to have inhaled deeply of the Joycean air; however, but the critical tendency has, I believe, overemphasized the Joycean presence, thereby creating a Procrustean Bed on which to impale and then misdiagnose the O'Brien corpus. No one can stay in the saddle more tenaciously than professor/scholars riding their hobby horses through primary and secondary sources to declare territorial imperatives and to establish the progeny, legitimate or otherwise, of their literary superheroes. Like Dermot Trellis in At Swim-Two-Birds, who "confined his reading to books attired in green covers" [ASTB 139], these overspecialized academics suffer terminally from a tunnel vision that precludes, or at best grants minimal recognition to, all writers except those they have isolated for apotheosis.

It is just this kind of excessive, obsessive scholarship and pedantry that O'Brien excoriates and ridicules in all of his novels, especially in The Third Policeman, which he began in 1938 while At Swim-Two-Birds was still in the publication process. Although it was rejected by several publishers and never published in his lifetime, O'Brien retained much of its material and reworked it into The Dalkey Archive, which was published in 1964 to capitalize on the success that At Swim-Two-Birds had achieved when it was republished in 1960. What Huxley and Heine did for At Swim-Two-Birds, Jaris-Karl Huysmans's A Rebour does for The Third Policeman and, to a certain extent, for The Dalkey Archive. Where Huxley and Heine provided role models, however, Huysmans's protagonist, Des Esseintes, provides the thesis for O'Brien's antithesis, de Selby, and together they create a dialectic which produces the hell that the novel's unnamed narrator must endure on a cyclical basis every sixteen years ad infinitum.

It is not until the novel's final pages that the reader, who probably has been taking the story too literally, discovers that this narrator died in the opening pages and has been wandering through a Kafkaesque and kaleidoscopic Hades the entire time. The narrator had murdered and robbed a wealthy neighbor to finance his publication of a beautifully bound, collected edition of the works of de Selby, whose absurd and abstruse ravings on every inconceivable topic have preoccupied the narrator's adult life, including the theory, quite possibly prompted by a similar notion in Die Harzreise, that the earth is sausage-shaped. The myriad parody and satire of At Swim-Two-Birds are restricted here to castigating the pathological narcissism and pseudo self-insight of Huysmans's Des Esseintes. The anonymous narrator of The Third Policeman and de Selby's two principal commentators, Hatchjaw and Bassett, are heroically mocked for their equally pathological absorption in de Selby's writings. This scholarship achieves new and grotesque depths when de Selby's sewage is analyzed to gain, paradoxically, greater awareness of his mind!

The Third Policeman is a drastic shift from the frequently chaotic technical innovations, combinations, and permutations of At Swim-Two-Birds to a more deliberately thematic and structural presentation. This is especially true when we realize that Niall Sheridan played Max Perkins to O'Brien's Thomas Wolfe and reduced the original manuscript of At Swim-Two-Birds by almost a third. Readers attracted to O'Brien through the recent expostulations of critics earnestly detecting the fabulators and metafictionists among twentieth-century novelists will be disappointed if they seek commensurate technical virtuosity beyond At Swim-Two-Birds. Just as Dermot Trellis pondered at the conclusion of At Swim-Two-Birds as to whether "Ars est celare artem" [314], although the opposite had been practiced throughout the novel's preceding chapters, O'Brien apparently believed that he had experimented sufficiently with the various aspects of the novel and would now try traditional techniques in The Third Policeman.

Twenty years later when O'Brien was writing The Hard Life and converting portions of The Third Policeman into The Dalkey Archive, it seems almost as though he had decided that his first novel was "all a joke for entertainment purposes" [TP 98], and that he would now prove to himself, the critics, and his readers that he could also be a quite serious and successful traditionalist. Although the metacritics have accelerated an interest in O'Brien that has been growing in this country since the early sixties, they may also be producing the next misconception of O'Brien's content and form à la the "propter-Joyce" ruse; videlicet, by establishing the presence of metafiction, fabulation, self-evident sham, etc. etc., in one novel, they will insist upon its ubiquity in all five novels. It thus becomes more and more obvious that, regardless of the critical stance, wherever O'Brien reigns, it aporias.

According to Robert Alter, much of this aporia occurs when the "novelistic self-consciousness has gone slack because fiction is everywhere and there is no longer any quixotic tension between what is fictional and what is real."(19)  If the "self-conscious," metafictional, fabulating novel is, by its very nature, supposed to "probe into the problematic relationship between real-seeming artifice and reality,"(20) then the problem with O'Brien, especially in terms of Joyce, may have been that he seriously misunderstood what he satirized, and later condemned Joyce's art and its relation to life because he, according to J. C. C. Mays, began "to take art as life and treat the literary literally,"(21) and thus to become what Mays has declared he was, a "literalist of the imagination."(22)  A similar interpretation of his work was recently offered by Niall Sheridan at the dedication of a plaque to Brian O'Nolan in Blackrock, Co. Dublin.  Sheridan explained that "much of his finest work inhabits a metaphysical universe called up by his subtle penetrating intellect and his powerful imagination."(23)  If Mays and Sheridan are correct, then it is almost metafictional justice that O'Brien is considered by many critics today to be Icarean in his obscene-clone fall from Joyce's artistic heights.

In his intelligent and persuasive essay comparing Joyce and O'Nolan on art and life, Mays argues that in O'Nolan "character tends continually to manifest itself through mimicry and interrelation" and to appear "as a function of style which is exhilarating and ingenious."(24)  Joyce, on the other hand, "takes life into art compulsively so as to recreate life at a proper distance."(25)  In At Swim-Two-Birds, The Third Policeman, its successor, The Dalkey Archive, The Hard Life, and The Poor Mouth (which mocks the romanticized renditions of the Gaeltecht and the Jansenistic orientation of its inhabitants), O'Nolan, as O'Brien, does treat his subject matter, which has been removed from its realistic context by his parodic and satiric intention, as if it were life itself. It is thus ironic, as with Kurt Vonnegut's "So it goes" in Slaughterhouse-Five, that O'Brien repeatedly exclaims in terms of the people and places he depicts in The Poor Mouth that "their likes will not be there again."  The line is also a satiric swipe at Tomás O'Crohan, who used a similar expression throughout his autobiographical work, The Islandman.  What O'Nolan misinterpreted in Joyce as arrogance and disdain for people and reality were, in fact, vital parts of Joyce's aesthetic process to insure the utmost objectivity.  The more enamoured the world became of Joyce, the deeper O'Nolan sank into a resentment that was ironically a negative version of the obsessions for de Selby that he condemned in The Third Policeman, and the more he encouraged future generations of readers and critics to compound and treble the of Joyce's presence in his own aesthetic principles and writings.

In 1951 O'Nolan published an article in Envoy in which he articulated his attitude to Joyce and thus perhaps hoped to exorcize his demonic presence. Fifteen years later, however, while working on the manuscript, "Slattery's Sago Saga"—which remained unfinished because, as one commentator with a flair for morbid understatement observed, "he was distracted by dying,"(26) —O'Nolan was still on the attack, trying to fly beyond his imagined, ineluctable Joycean nets and in the process leave them in shreds with himself "an austere and chastened character saddened as it has been by the contemplation of human folly,"(27) and by "the sad extremities of human woe" [ASTB 255], his heart going like mad saying yes I said yes I will yes.

## NOTES

1.    William H. Gass, Fiction and the Figures of Life  (Boston: Nonpareil Books, 1978), 25.

2.    Robert Scholes, Fabulation and Metafiction (Urbana: University of Illinois Press, 1979).

3.    Robert Alter, Partial Magic:  The Novel as a Self-Conscious Genre (Berkeley and Los Angeles:  University of California Press, 1975), 223.

4.    Steven G. Kellman, The Self-Begetting Novel (New York:  Columbia University Press, 1980), 4.

5.    Robert Martin Adams, After Joyce:  Studies in Fiction After Ulysses (New York:  Oxford University Press, 1977), 190.

6.    Flann O'Brien, At Swim-Two-Birds (1939; reprint, New York: New American Library, 1976), 274.  Further reference to this work will appear in the text, identified by ASTB and the page number.

7.    Anne Clissman, Flann O'Brien, A Critical Introduction to His Writings (New York:  Barnes and Noble, 1975), 86.

8.    Niall Sheridan, "Brian, Flann and Myles," in Myles:  Portraits of Brian O'Nolan, ed. Timothy O'Keefe (London:  Martin Brian and O'Keefe, 1973), 39.

9.    Brian O'Nolan, "A Bash in the Tunnel," Envoy 5, no. 17 (April 1951):  11.

10.    Flann O'Brien, The Dalkey Archive (1967; reprint, New York: Penguin Books, 1977), 111.  Further references to this work will appear in the text identified by DA and the page number.

11.    Sheridan, "Brian, Flann and Myles," 34-36.

12.    Aldous Huxley, Point Counter Point (1928; reprint, New York: Harper and Row, 1965), 10.

13.    Ibid., 64.

14.    Ibid., 301-302.

15.    Flann O'Brien, The Third Policeman (1967; reprint, New York: New American Library, 1976), p. 70.  Further references to this work will appear in the text identified by TP and the page number.

16.    Clissman, Flann O'Brien, 86.

17.    Huxley, Point Counter Point, 301.

18.    Heinrich Heine, Pictures of Travel, vol. 3 of The Works of Heinrich Heine, trans.  Charles Godfrey Leland (New York:  Croscup and Sterling Co., n.d.), 60.

19.    Alter, Partial Magic, 223-224.

20.    Ibid., x.

21.    J. C. C. Mays, "Brian O'Nolan and Joyce on Art and on Life," James Joyce Quarterly 2, no. 3 (Spring 1974):  244.

22.    J. C. C. Mays, "Brian O'Nolan:  Literalist of the Imagination," in Myles:  Portraits of Brian O'Nolan, ed. Timothy O'Keefe (London:  Martin Brian and O'Keefe, 1973), 77-119.

23.    Niall Sheridan, "Plaque inaugurated to Myles na Gopaleen," Irish Times, 2 April 1981.

24.    Mays, "Brian O'Nolan and Joyce," 244.

25.    Ibid., 243.

26.    Stephen Jones, Introduction to A Flann O'Brien Reader (New York:  Viking Press, 1978), xvii.

27.    Myles na Gopaleen, The Best of Myles, ed. Kevin O'Nolan, (London:  MacGibbon and Kee, 1968), 340.

## 14

## "*Non Serviam*": James Joyce and Modern Irish Poetry

### *Robert F. Garratt*

Unlike their predecessor's fifty years before, Irish poets at mid-century did not want for tradition; indeed they found it lay thick all about them. The difficulty came rather in continuity, "the recognition," as Thomas Kinsella says, "of the past in ourselves," and the attempt to identify with tradition.(1) One aspect of this tradition, Revivalism, seemed easily expendable, since it had worked itself into a cliche. The Ascendancy tradition, on which Yeats directed future poets to cast their eyes, likewise could be rejected. While offering a conservative critique of the Revival, it alienated most lower- and middle-class Catholic poets. Yeats himself, an essential part of the Irish literary tradition, proved to be more problematic for younger writers. A major figure and a great talent always presented problems for those writers who follow him, not only in the personal oedipal struggle which Harold Bloom suggests in The Anxiety of Influence,(2) but even more profoundly, as another part of an already burdensome literary tradition which W. Jackson Bate has identified.(3) Moreover, the close proximity of a great talent can produce a quiet and subtle kind of influence, more difficult to discuss or analyze, which Stephen Spender describes as "the felt presence of one poet in the sensibility and attitudes of other poets."(4) Poets are more likely to feel this in a small country like Ireland where attempts to establish a literary tradition are conscious and recent. Yeats's insistence in his later poetry upon redefining that tradition in a particularly narrow way allowed younger writers to reject him on ideological grounds and to look elsewhere for a father figure who might provide continuity.

Irish poets found that figure in James Joyce, a surprising choice perhaps when one considers Joyce's early exile from Ireland and his international reputation as a novelist. Yet Joyce seems a natural father on many levels. His choice of lower- and middle-class life as the marrow of his art deconstructs romantic Ireland, as Denis Donoghue rightly claims,(5) opening the possibility for others to deal realistically with Irish life. The treatment of Catholic and urban experiences in particular offered writers new possibilities. Joyce's self-imposed exile became an emblem of the writer's plight in a society which is at the core puritanical and backward. Most important perhaps, Joyce's great achievements came in prose and for that reason did not impose upon younger poets in the direct and obvious way that Yeats's word did. This new generation--Austin Clarke, Patrick Kavanagh, and Kinsella, among others--read Joyce as a master of fiction and as a realist, both of which safely distanced him from Yeats. Moreover, these younger

writers chose to see Joyce as the expression of their own experiences
and the embodiment of artistic struggle in the modern world.(6)

## "FILTHY STREAMS"

Joyce's attack on Yeats and on the Revival came early in his career and appears in summary form in "The Holy Office," a witty satirical broadsheet composed in 1904 and circulated in Dublin in 1905.  The
poem announces his intention to travel a different road:  "But I must
not accounted be / One of that mumming company," and ridicules these
followers of the Revival, among them Yeats, Lady Gregory, J. M. Synge,
Oliver Gogarty, AE (G. W. Russell), Padraic Colum, and Seamus O'Sullivan.  The disrespectful stance is more than levity aimed at toppling
the Olympians; it also paves the way for the manifesto declaring Irish
literary independence.  Bringing "the mind of witty Aristotle" to the
lowlife of Ireland, he will embrace life in all its forms; recognizing
its corruption, he will not turn his back on the distasteful.

> That they may dream their dreamy dreams
> I carry off their filthy streams
>         . . . . . . . . .
> Thus I relieve their timid arses,
> Perform my office of Katharsis.
> My scarlet leaves them white as wool.
> Through me they purge a bellyful. [CW 151]

The reference to Aristotle's notion of purgation or purification indicates Joyce's willingness to deal with the fallen and with the sinners.
In the context of Irish literature, he opts for the treatment of Irish
experience, both as it is reflected living under foreign domination and
in the Catholic preoccupation with sin; he rejects the mystical and romantic Celtic Twilight.  Aristotelian catharsis also implies the tragic
hero whose fall will purge the audience's feelings of guilt, pity, and
remorse.  These elements surface in the final lines in the figure of
the hero-artist which will be developed later in Portrait.  Here the
portrait of the artist develops in comparison with Yeats and the Reviv-
alists, "that motley crew" that hates his strength.

> Where they have croached and crawled and prayed
> I stand the self-doomed, unafraid,
> Unfellowed, friendless and alone,
> Indifferent as the herring-bone,
> Firm as the mountain-ridges where
> I flash my antlers on the air. [CW 152]

One need not look far to see the importance of this isolation in Portrait and in Ulysses.  But in 1904 it serves as the defiant pose of a
young artist struggling to find his own voice; it is the platform from
which he can attack the impulses of the herd to group and move together.

In a series of reviews and essays written between 1902 and 1904,
the "unafraid and unfellowed" critic justifies his heroism by standing
alone against all literary task and momentum.  He declares that nationalism in poetry too often discourages invention, producing an expression which "the writer has not devised, he has merely accepted" [CW
84-87].  In "The Day of the Rabblement," he warns that in joining a
national movement the artist risks "the contagion of its fetichism and
deliberate self-deception [CW 71].  He criticizes Lady Gregory's Poets
and Dreamers and in the process manages to squeeze in a deft comparison
which damns Yeats with faint praise.

In fine, her book, wherever it treats of the "folk,"
sets forth in the fulness of its senility a class of
mind which Mr. Yeats has set forth with such delicate
scepticism in his happiest book, "The Celtic Twilight."
[CW 104]

In a review of Stephen Gwynn's Today and Tomorrow in Ireland, Joyce ex-
poses the paucity of imagination in all the Revival writers save Yeats
[CW 91]. Furthermore, he raises the question of motivation. In "A
Mother," a story from Dubliners which demands to be read against the
background of the Revival, Joyce shows the inevitable result of the
artist trading in the crowd's marketplace. Yeats's mistake was to imagine that his literary movement could become truly popular and raise
the cultural level of Ireland. Instead, as "A Mother" indicates, the
movement loses out to the rabble and pettiness of the mob. Art and
artistic values are victims of the commercial exploitation and the
shallowness of a fashionable interest in Irish culture.(7)
    Joyce's strategy looks two ways at once: toward the myopic in-
wardness of national literature, and toward the justification and promotion of Joyce's own literary ideals. Joyce's criticism is outrageous
and even audacious, particularly when at this stage there were little
more than ideals behind these pronouncements; Chamber Music was not to
appear for three more years, and Dubliners did not appear until 1914.
Yet, given the hindsight enjoyed by the poets of Kavanagh's or Kinsella's generations, it is precisely the audacity of the young, unpub-
lished Joyce that makes his authority so great. His critique of Revivalism as early as 1902 establishes him as the first important Irish
writer to recognize its limitations.(8)
    As significant as this stance becomes for some literary histori-
ans, however, it does not establish Joyce's paternity for post-Yeatsian
poetry. Yeats, after all, had rejected Revivalism and shared many of
Joyce's views about the tyranny of puritanical Ireland, as poems such
as "September 1913" and his diaries and autobiographies make clear.
But Yeats lacked Joyce's consistency on the matter; indeed, Joyce himself recognized a "treacherous instinct of adaptability" in Yeatsian
poetics [CW 71]. Furthermore, Yeats's mythologizing of Ascendancy Ireland restricted the Irish experience to a minority. Joyce, on the
other hand, would tap the mainstream of modern Irish life, the rising
bourgeoise, and treat it realistically, even ironically, becoming, in
Thomas Kinsella's phrase, "the first major Irish voice to speak for
Irish reality since the death of the Irish language."(9) Joyce's importance stems from subject matter in two interesting ways: first, it
opens up lower- and middle-class life for literary treatment; and second, it provides continuity with that literature, essentially Gaelic
and Catholic, which reflects the life of the dispossessed and downtrod-
den in the sixteenth, seventeenth, and eighteenth centuries. Joyce's
pioneer effort in holding a mirror up to modern Irish life gave the
poets of the 1940s and the 1950s an alternative to Yeats's directive in
"Under Ben Bulben," an alternative which was to prove familiar and
helpful. Clarke recognized in the Portrait his own youthful experiences with the Jesuits; Kavanagh saw in Joyce's special use of locale a
strategy he could adapt to treat rural Ireland;(10) Kinsella read Joyce
as the writer who makes urban literature possible.(11) The antiroman-
ticism implicit in Joyce's treatment of Dublin's mean streets not only
provides an alternative to Yeats's romantic Ireland, but also shows to
what extent ordinary experience can be transformed into art.

THE CREATED CONSCIENCE OF RACE
    In his famous exchange with the publisher Grant Richards over the

fate of <u>Dubliners</u>, Joyce wrote prophetically about the effects of his work, particularly on Irish poetry.

> I believe that in composing my chapter of moral history in exactly the way I have composed it I have taken the first step towards the spiritual liberation of my country. [<u>L</u> I 62-64)]

These remarks were to educate Richards about the intention of <u>Dubliners</u>: the stories were realistic portraits of Dublin life and demanded the "ashpits, weeds, and offal" of city life and specific locations of shops and pubs.  Only such realism could counter the fabulous and romantic account of Irish life with one which would serve as a "polished looking glass," wherein his fellow citizens might see themselves and their world.  The long-range effect, however, went beyond an apologia for the aesthetics of fiction.  The liberation provided by Joyce's critical remarks, supported so powerfully by the practice of his stories and novels, allowed a number of middle-class Catholic poets the authority and the example they needed to write from experience and from the heart.  Clarke's account of his struggle between doubt and faith in <u>Night and Morning</u> takes its shape from the treatment of Catholicism in <u>Portrait.</u>  Similarly, Kavanagh's celebration of the local and his depiction of the spiritual and emotional death-in-life of rural Ireland in "The Great Hunger" grew out of his reading and appreciation of Joyce's scrutiny of Dublin.  Kinsella, writing in the 1960s, saw in Joyce's treatment of the common and the ordinary a focus that accommodates both the Gaelic and the English sides of Irish identity.

For Clarke, as for others of his generation, Joyce's startling originality came in the treatment of Irish Catholicism.  The exploration in <u>Portrait</u> of so many aspects of Catholic youth and adolescence caused Clarke to read it as a cardinal text.  The Joycean artist-hero cannot be held responsible by any force other than his own imagination and sensitivity.  Yet religion seeks to dominate the intellect and becomes a net restricting artistic flight.  In the context of this conflict, Stephen's "Non serviam," developing out of the logic of a <u>Kunstlerroman</u>, sheds light upon a preoccupation among twentieth-century Irish writers.  Clarke wrote about the powerful effect religion had upon his imagination, particularly upon his sense of sin and guilt.  Religious themes and the treatment of Catholic life recur throughout Kavanagh's poetry.  Kinsella describes the Catholicism of his youth as "so pervasive that it hardly counted as an influence at all; it was a reality like oxygen."(12)

Subject matter alone, however, did not determine Joyce's importance as the great liberator, although his depiction of what Kinsella calls "the eloquent and conniving and mean-spirited tribe of Dan" represents its own form of liberation, pulling free from the dominant Ascendancy perspective.(13)  Joyce extracted the marrow of his art from the bones of average Dubliners.  In doing so, he broke ground as no Irish writer had done before him, demonstrating that the artist could find his inspiration from a life which under Yeatsian dictum was without meaning; he encouraged writers by his example to sense in negative feelings about nationality and religion a positive artistic potential.

What stunned Clarke and what subsequently moved Kavanagh and Kinsella was Joyce's controlled forging of oppressively negative experiences into artistic triumphs:  the torpid life of the Dublin streets, the seedy details of middle-class neighborhoods, and most important, the intellectual and moral stagnation in Irish life could be transposed by the inventive yet objective imagination of the artist.  The crucial conflict in <u>Portrait,</u> the tension over Stephen's choice between religion and art, builds upon the gradual establishment of the independence of the artist.    When Stephen refuses to cry out when struc unjustly, he assumes a defiance that will culminate in his refusal to serve that in which he no longer believes.    His imaginative independence and integrity make possible a new working of raw material, an acceptance of the city as a paysage moralisé.    Thus Joyce not only opens up the Catholic and the urban experiences to the writers who follow him, but he also offers the heroic posture of the artist, whose creative energy converts the commonplace into the significant and even the universal.

JOYCEAN PRACTICE
Joyce's presence in modern Irish poetry surfaces in two different ways, through allusion and through subject matter.    Allusions to Joyce in Kinsella's poetry establish an important ethos that extends the authority of the poetic voice.    In a crucial passage in "Nightwalker," the poet, walking near the Martello Tower, declares his affiliation with Joyce:

> Watcher in the tower, be with me now
> At your parapet, above the glare of the lamps.
> Turn your milky spectacles on the sea
> Unblinking; cock your ear.(14)

The invocation appeals directly to a Joycean intelligence to gather all that surrounds the nightwalker and to aid in shaping and ordering impressions and memories.    "Nightwalker" depicts the alienation of the poetic sensibility from its surrounding world.    The "Father of Authors" has led the way by showing that art can be created out of isolation and alienation.    Like romantic idealism, corruption and disappointment serve art extremely well.    As Kinsella implies in section 1, out of the base and common we construct our monuments:    "Clean bricks / Are made of mud; we need them for our tower."

The pursuit of the real, however discomforting or distasteful, directs many of Kinsella's poems, including "Phoenix Park," Notes from the Land of the Dead, and many of the later poems from One and A Technical Supplement.    The acceptance and understanding of experience that informs these later poems came early in Kinsella's career with another important Joycean allusion.    The portrait of the artist at his attic window gazing out at the city stretched out below in "Baggot Street Deserta" reveals much about the strategy that will be at the heart of his work.    The poet accepts his "call of exile" and, isolated, will both inflict and endure the mental sting involved in "obsessed honest" with the "business of the bordermarches / of the Real."    The essential condition of this real world for Kinsella is its mysterious alienating chaos which the artist must attempt to contact and order.

> The slow implosion of my pulse
> In a wrist with poet's cramp, a tight
> Beat tapping out endless calls
> Into the dark.(15)

The setting among the streets of Dublin, the obsession with honesty, the interest in the real, and the effort to order recollections and thoughts suggest a Joycean tenor in the poetry, an acknowledgment of the modern world which reverberates throughout all of Kinsella's poetry.

Clarke and Kavanagh, in their different ways, develop a Joycean direction in their use of setting and in their scrutiny of the

twentieth century Catholic consciousness.  Clarke's use of Dublin in
many of his later poems owes much to Joyce.  The details of the city,
with specific locations and buildings properly placed, display an ac-
curacy that Joyce insisted upon.  The following from "Mnemosyne Lay in
Dust" is characteristic.

>            the Phoenix Park,
> Along the People's Garden . . .
> The Wellington Monument . . .
> The Fifteen Acres, the Dog Pond . . .
>
> They crossed over Kingsbridge.
> The Guinness tugs were roped
> Along their quay, cabs ranked
> Outside the Railway Station . . .
>                          Up Steeven's Lane
>
> He walked into his darkness.
> Classical rustle of Harpies,
> Their ordure at Swift's Gate.(16)

Clarke frequently recalls with Joycean precision the Edwardian city of
his youth in order to measure the price of modernizing Dublin for mid-
twentieth-century commerce and traffic.  The older city of the imagination reflects traditional values which the modern city has discarded.

> Mayor, Alermen and councillors detect Georgian crack and
> strain in Merrion Square; Before they can be found.
> Young architects Copy out modern plans with ruler,
> square.  Contractors nod.  Has anyone been squared?  Of-
> ficial, night-student from our Technical School?    Iron
> balustrade, high fanlight, storey, Are gone.  New glass
> and concrete end their story.(17)

Kavanagh's use of place is less satirical but equally pronounced.
There are a number of Dublin poems in Kavanagh's canon, but his in-
triguing use of setting comes in the details of his boyhood home in
rural Monaghan, growing out of the poet's declaration, "I have lived in
important places."  Location, the names of roads and fields, the celebration of the parish, all of these serve to create the details of a
poetic kingdom.  But Kavanagh's treatment of his rural parish eschews
Yeatsian romance in favor of Joycean realism.  The portrayal of the
grim details of rural life in "The Great Hunger" prove Kavanagh's interest in the reality of experience.  Moreover, the portrait of Paddy
Maguire, the poems's protagonist, owes much to Joyce's many still-lives
in Dubliners.  The slow, steady evaporation of Maguire, life-forces
make him the rural counterpart of Farrington, Little Chandler, Mr.
James Duffy, and other paralyzed Dubliners:

> Watch him, that man on a hill whose spirit
> Is a wet sack flapping about the knees of time.
> He lives that his little fields may stay fertile when
> his own body
> Is spread in the bottom of a ditch.(18)

Maguire's failure is one of imagination, and Kavanagh alludes to Portrait to emphasize the difficulty.  Maguire believes that he has
slipped the nets holding men back-- "he laughed over pints of porter /
Of how he came free from every net spread / In the gaps of experience"

--but because of his complacency and lack of vision he succumbs to them. With "The Great Hunger," Kavanagh opts for the reality of experience rather than the romantic portraits of the land and the peasant seen so often in the poetry of the Revival.

## RELUCTANT FATHER

The prominence of Joyce in modern Irish poetry reflects more the temperaments and needs of a new generation of writers than it does Joyce's interest in bequeathing poetic patrimony. Unlike Yeats, who prescribed a poetic strategy for future generations, Joyce remained cut off from Irish letters, refused to join the Irish Academy in 1932, and offered little commentary on the work of younger writers.(19) Yet he seemed a natural choice for a generation of lower- and middle-class writers whose religious experiences, education, urban orientation, political disillusionment, and poetical opposition to both Yeats and Revivalism were reflected in Joyce's life and work, especially the early fiction. In expressing their world and transforming their experiences, Joyce provided these younger poets with new potential, taught them to accept their own identities and cultural orientation, and presented them unknowingly with a father-figure less austere and threatening than Yeats. In the end it was precisely his unwillingness to participate in the affairs of the Irish literati which made him so appealing as a paterfamilias; by being removed from the scene he provided a symbolic authority and example without a restrictive presence. Moreover, his choice of genre gave the same comfort. The treatment in fiction of religious doubt, alienation from society, and memories of oppressive schooling invited similar treatment in poetry. Similarly, the techniques of realism, the use of setting, and the depiction of psychological realism in the novels and the short stories might be adapted for poetry.

While both Joyce and Yeats looked upon Catholic lower-middle-class Ireland with a critical eye, Joyce looked from within, making his separation the rebellion of one who knew firsthand the conditions that proved unacceptable. The very posture of rebellion assumed a familiarity with those forces he repudiated: the Church, the home, the fatherland. Yeats, on the other hand, remained apart from that which he criticized. His Protestant inheritance predisposed him toward values of the privileged ascendancy; as a result, he saw in the English literary tradition as much meaning and importance as the Irish one he sought to create. Yeats recognized this distance, commenting late in his life on his peculiar cultural perspective, that despite his Irish ancestry and his work for Irish literature, he owed his soul to Shakespeare, to Blake, and to the English language in which he spoke and wrote. This ambivalence stands behind his famous remark about his Anglo-Irish perspective, "My hatred tortures me with love, my love with hate," and the well-known repudiation of the younger poets as "Base born products of base beds." While Yeats turned his alienation into a powerful poetic statement, he nonetheless removed himself from the mainstream of modern and contemporary Irish literature.

This divided tradition states the essential condition of the modern Irish mind, literary or not, and demonstrates why the promises of the Revival died so hard in Ireland. The Irish literary tradition proffered a sense of identity which became the preoccupation of Irish writers of the early twentieth-century; that identity still confounds contemporary poets like Seamus Heaney and Derek Mahon. Modern poetry in general is haunted by the divided mind, a reflection of man cut off from his past, confused about meaning, and attempting to reconcile himself to his solitude. In the Irish literary tradition that reconciliation is defined in cultural and national terms. The struggle for reconciliation becomes embroiled in the question of identity. Yeats's

ultimate impossible acceptance of Anglo-Irish tradition not only made
it difficult for most writers to follow him, but also reinforced the
differences between two elements of Irish society. Joyce, whose understanding of this condition is implicit in Stephen's connection of Irish
art with servitude, recognized the difficulty for the Irish writer who
inherits a fractured tradition. But Joyce did not wait until Ulysses
to demonstrate this rift; it appears both in Dubliners and in Portrait.
In "The Dead" Gabriel Conroy's anxieties about cultural identity show
Joyce's early awareness of the problem. The difficulty develops in
Portrait to become a major theme. Stephen confesses to himself that
the English tongue is not his own, but this understanding does not
drive him into the arms of the Gaelic League. In the diary section of
the end of chapter 5, he expresses a reluctance about the native Gaelic
tradition. The old man from the west of Ireland who speaks Irish,
smokes a pipe, and lives in a cabin offers him no comfort:

> I fear him. I fear his redrimmed horny eyes. It is
> with him I must struggle all through this night till day
> come, till he or I lie dead, gripping him by the sinewy
> throat till. . . . Till what? Till he yield to me?
> No. I mean him no harm. [P 252]

Joyce, who could not identify with the dying Gaelic culture, nor
accept completely the imposition of an English one, accommodated both
and in a sense used the fragmentation of Irish literature as a metaphor
for the reality of the modern condition. By accepting this condition,
and more important, by insisting on a personal vision which focused upon cultural and spiritual isolation, Joyce offered the next generation
of poets the means to restore life to a poetic tradition.

NOTES

1.    Thomas Kinsella, Davis, Mangan, Ferguson? Tradition and the
Irish Writer (Dublin: Dolmen Press, 1970), 7.

2.    Harold Bloom, The Anxiety of Influence (New York:    Oxford
University Press, 1973).

3.    W. Jackson Bate, The Burden of the Past and the English Poet
(Cambridge:  Harvard University Press, 1970).

4.    Stephen Spender, "The Influence of Yeats on Later English
Poets," Tri-Quarterly 4 (1965):  84-87.

5.    Denis Donoghue, "Romantic Ireland," in Yeats, Sligo and Ireland, ed. A. Norman Jeffares (England:  Bucks Gerard Cross:  Colin
Smythe, 1980), 30.

6.    Austin Clarke states that Portrait "had long since become
confused with my own memories"; see Twice Round the Black Church (London, Routledge and Kegan Paul, 1962), 26. Clarke and Patrick Kavanagh
both admired Joyce's stance in dramatizing the artist's ability to
speak out.

7.    Herbert Howarth, in The Irish Writers (New York:  Hill and
Wang, 1958), 253-54, suggests that in name-play Joyce debunks Yeats's
popular ideal in the play Cathleen ni Houlihan by splitting Kathleen
from Holohan and having them argue over money.

8.    Frank O'Connor, A Backward Look (New York:    Capricorn Books, 1968), 194–96.

9.    Kinsella, Davis, Mangan, Ferguson? 65.

10.    Kavanagh's acceptance of parochialism-- "a mentality which is never in any doubt about the social and artistic validity of his parish" --and his reference to Joyce as one of the two great Irish parishioners (the other was George Moore) are important to his overall aesthetic thinking; see Kavanagh's Weekly, 24 May 1952, facsimile ed. (The Curragh, Co. Kildare, Ireland: Goldsmith Press, 1981).

11.    Kinsella, Davis, Mangan, Ferguson? 64.

12.    John Haffenden, Viewpoints:    Poets in Conversation (London: Faber and Faber, 1981), 100.

13.    Kinsella, Davis, Mangan, Ferguson? 65.    Kinsella seems reluctant to name this group, but he means the Catholic bourgeoisie.

14.    Thomas Kinsella, Poems, 1956-1973 (Winston-Salem, N.C.:    Wake Forest University Press, 1979), 108.

15.    Kinsella, Poems, 1956-1973, 30.

16.    Austin Clarke, Collected Poems (Dublin:    Dolmen Press, 1974), 350-51.

17.    Ibid., 416.

18.    Patrick Kavanagh, Collected Poems (London:    MacGibbon and Kee, 1967), 35.

19.    Austin Clarke suggests that Joyce had no interest in reading Clarke's poetry and asked him only about places and persons in Dublin; see Twice Round the Black Church, 24-27.    Deirdre Bair in Samuel Beckett (New York:    Harcourt, Brace, Jovanovich, 1978) reports that Joyce gave Beckett's work only cursory recognition; see especially pp. 93-95, 180.

# 15

# Joyce, Heaney, and "that subject people stuff"

## Lucy McDiarmid

> What is a ghost?  Stephen said with tingling energy.
> One who has faded into impalpability through death,
> through absence, through change of manners. [U 188]

Dead writers tend to speak in the imperative mood.  The shade of Brunetto Latino, warning Dante of the "envious, proud, and avaricious"
Fiesolans, orders, "See that you root their customs from your mind,"
and closes by requesting the poetic immortality which is his due:
"Remember my Treasure, in which I still live on."(1)  The ghost of
Yeats, sounding more like a seventeenth-century divine than an Irish
poet, predicts that Eliot's "thoughts and theory" will be forgotten,
and admonishes, "pray they be forgiven / By others, as I pray you to
forgive / Both bad and good."(2)  And in Seamus Heaney's "Station Island, XII," which is modelled on these passages from the Inferno and
"Little Gidding," the ghost of Joyce utters a series of commands to the
poem's speaker: "Get back in harness . . . Cultivate a worklust . . .
don't be so earnest . . . strike your own note . . . Swim / out on your
own."(3)  One of a sequence centered on the Lough Derg pilgrimage, the
poem was originally published under the title "A Familiar Ghost" in the
Irish Times on Joyce's hundredth birthday.  Here and in the poem Heaney
invokes Joyce in order to define himself.  With all the authority of
his predecessors Latino and Yeats, yet in a voice distinctly his own,
"cunning, narcotic, mimic, definite / as a steel nib's cursives," Joyce
tells the younger man not only how to be a writer, but how to be an
Irish writer.  The poem is an example of that quintessentially Joycean
event, the discovery of the true father, but with this wrinkle:  the
father tells the son not to look for fathers.
   The characters, of course, are not Joyce and Heaney, but "Joyce"
and "Heaney."  Joyce--or, strictly speaking, his ghost--speaks Heaney's
notion of what Joyce would say to the poet as he steps off the boat
from Station Island in Lough Derg, having completed the pilgrimage
("But we had done with peregrinatio").  And the poem's speaker is no
more to be identified with Heaney than Chaucer-pilgrim is to be identified with Chaucer-poet.  Heaney is a wide-eyed enthusiast:  "Hail Glorious Saint Patrick!" he sings, in the traditional song of the pilgrimage, a song for the many.  But the song "warped as it lifted off in
gusts of wind."  The poem's language reveals at once another, more
critical consciousness, one which describes the pilgrims on the boat as
"Close-packed" and "like a band / of starved monks."  This proximity is
imprisonment, a community which binds and starves the individual.

Against such constraints Joyce battled all his life:  his attitude already informs the poem's imagery even before he appears.

It is Joyce who offers a hand "scribe-cold and bony" to the "convalescent" speaker, helping him off the boat.  The ghost's guidance is as much chastisement as encouragement.  He refers with great disdain to the "pious exercise" and "your peasant pilgrimage."  "I was at nobody's service / the way you are at theirs," he announces, echoing Stephen Dedalus's echo of the satanic non serviam:  "I will not serve that in which I no longer believe, whether it call itself my home, my fatherland, or my church" [P 246-47].  To be "at service" to the community is to be its slave, to surrender and deny individual identity for the sake of some putative larger good.  "This was a backsliding enterprise" because Heaney-pilgrim let his artistic self be stifled by a group whose beliefs he did not share.  Going on the pilgrimage was a gesture of false deference, mechanical and insincere.  "You lose more of yourself than you redeem / doing the decent thing," warns the ghost, and what is lost is the independent expressive self, which becomes as "warped" as the pilgrims' singing.  The word "decent" is used with similar derogation in A Portrait of the Artist as a Young Man to describe the pressure of social groups on Stephen Dedalus.  A "worldly voice" tells him to "be a decent fellow," to help his family, his friends, and his country, but for Stephen as for Heaney in this poem such a call is "hollowsounding" [P 8].

Yet the denial of a "service" that warps the imagination does not entail the severance of all relation to a community.  It does not sanction or encourage the notion of being a poète maudit.  Stephen himself, after all, is going to "forge in the smithy of [his] soul the uncreated conscience of [his] race" [P 253].  He sees himself explicitly as an Irish artist and identifies with his "race" (even if, in the final ecstatic entry of his diary, he does seem to ignore the fact that Irish literature was by no means "uncreated" at the time of his writing).  "You've listened long enough.  Now strike your note," Joyce's ghost remarks, so some "listening" must be necessary.  But how, as he puts it, can the artist write "for others but not . . . with them"?  The way the ghost recommends is to write "for your own joy in it," to write not for any civic obligation but for the pleasure of creating.  The language he uses suggests that such artistic activity becomes, itself, a form of redemption as valuable for the community as religion:

> When I refused to take the sacrament
>     I made my life an instrument of grace
>     so all of you had more abundant life.

Joyce, as Heaney envisions him, does not set up "profane" art against religion, but true voice against false, "I made my life an instrument of grace" against "Hail Glorious Saint Patrick!"  When the artist creates purely for his own "joy," his whole life becomes an "instrument of grace" for his society.  He does not need to engage in "pious exercise."

Heaney-pilgrim's first response to the ghost is a gush of excitement.  With the reverence Stephen accords to the fabulous artificer, Heaney addresses Joyce as "Old father."  In the next breath he also calls out "mother's son," and the two phrases together suggest a fusion--and confusion--of Joyce and Stephen Dedalus.  The pilgrim is evidently eager to worship.  He needs a religious authority, and, chastized for his pilgrimage, he now proceeds to create a new religion, with Stephen's diary elevated to the position of sacred text:

there is an entry in Stephen's diary for April the thir-
teenth, a revelation

set among my stars.  That day's my birthday and those
words are vagitus in my ears, the collect for a new
epiphany,

the Feast of the Holy Tundish!"

The tundish, of course, is the subject of discussion between Stephen
and the dean of studies in the last chapter of Portrait.  When Stephen
uses the word tundish for funnel, the dean takes it to be a quaint
Irishism:

> ---Is that called a tundish in Ireland?  asked the dean.
> I never heard the word in my life.
> ---It is called a tundish in Lower Drumcondra, said
> Stephen laughing, where they speak the best English.
> ---A tundish, said the dean reflectively.  That is a
> most interesting word.  I must look that word up.  Upon
> my word I must.

Stephen is reminded that his language is that of his colonial rulers:

> His language, so familiar and so foreign, will always be for
> me an acquired speech.  I have not made or accepted its
> words.  My voice holds them at bay.  My soul frets in the
> shadow of his language. [P 188-89]

But at the end of Portrait the "fretting" changes to a more active ir-
ritation.  This is the entry for April 13th:

> That tundish has been on my mind for a long time.  I
> looked it up and find it English and good old blunt Eng-
> lish too.  Damn the dean of studies and his funnel!
> What did he come here for to teach us his own language
> or to learn it from us?  Damn him one way or the other!
> [P 251]

Stephen is right, of course; good old blunt Shakespeare uses the word
in Measure for Measure (3.2).
      In proclaiming April 13th the "Feast of the Holy Tundish," Heaney-
pilgrim identifies with Stephen's resentment of the English dean and
the English language, and attempts to transform Stephen's adolescent
rebellion into a religion.  The conjunction of Heaney's birthday and
the date of Stephen's diary entry seems a miraculous coincidence to the
superstitious pilgrim.  He hears the words as a birth-cry (vagitus)
heralding the beginning of a substitute Christianity, with its own "epiphany."(4)  The tundish, an inverse chalice, centers this holiday's
ritual on a defiance of English authority.
      Joyce's ghost doesn't appreciate this worship.  The pilgrim has
deified, or at least canonized, a man behaving like a child, a young
man Joyce himself treated ironically.  The ghost becomes impatient with
such inappropriate adulation.

> "Who cares,"
> he said, "any more?  The English language belongs to us.
> You are raking at dead fires, a waste of time for some-
> body your age.

> That subject people stuff is a cod's game, infantile--
> like your peasant pilgrimage."

The "dead fires" Heaney is raking at identify him with the naive dean of studies. In worshipping Stephen's defiance, Joyce says, Heaney defines himself as a child in relation to parent England. He is attempting to keep alive a linguistic antagonism centuries out of date. Stephen--so Heaney imagines Stephen's creator thinking--was being childish in that diary entry, and the wide-eyed pilgrim wants to perpetuate, and ritualize, his complaint. The tundish is a reminder of Stephen's frustration with his colonial position, and Heaney's wish to turn it into a sacred symbol signifies an obsession with that position. The reverence for Stephen's diary is the flip side of the antagonism to England. In either case, the child's attention is focused on authority. In choosing to worship, or model himself on, Stephen Dedalus, the pilgrim is not proclaiming his autonomy and his independence of all the "nets" Stephen wanted to escape. On the contrary, he is defining himself as a dependent, someone in a permanent stance of rebellion. To be denying ties to authority is still, of course, to see himself in a colonial relation.

In the poem's final imperatives Joyce plays an active Dedalus to Heaney's passive Stephen: "The way of the blunt / sleek dolphin has to be your way: swim / out on your own." Like the murdered fisherman of Heaney's earlier poem, "Casualty," recalled as "Plodder through midnight rain," Joyce's ghost goes striding off in the rain, the "shower in a cloudburst." In their autonomy and defiance of political restrictions both Joyce and the fisherman serve as models for the poet. Like Stephen Dedalus, the fisherman will not serve: he goes "out drinking in a curfew / Others obeyed." The description of the funeral in the second section of "Casualty" is reminiscent of the pilgrimage:

> Coffin after coffin
> Seemed to float from the door
> Of the packed cathedral
> Like blossoms on slow water.(5)

Like the pilgrims, the people at the funeral are imprisoned in a community, "braced and bound / Like brothers in a ring." The fisherman will not be restricted by crowds like this one; he breaks "our tribe's complicity." In both poems the mild speaker admires his tougher, more independent subject, a dead man who walks off at the end very much alive and forceful. His deliberate, determined movement away from a crowd and into water is associated with creative activity. At the end of "Casualty," Heaney remembers a time when the man took him fishing:

> I tasted freedom with him.
> To get out early, haul
> Steadily off the bottom,
> Dispraise the catch, and smile
> As you find a rhythm
> Working you, slow mile by mile,
> Into your proper haunt
> Somewhere, well out, beyond.(6)

The poet's proper haunt, like the fisherman's, is "somewhere, well out, beyond." Just as fishing, with its "rhythm," blends into poetry-writing here, so writing poetry, in "A Familiar Ghost," becomes a fish's free movement outward over water:

                    swim
           out on your own and fill the element
           with signatures on your own frequency,
           echo-soundings, searches, probes, allurements,
           elver-gleams in the dark of the whole sea.

The order to "swim" may echo Dante's description of the poet Guido
Guinizelli, whom he meets in canto XXVI of the Purgatorio (ll 73-135).
After requesting Dante to say the Lord's Prayer for him, he disappears
"Come per l'acqua pesce andanda al fondo"--"as a fish does to the dark
depths of the sea" (Ciardi).
     "A Familiar Ghost" is "Casualty" made heroic, the dead man here
more victor than victim.   The Dantesque allusions give greater power
and energy to the poet's model.  "Casualty" ends with a poignant, nos-
talgic apostrophe---

           Dawn-sniffing revenant,
           Plodder through midnight rain,
           Question me again.

--but Heaney's parting with Joyce is sterner.  Something of Brunetto
Latino's proud, independent bearing is reflected in the lines describing Joyce's stride:  "As he moved off quickly / the downpour loosed its
screens round his straight walk."
     The ghost, like all ghosts, speaks to some extent for his author:
he is older Heaney addressing younger Heaney.   His contempt for the
pilgrimage and for the speaker's rebellious stance has bearing on a
number of poems Heaney wrote in the early seventies, poems which have
as their focus "that subject people stuff."   The relation of England to
Ireland in these poems tends to be that of brute domineering male to
helpless female, rather than parent to child, but the psychological--
and literary--subjugation of Ireland to a cruel authority remains the
same.  "Traditions" (from Wintering Out, 1972) seems directly inspired
by Stephen's grievance in Portrait ("His language, so familiar and so
foreign, will always be for me an acquired speech"):

           Our guttural muse
           was bulled long ago
           by the alliterative tradition,
           her uvula grows
           vestigial.(7)

The Irish muse was "bullied," was "John-Bulled," and impregnated by the
English language, her sounds and her poetry transformed.   The uvula
isn't needed in English as it is in Irish for sounds like the broad "d"
in Dia dhuit.  The "cherished archaisms" which are "correct Shakespear-
ean," mentioned in the poem's second section, are just such words as
"tundish."   The "Traditions" of the title are "vestigial" Irish traditions and hybrid colonial ones.   In the later poem "Ocean's Love to
Ireland" Sir Walter Raleigh's rape of a young English girl is a figure
for colonial domination:

           Speaking broad Devonshire,
           Raleigh has backed the maid to a tree
           As Ireland is backed to England
           And drives inland.(8)

Raleigh's dialect is important because it is the guttural muse who he
is "bulling": one language rapes another.  As the third section says,

"The ruined maid complains in Irish." Her complaint, in her native language, is a poetry of subject people; it is a complaint against her oppressor, voiced in a language which will soon virtually disappear. The result of the rape is immediately audible in the poem:  "Iambic drums / of English beat the woods." Heaney has introduced a perfect blank verse line between two lines to embody the iambic drums.  The ruined maid is Ireland, and what happens to her happens to the whole country, "the ground possessed and repossessed."

"Act of Union," the most famous of these "subject people" poems, combines in its title the sexual act and the political act by which the Irish parliament was dissolved in 1800 and Irish representation transferred to a union parliament in Westminster.  Again, Ireland is the female impregnated by male England.  In this minor variation on the theme, the colonial relation is more ambiguous:

> Conquest is a lie.  I grow older
> Conceding your half-independent shore
> Within whose borders now my legacy
> Culminates inexorably.(9)

Ireland is not entirely "subject," and the baby to be born will fight his father for his mother's sake: "His heart beneath your heart is a wardrum / Mustering force."  The analogy on which "Act of Union" is based keeps alive the colonial terminology; whatever concessions its speaker makes to the "half-independent" shore, it persists in seeing an England "imperially male" and an Ireland like the raped Renaissance girl, whose childbirth will leave her "raw, like opened ground, again."

All of these poems were published between 1972 and 1975, and all celebrate the Feast of the Holy Tundish.  An essay Heaney wrote in 1978 shows a marked change, and anticipates the poem about Joyce.  In "The Interesting Caset of John Alphonsus Mulrennan," Heaney discusses the Irish sense of loss of a native language and refers to the "linguistically fractured" tradition.(10)  Heaney quotes the whole exchange between Stephen Dedalus and the dean of studies, and observes that Stephen "feels excluded from the English tradition."  The loss is the loss of the ruined maid, of the guttural muse's virginal state before she was "bulled," of precolonial Ireland.  One way various literary figures have coped with the feeling of loss, says Heaney, is to reach back in Irish culture to a time or tradition existing before English domination.  Hence Mangan and Ferguson and "their efforts to restore the old mythology and poetic idiom by translation and imitation."  Hence, later, Yeats, Douglas Hyde, Synge, Lady Gregory, and their "counter-culture," based, as Yeats says in "The Municipal Gallery Revisited," on "contact with the soil."(11)  Hence also Austin Clarke and his "attempt to reproduce in English the musical lingering effects of verse in Irish."

Of these efforts to regain what was lost culturally before the colonial subjection of Ireland, Heaney writes,

> What each version of Irish tradition does, then, is to
> venerate ancestors of some kind, to posit an original
> place and an original language and culture and to pine
> for its restoration, or at least to judge present condi-
> tions in the light of this lost ideal.  Whether Anglo-
> Irish or Catholic Gaelic or Protestant Planter, each
> tradition intersects with a social and political vision.
> Each is symptomatic of the fracture in the island's his-
> tory.  Each is a tradition with a small t pining for a

> more inclusive and ample possibility. Each is stay-at-
> home, inwardlooking, pious, exclusive and partial.(12)

Each, in other words, is like Heaney on his pilgrimage.  The revival-
ists are like orphans fantasizing about unrecorded families.  They
"venerate ancestors" they never knew, longing to be part of a family
and a history.
    At this point in the essay Heaney reintroduces Joyce as a writer
who is not--quite literally--"stay-at-home," and certainly not pious.
Joyce acts like an adult, accepting the present and not pining for a
mythical past.

> His tower will be on Dublin Bay, watching the ships that
> link Ireland with the modern world beyond, not like
> Yeats's Norman tower in Ballylee, linking the poet with
> the Gaelic peasantry of Raftery and the Anglo-Irish her-
> itage.(13)

Joyce teaches a mode of adjustment to that fractured linguistic tradition.  His "achievement," says Heaney, "reminds me that English is by
now not so much an imperial humiliation as a native weapon."  This suggestive final sentence signals the end of the "subject people" stance.
If the English language is a "native weapon," it is no longer seen as
an "acquired speech" which the voice "holds . . . at bay."  It is in-
digenous now.  The imagery keeps the colonial analogy alive; "native
weapon" still implies a revolution against established authority.  But
fighting back is at least the beginning of autonomy.
    "A Familiar Ghost" dismisses such a cast of mind with its depre-
cating phrase "subject people stuff."  This new poem affiliates itself
with Tradition with a big T.  Unlike the pilgrimage it describes, the
poem is anti-provincial, and itself embodies the values the ghost
speaks for.  It looks outward to a European literary tradition rather
than inward to a native Irish one.  It looks, for example, to Dante.
The poem is clearly modelled on Dante's encounters with the ghosts of
the dead in the Inferno and the Purgatorio, particularly the encounter
with his revered master Brunetto Latino in the fifteenth canto of the
Inferno.  Dante, as well as Joyce, is Heaney's "guide."  The Lough Derg
pilgrimage puts the poem in a purgatorial context.  Heaney, who has
translated passages from Dante, sustains the aba bcb rhyme scheme of
the terza rima.
    But the determination not to be insular is even more striking in
the allusions to T. S. Eliot:  it's much easier for an Irish writer to
invoke a medieval Italian poet than a twentieth-century English one.
In its title the poem proclaims its relation to "Little Gidding," where
Eliot, fire-watching during the Blitz, meets a "familiar compound
ghost," a compound of Yeats, Joyce, and Dante, among others.(14)  (At a
reading in Boston in 1982, Heaney read the second part of "Little Gidding" before reading "A Familiar Ghost.")  The poetic master Eliot
meets sternly forces him to acknowledge, as Heaney's guide does in his
turn, the narrowness of his vision:

> I am not eager to rehearse
>     My thoughts and theory which you have forgotten.
>     These things have served their purpose: let them be.
> So with your own.(15)

(Like Joyce, Eliot was interested in Hamlet and his ghost, as his echo
testifies:  the familiar ghost "faded on the blowing of the horn," the
all-clear.)  To use Eliot with respect and admiration, as Heaney's poem

does, is to get beyond provincial antagonisms to that larger Traditionwhich Eliot himself reverenced so much. After all, who more Anglo than the man who announced, in 1927, that he was "Classicist," "Royalist," and "anglo-catholic"? And perhaps, in the allusion, a fraternal relationship is hinted at: as an American, Eliot was a "colonial" subject himself, trying to get beyond his nation's insularity to the European tradition he, too, found in Dante.

Heaney's naive speaker may be fixated on the Holy Tundish, but the clever author of the poem is in touch with English and European literary traditions. He is "outward-looking" and cosmopolitan, not a subject person but a native of the world. "A Familiar Ghost" is a poem of liberation: in its language is liberated from politics, imagination from "pious exercise," personality from the imprisoning "Close-packed" band of pilgrims, whose society starves the body and warps the voice. And the liberation is purely Joycean: Guido Guinizelli asks Dante to pray for him, Arnaut Daniel dives into the fire that refines, the ghost in "Little Gidding" urges restoration by "that refining fire / Where you must move in measure, like a dancer." Heaney's pilgrim moves in measure at the start of the poem, singing "Hail Glorious Saint Patrick!" with all the others. What Joyce commands is a movement without "measure," idiosyncratic and unpredictable: "Fill the element / with signatures on your own frequency."

As Harold Bloom has observed, every poet creates his precursors. The ghost in the poem is Heaney's re-creation of Joyce. But Joyce had a hand in the creation of the poem; it could not have been written without his example. "I made my life an instrument of grace / so all of you had more abundant / life," he says, and that abundance helped bring forth this poem. If Hamlet's grandson can be Shakespeare's grandfather, then Heaney and Joyce must be similarly related. Within the poem, Joyce acts as father to Heaney; he guides the pilgrim and offers practical advice, he is addressed as "old father," and, finally, he rejects the paternal role foisted on him. But Heaney wrote the poem, and is in that sense father to Joyce's ghost. Historically, however, Joyce preceded and prepared the way for Heaney, as an Irishman writing happily in English. The real Joyce, then, is the grandfather of his own ghost. But the real Heaney, creating the ghost who fathers his pilgrim, becomes grandfather to his own younger self. Able to play both father and son, Heaney establishes here his autonomy as a fellow member of Tradition, a colleague among colleagues.

## NOTES

1. Dante, The Inferno, trans. John Ciardi (New York: New American Library, 1954), 137, 139 (canto, XV, 11.69, 118).

2. T. S. Eliot, "Little Gidding," in Collected Poems 1909-1962 (New York: Harcourt, 1963), 204.

3. Seamus Heaney, "A Familiar Ghost," in James Joyce: A Special Supplement of the Irish Times, 2 February 1982, 1. The poem has since been reprinted in James Joyce and Modern Literature, ed. W. J. McCormack and Alistair Stead (Boston: Routledge and Kegan Paul, 1982) a revised version appears in Heaney, Station Island (London: Faber and Faber, 1984), 92-94.

4. Samuel Beckett, whose birthday is also April 13th, uses the Latin word vagitus to mean birth-cry in his short play Breath. I am grateful to Suzette Henke and Deirdre Bair for this information.

5.    Seamus Heaney, "Casualty," in Field Work (New York:    Farrar Straus, 1979), 22.

6.    Ibid., 24.

7.    Seamus Heaney, "Traditions," in Wintering Out (London:    Faber and Faber, 1972), 31.

8.    Seamus Heaney, "Ocean's Love to Ireland," in North (London: Faber and Faber, 1975), 46.

9.    Heaney, "Act of Union," in North, 49.

10.    Seamus Heaney, "The Interesting Case of John Alphonsus Mulrennan," Planet:    The Welsh Internationalist 41 (January 1978): 35.    I am grateful to John Wilson Foster for calling my attention to this essay.

11.    Heaney, "The Interesting Case," 36.

12.    Ibid., 39.

13.    Ibid.

14.    But see also Stephen's use of "familiar" as attendant spirit: "My familiar, after me, calling Steeeeeeeeephen" [U 20].

15.    Eliot, Collected Poems, 203-4.

# Part V

## Joyce's Centenarian Contemporaries

# 16

# The Two Patricks: Galltacht and Gaeltacht in the Fiction of Pádraic Ó Conaire

*Philip O'Leary*

Writing in An Claidheamh Soluis (The Sword of Light) in 1906, Pádraic Pearse issued a ringing challenge to the fledgling Irish language literary movement: "We want no Gothic revival. We would have the problems of today fearlessly dealt with in Irish."(1) No Gaelic writer answered that call more promptly or more creatively than did Pádraic Ó Conaire. In "Nóra Mharcuis Bhig," a story that took the first prize at the Oireachtas of 1906, the very year of Pearse's editorial, Ó Conaire was already coming to grips with a conflict still unresolved by Irish-language writers: how to capture urban, English-speaking life in the language of the remote countryside.(2) He was perhaps uniquely qualified to bridge this gap, in that from early in his life he had experience of both town and Gaeltacht. Born in Galway in 1882 of parents with close Gaeltacht ties, in 1893 upon the death of his mother he was taken to live in Ros Muc, the Ros na gCaorach of Pearse's Gaeltacht idylls. From 1897 to 1899 he was away at school, for the most part at Blackrock College near Dublin, and in 1899 he left Ireland for a civil service post in London, where he remained until 1914.(3) He began writing, apparently under the inspiration of the London branch of the Gaelic League, in the early years of this century; his story "Páidín Mháire" won an Oireachtas prize in 1904. In 1910 his novel of Irish exile life in London, Deoraíocht (Exile), won another Oireachtas prize and was, as Máirtín Ó Cadhain said, "for long our outstanding novel."(4)

Predictably, Ó Conaire's groundbreaking attempts to bring Irish prose into the twentieth century met with some resistance. Looking back on Deoraíocht in 1922, "Conall Cearnach" (Feardorcha Ó Conaill) wrote: "Pádraic Ó Conaire did a bold thing writing about London in Conamara Irish. There is only one thing wrong with this—it's not natural. Writing in Irish about certain matters in life is like writing about them in Latin."(5) For the new generation of Irish language enthusiasts rising up with the Revival, however Ó Conaire's work was a revelation. Liam Ó Briain writes:

> Although Pearse began on his stories at exactly the same
> time, and although they are fine and beautiful, he
> didn't provide the same jolt out of the time of the old
> storytelling and into the twentieth century, into the
> bare, ugly reality of life as it was around the people
> of the Gaeltacht and the Galltacht, the jolt that was
> necessary if our movement was to show any seriousness.

It is not possible to understand today, what great courage it took to write something like "Nora Mharcuis Bhig"
at that time.(6)

Similarly, Leon Ó Broin has written of Ó Conaire's later collection
Seacht mBua an tEiri Amach (Seven Triumphs of the Rising): "It opened
my eyes and raised my spirit. Before that book was published, the idea
was lodging itself in my mind that Gaelic literature had no destiny except to be forever discussing the worn-out subjects of the countryside."(7)  Cathaoir Ó Braonáin's judgment on the same story collection
is definitive: "Pádraic Ó Conaire has killed Cock Robin, and we who
see him die must be grateful for the arrow."(8)
    The mere fact of their setting thus made milestones of Ó Conaire's
urban stories in their own time.  Today, however, we must look beyond
their undeniable historical importance to see just how Ó Conaire presented city life and especially its impact on those coming to it from a
rural, particularly a Gaeltacht, background.  Ó Conaire's cities, and
to some extent even his towns, are hostile places; in W. P. Ryan's description, they are "an unloving and unlovely environment,"(9) at times
not all that far removed from the stereotyped centers of sin warned
against by Irish writers of anti-emigration tracts.  Ó Conaire was extremely aware, partly from hard-won experience, of urban poverty.(10)
The down-and-out narrator of the early story "'Fan go Fóill'" ("'Hold
On a Bit'") describes the hopelessness of life among the London unem-
ployed: "It's many a wonder I saw at that time.  Big strong men who
had no chance to get work begging for charity at the side of the
street. . . .  Women being tormented, children being beaten.  And the
Man with the Hooves sitting on high mocking them all."(11)  Even more
grim is his picture in Deoraíocht: of people starving in London:

> They were thin and weak.  There was a look in the eyes
> of some of them when they saw the food like the look in
> the eyes of a tiger.  They were perished with the cold
> and the hunger.  They bolted the food with the sweat
> falling from them with the heat of the coffee and their
> exertion in drinking it.  It was so long since they had
> had a good meal that some of them couldn't keep the food
> in their stomachs.(12)

Later in the novel he describes elderly poor people picking through
hotel garbage cans for food:

> when some of them would come on a piece of bread or
> meat, you'd see them seizing it with their thin fingers
> and cleaning the filth from the grimy food with their
> fingernails.  As they bent over those tin containers in
> the half-light of the morning with the big hotels look-
> ing down on them derisively, they were like a flock of
> terrible, hungry, huge wild birds picking a person's
> bones in a desert with their large, bony claws. [75]

This reference to a "desert" indicates a perceptive and far-reach-
ing insight into urban life on Ó Conaire's part.  Although Breandán Ó
Doibhlin in his influential essay "An Coimhthios: Gne den Aigne Idirnáisiúnta i Litríocht na Gaeilge" ("Alienation: An Aspect of the International Mind in Gaelic Literature") has downplayed the significance
of the theme of alienation in Ó Conaire's work,(13) Bernard Ó Maoldomhnaigh feels that in Deoraíocht Ó Conaire is "seeking a natural expression for a social problem—the alienation felt by a person who is set-

tled in a place where he is cut off from the life around him."(14)   Indeed Pádraig Ó Croiligh sees Ó Conaire as using the condition of exile
that was the fate of so many young people in the Gaeltacht as a symbol
of modern alienation:

> But Pádraic isn't concerned with the problem of exile
> per se; for it is a kind of symbol for a problem that
> everyone has, the problem of the person in relation to
> himself and to his fellow person . . . This is a problem
> that is part of this new urban life of ours, a problem
> that is discussed frequently nowadays and called aliena-
> tion.(15)

What makes their sense of alienation so painful for Ó Conaire's
Gaeltacht exiles is their inability to take advantage of the possibilities for diverse human companionship seemingly offered by the city after the isolation of their rural homes.  Ó Conaire's desert is a dense-
ly populated one.   In one of the stories in Scéalta an tSairsint Rua
(Stories of the Redheaded Sergeant), he describes a London boarding
house as "as full of people as an egg is of meat,"(16) and pictures of
urban overcrowding and lack of privacy are common in his fiction.  For
example, Nóra Mharcuis Bhig and her roommate live "in an extremely
large house in which the people were piled on top of each other."(17)
Yet despite the proximity of so many people, Ó Conaire's characters
find it impossible to establish any real communication or intimacy with
others.  Having come to the city to escape some of the penury and con-
striction of rural life, they find themselves trapped again in the spe-
cious freedom of urban indifference or outright hostility.
    In Deoraíocht, the protagonist and narrator Mícheal Ó Maoláin is
amazed and ultimately outraged when Londoners pay no attention to him
as he painfully learns to walk again after having been mutilated in a
traffic accident:

> Everyone had his own story, and I had my own big, sad
> story.  I began thinking.  I had to get through the rest
> of my life in this wretched condition.  I began to re-
> sent these people who were going by me actively and
> quickly, able to use their legs.  I thought they should
> at least look at me.  A person who was learning to walk
> again.  A person who had been at death's door and had
> escaped. [2]

The antinationalist detective in "Bean an tSiopa Seandachta" ("The Woman in the Antique Shop") from the Seacht mBua an tÉirí Amach collection, a man for whom the anonymity of Dublin has been a protection
throughout his career, becomes the victim of this same impersonality
when, guilt-stricken, he suffers a virtual breakdown after the Rising
he has helped to betray.  Walking the streets of the city, he seeks in
vain for a cure he knows would be surer than drugs, "a little word of
praise, a little word that would make him vigorous and alive
again."(18)  Unable to find sympathy, even from his fellow detectives,
he is driven to suicide.  Urban indifference and lack of empathy turn
to genuine callousness in "'Fan go Fóill,'" when the commotion surrounding the death of an Irish exile occasions only mockery and com-
plaints about being disturbed from his fellow occupants of a London
flophouse: "The people who had been around us shortly before were falling asleep again.  Some of them grumbling that they had been awakened.
Others ridiculing the Scotsman because he had gone for the priest."(19)

Indeed the image of London as actively hostile rather than merely indifferent is central in Deoraíocht. At one point the starving Ó Maoláin reflects:

> In other towns when a person is in trouble, when he is ashamed and downcast and humbled, it doesn't seem to him that the things around him--the houses, the walls, the street itself--are trying to do anything to him, but in London a person like that thinks that the big gloomy houses would knock him down, that they would fall on him to crush him into the ground--if they thought it worth their while to make the effort for something so contemptible. [75]

This feeling of animate hostility is strengthened by Ó Conaire's choice of imagery in the novel. In one of the better-known scenes in the book Ó Maoláin sees a city park frequented by the homeless as "a great hideous giant with an ugly blotchy disease that was rotting his flesh and eating into him to the bone, and that could be seen in big black spots coming out through the skin. And with the pain he felt from the sickness his skin was grey . . . and his flesh was writhing, causing those black spots to quiver now and again" [69-70]. One instance of Ó Conaire's use of animal imagery, his picture of the elderly poor searching garbage cans as vultures, has already been cited; such imagery dominates Deoraíocht. For example, he later sees the vagrants in the park described above not as diseased sores on a giant's body, but as "jellyfish left on the beach after the tide" [126]. Loungers around a public-house door are compared to "the horseflies that suck the blood of horses and cows" [73]. The windows of surrounding buildings seem to Ó Maoláin like "the eyes of an evil animal displeased with the human race" [124]. The Thames becomes "a hideous monster" and ultimately London itself is seen as "that monster with thousands of lights, thousands of eyes, thousands of precious stones flashing in its skin" [74]. Such savage imagery is not, moreover, limited to the nightmarish world of Deoraíocht. Nóra Mharcuis Bhig, half asleep on her way to Dublin for the first time, imagines the train to be "some wild animal . . . a fiery dragon taking her to some horrible desert" [Nóra 7]. In like manner, in "An Ceol agus an Cuimhne" ("The Music and the Memory"), the storm outside a shabby London boarding house is described as being like "thousands of mad wild animals trying to get a grip on you."(20)

Yet while Ó Conaire describes his urban landscapes with vividly concrete imagery, he offers few precise geographical references which would enable the reader to fix his settings on a map. The contemporary critic Feardorcha Ó Conaill found it hard to identify the city of Deoraíocht with the London he himself knew, and Tomás Ó Broin has written of the "vague, unworldly atmosphere" of Ó Conaire's London and Galway in Deoraíocht. Ó Broin writes: "We don't encounter any of the usual names known throughout the world, Hyde Park, Marble Arch, Piccadilly. It is no exaggeration to say that Ó Conaire is trying to make the city unrecognizable."(21) Although Ó Conaire does provide precisely detailed geographical indicators in his Dublin story "Bean an tSiopa Seandachta" --indeed Eoghan Ó hAnluain has said of one of its passages that idt is "the closest thing we have in Irish to the usual Joycean description"(22) --this is a story based partly on undercover police work and thus requires attention to hard facts. On the whole, Ó Conaire's cityscapes, whether of London, Dublin, or even Galway, are vaguely defined, and this vagueness contributes, of course, to his characters' sense of uneasiness, of being out of place, out of touch with their immediate surroundings.(23)

Even more striking than Ó Conaire's omission of the names of
streets or sections is his consistent tendency to deny names to his urban characters.  While his rural characters have names that serve to
identify not only themselves but also their roots--for example Páidín
Mháire (Páidín, Máire's son) or Nóra Mharcuis Bhig (Nóra, the daughter
of Little Marcus)--his urban characters either have no names at all or
are known solely or mostly by descriptive epithets like "An Fear Mór"
("The Big Man"), "An Bhean Rua" ("The Redheaded Woman"), or "An Bhean
Ramhar" ("The Fat Woman").  Tomás Ó Broin writes of the characters in
Deoraíocht: "It is possible to say that one notes some abnormality in
them, for the same brief description is used almost every time they are
encountered; it is probable that the aim of this repetition is to make
the reader think of puppets."(24)  Wandering an undefined but actively
unsympathetic urban desert and having lost a clear sense of who they
are and where they came from, Ó Conaire's city characters search in
vain for an understanding face in the crowd.

The author's favorite device for conveying this sense of isolation
in the midst of company is what Pádraig Ó Croiligh has called "the major symbol of the window," pointing out that windows make possible a
superficial contact between people while obstructing true communication.(25)  In story after story Ó Conaire's characters, boxed up in
tiny, shabby, cell-like rooms,(26) stare from windows at a world from
which they are cut off yet in which they yearn to share.  Shortly after
her arrival in London, Nóra Mharcuis Bhig, desperately homesick and in
need of human warmth, gazes longingly at passersby outside her board-
ing-house window, but when she goes out into the streets, the crowds
offer her no comfort: "The same thoughts were pressing in on her outside on the street amongst the people as had been inside" [Nóra 9].  In
Deoraíocht, Ó Maoláin likewise spends hours at his window watching a
world with which he shares no understanding: "When I sat by the window
looking out at the street and at the people going by, the loneliness
and homesickness would be so great that I would have to get up and go
out amongst people.  But I was so gloomy and sorrowful that I thought
that they were all mocking me, that they loathed me, that they hated
me" [9].  At one point Ó Maoláin is deluded into believing that he has
reached a true empathic understanding of a neighbor he has only watched
through the window kissing his wife.  One night the falseness of this
perception is made clear to him when he discovers that the man has
beaten his wife to death in a drunken rage [103, 124].

Ó Conaire's most complex use of window symbolism occurs in the
story "Neill."  The main character is a Galway woman who has spent
hours of every day for the past nineteen years looking out her window
into the window of the woman who stole her fiancé and whose humiliation
is the object of her life.  Virtually all of Neill's contact with the
world is through her window, and she has thus lost her sense of reality
as well as all possibility of communication or human sympathy.  Even
when she wishes at one point to reach out to the woman whose life she
has finally ruined, she remains the watcher at the window: "She saw
Brighid Ní Ruadháin in the room going back and forth, ceaselessly.  She
saw her white, tormented face, but when the other woman saw her, she
left the window.  And when Neill saw her going away she felt a strong
urge to go to her and to seek her forgiveness.  But she did not
go."(27)

When Ó Conaire's urban characters do manage to leave their windows
to attempt to make contact with other people, that contact usually remains merely superficial, for they lack either depth of spirit or the
honesty to reveal their true feelings.  Ó Conaire contrasts this shallowness with primitive Gaeltacht passion and sincerity as expressed in
the keen in "An tSochraid cois Tuinne" ("The Funeral by the Sea"):

"Some of us in this new age think it shameful to look too deeply into
the heart of a person who is emotionally moved, for we think that it is
not permissible for us to probe some of the mysterious secrets of this
life or to reveal the mysterious secrets in our own hearts to friend or
to enemy. These people didn't think that way."(28)   Indeed it could be
said of many of his urban characters that they have neither true
friends nor real enemies.   Even when a marriage fails, as happens in
"M'Fhile Caol Dubh" ("My Slender Blackhaired Poet"), no deep emotion is
involved.   The wife says of her now loveless marriage, "My husband--
what can I say but that the pair of us were tired of each other--yes,
that's the most suitable word . . . Lack of interest and emotional
weariness were destroying life for the two of us."(29)   Her life, mat-
erially quite comfortable, is spiritually barren:   "There are hundreds
and hundreds of us rich women living pleasant insignificant lives--
shopping in the afternoon, tea, with criticism of neighbors and friends
afterwards, the train home, dinner, the man of the house snoring over
the newspaper."(30)   Of course such an existence destroys any chance of
meaningful thought or accomplishment, and in Ó Conaire's parable about
the temptation and ultimate prostitution of an artist, "Ná Lig Sinn i
gCathú" ("Lead Us Not Into Temptation"), the sculptor's only hope for
personal and creative integrity is to abandon the city:   "The life he
had spent, towns, amusement, the company of beautiful women--they were
all nothing compared to the work he had to do."(31)   Lured back into
the city by the woman he loves, he becomes enmeshed again in "the en-
chantments of the world" and his vision is irredeemably corrupted.(32)
     Such a view of the debasing and soulless influence of twentieth-
century urban life, especially that of England, would have gratified,
while it simultaneously properly horrified, many of the rural primitiv-
ists of the early years of the language revival.(33)   Escape to a pas-
toral Gaelic utopia was not, however, Ó Conaire's solution to the ma-
laise of city life, and his boldness in introducing urban themes into
modern Gaelic literature was matched by his courage in depicting the
failings of rural and particularly of Gaeltacht society.   None of Ó
Conaire's urban exiles comes to the city of his or her own free will;
all are driven there by some deficiency in the home environment, the
most obvious being rural poverty.   In essays such as "Ceisteanna a
Bhaineas le Buanú na Gaeilge sa nGaeltacht" ("Questions Relating to the
Preservation of Irish in the Gaeltacht"), he discusses the grinding
poverty of native speakers, describing their struggle to even feed
their families as "a constant striving to do what can't be done,"(34)
while in stories such as "Páidín Mháire" he captures unforgettably the
misery of peasants living with the ever-present specter of a shameful
death in the poor house.(35)
     Yet in the Gaeltacht as in London, material poverty is not the
most painful deprivation for the sensitive spirit.   With an honesty
still not universal in Gaelic fiction, Ó Conaire faced up to the isolation of Gaeltacht life with its attendant provincialism and narrow-
mindedness.   For example, his "An Scoláire Bocht" ("The Poor Scholar")
begins as a rather touching story of a young man's awakening to the
significance of native learning under the tutelage of a wandering
teacher.   By the story's end, however, the young man has broken the
heart and spirit of his teacher by burning a treasured manuscript on
the order of an ignorant priest fearful of Protestant proselytism
through Gaelic books, and has even begun to wonder whether all reading
might be sinful.(36)
     This blind fear of the Church is matched and even exceeded by ru-
ral fear of the opinion of the neighbors, a fear that acts as a stulti-
fying force for conformity.   Dread of public opinion is treated comi-
cally in "Rún an Fhir Mhóir" ("The Big Man's Secret"), in which the

narrator worries more about the possible shameful arrest of his kinsman than about the murder he thinks the man has committed: "If he had so great a need to kill his first wife, wouldn't it have been proper for him to do it in secret, without an uproar and without drawing this shame down on himself and on his friends and relatives?"(37)  The theme is dealt with more tragically in "Nóra Mharcuis Bhig," in which Nóra's father feels more shame and humiliation than sadness at the failure and exile of his two sons: "They had shamed him.  The people were making fun of him.  He was the laughing stock of the village" [Nóra 4].  When Nóra returns from London an apparent success, his reaction is not primarily joy at having her home, but rather gratification concerning his personal vindication and his enhanced social standing: "If his sons were no good, his daughter was splendid.  She was an example to the whole parish" [Nóra 13].  When she finally gives in to temptation and gets drunk at a local fair, her father makes no attempt to understand or help her, wishing instead to get her away from the judging eyes of the village as quickly as possible:  "If those are the habits you learned in England, it's there you'll have to practice them" [Nóra 16].  This, for Nóra, is a sentence to degradation rather than a chance for personal liberation, yet home offers her nothing either.  O Conaire's comment on a somewhat different situation is relevant to the sufferings of his urban exiles:  "The person between two worlds is greatly to be pitied."(38)

Nevertheless, despite his clear awareness of the physical and spiritual shortcomings of rural life, O Conaire does show a positive side to the country environment almost entirely lacking in his depiction of the city.  Gaeltacht people are capable of a warm friendliness and hospitality even to total strangers, as they show in their support of the wandering teacher, especially after his accidental blinding, in "An Scoláire Bocht," and even their well-developed interest in the affairs of others can have a benevolent side.  In "Fearfeasa agus an Fathach Fada" ("Fearfeasa and the Tall Giant"), Gaeltacht people are described as "curious people . . . but well-mannered people also."(39)  The involvement of his neighbors in the problems of "The Big Man" in the comic "Rún an Fhir Mhóir" is largely motivated by a desire to help, and they identify themselves as "friends who came here for your good, friends who came here to help you, whatever crime you have committed."(40)  Nonetheless it is impossible to escape the conclusion that O Conaire felt that for the sensitive, independent personality, such group unity and support were inadequate consolations for the loss of the freedom to develop in one's own direction and to satisfy one's individual emotional needs.

A word must be said here about O Conaire's attitude to city life as shown in his later sketches and essays, for it is primarily these that have been most frequently collected and anthologized in Ireland and that have reached a wider audience through the translations reprinted by the Mercier Press, Field and Fair and The Woman at the Window.(41)  In his late pieces, written after his return to Ireland in 1914 when he was eking out a precarious living as Gaelic literature's first full-time man of letters, the city is only referred to briefly as the stereotypical center of "sadness and anxiety and heartfelt sorrow,"(42) where people are "smothered"(43) and whose attractions are "only airy toys compared to the joyful life you could have here with me in my old quarry, far from people and from the false civilization of this day and age."(44)  Still, even in these late sketches, often written with an eye on the shillings they would bring in and at times shamelessly recycled under different titles, O Conaire never attempted to present a rural utopia he knew to be false.(45)  Rather, his quite obviously unsatisfactory, albeit lyrical, alternative to city corruption and shallowness is a life on the open road impossible for virtually all of his readers: "Come with me and your bruised heart will be lifted, your spirit expanded, your melancholy cured, and the pair of us will welcome the spring and the world's return to life."(46)

Writing in 1923, Ó Conaire indirectly justified his own artistic career while in effect restating Pearse's 1906 challenge to what he saw as his increasingly timid fellow Gaelic writers: "No language survives but the language in which there is a literature in tune with its time, and our own language will not survive either unless harder and more sincere work is done in the field of literature."(47)  It is due in no small measure to Sean-Phádraic's (Ó Conaire's) own work in that field that Irish language literature lives and thrives today, struggling still to deal honestly with those painful modern questions he was the first to face.  Seán Ó Ríordáin's tribute to Daniel Corkery is in many ways even more true of Pádraic Ó Conaire:  "Arise and sing to him our heartfelt gratitude, / He showed the way."(48)

## NOTES

1.    Pádraic Pearse, "About Literature," An Claidheamh Soluis, 26 May 1906, 7.

2.    For example, in 1972 Diarmaid Ó Súilleabháin discussed "the schizophrenic condition of the Gaelic novelist" attempting to write in Irish of things belonging to an English-speaking world, and asked, "Is diffidence in face of this schizophrenia the cause of the scarcity of Gaelic novels?"; see "An Uain Bheo: Focal ón Ú'dar" ("An Uain Bheo:  A Word from the Author"), Irisleabhar Mha Nuad vol. 7 (1972):  67.  Perhaps Pádraig Ua Maoileoin provides an answer to this question in "Scríbhneoirí Chorca Dhuibhne" ("Writers from Corca Dhuibhne"):  "If I had any courage, I'd be writing about Dublin because that's what I understand best"; see his Ar Leithéidí' Arís (Our Like Again) (Dublin: Clódhanna Teoranta, 1978), 58.  All translations in this essay whether of primary or secondary sources are my own.

3.    The best source of biographical information on Ó Conaire remains Áine Ní Chnáimhín, Pádraic Ó Conaire (Dublin:  Oifig an tSolathair, 1947).  A new biography is, however, sorely needed.

4.    Máirtín Ó Cadhain, "Irish Prose in the Twentieth Century," in Literature in Celtic Countries, ed. J. E. Caerwyn Williams (Cardiff: University of Wales Press, 1971), 147.

5.    "Conall Cearnach," quoted by Muiris Ó Droighneáin in Taighde i gComhair Stair Litridheachta na NuaGhaedhilge o 1882 Anuas (Research Towards a History of Modern Gaelic Literature since 1882) (Dublin:  Oifig Diolta Foillseachain Rialtais, 1936), 148.  Críostóir Mac Aonghusa has said that Gaeltacht people have also had doubts about Ó Conaire's work:  "When some of his stories are read to the people of the Gaeltacht, they show no interest in them at all other than to say "He's a dirty man."  And remember that these people find no fault with the strong language of the old stories.  The 'strangeness' of Pádraic's stories explains their aversion to him"; see "Pádraic Ó Conaire," Comhar (December 1956): 22.

6.    Liam Ó Briain, in Pádraic Ó Conaire:  Clocha ar A Charn (Pádraic Ó Conaire:  Stones on His Cairn) ed. Tomás de Bhaldraithe (Dublin:

Clóchamhar Teoranta, 1982), 62.

7.    Leon Ó Broin, Clocha ar A Charn,   23.

8.    Cathaoir Ó Braonáin, review of Seacht mBua an Éirí Amach, by Pádraic Ó Conaire, Studies 7 (1918): 520.

9.    W. P. Ryan, The Pope's Green Island (Boston:  Small Maynard and Co., 1912), 287.

10.    Ní Chnáimhín, Pádraic Ó Conaire, 37-43, 51-53.

11.    Pádraic Ó Conaire, "'Fan go Fóill,'" in Nóra Mharcuis Bhig agus Scéalta Eile (Nóra Mharcuis Bhig and Other Stories) (Dublin:  Conradh na Gaeilge, 1909), 33.

12.    Ó Conaire, Deoraíocht, ed. Mícheál Ua Nunáin (Dublin, 1973), 23.  Further references to this work will appear in the text.  It seems likely that Liam O'Flaherty modelled his scene in The Informer in which Gypo Nolan feeds the poor on this scene in Deoraíocht in which Ó Maolain gives out food.

13.    Breandán Ó Doibhlin, "An Coimhthíos:  Gné den Aigne Idirnáisiúnta i Litríocht na Gaeilge," Irisleabhar Mhá Nuad 6 (1971): 18.

14.    Bernard Ó Maoldomhnaigh, "Anam ar Strae:  Staidéir ar Deoraíocht" ("A Soul Astray:  A Study of Deoraíocht"), Irisleabhar Mhá Nuad 6 (1971):  107.

15.    Pádraig Ó Croiligh, "Go nGoilleann an Bhróg:  Samhlaíocht Phadráig Uí Chonaire" ("Until the Shoe Pinches:  The Imagination of Pádraic Ó Conaire"), Irisleabhar Mhá Nuad 3 (1968):  60.  See also Pádraigín Riggs, "An Deoraíocht i Saothar Uí Chonaire" ("Exile in the Work of Ó Conaire"), in Pádraic Ó Conaire:  Léachtaí Cuimhneachain (Pádraic Ó Conaire:  Commemorative Lectures), ed. Gearóid Denvir (Inveran: Cló Chonamara, 1983), 19-29.

16.    Pádraic Ó Conaire, "Dealg sa mBeo" ("A Thorn in the Flesh"), in Scéalta an tSáirsint Rua (Dublin:  An Preas Náisiúnta, 1941), 91.

17.    Pádraic Ó Conaire, "Nóra Mharcuis Bhig," in Nóra Mharcuis Bhig agus Scéalta Eile, 8.  Further references to this story will appear in the text identified by Nora and the page number.

18. Pádraic Ó Conaire, "Béan an tSiopa Seandachta" ("The Woman in the Antique Shop"), in Seacht mBua an Éirí Amach (Dublin:  Sairseal agus Dill, 1967), 141.

19.    Ó Conaire, "'Fan go Fóill,'" in Nóra Mharcuis Bhig, 36.

20.    Pádraic Ó Conaire, "An Ceol agus an Cuimhne" ("The Music and the Memory"), in Síol Éabha (The Descendants of Eve) (Dublin:  Mártan Lester, 1922).

21.    Tomás Ó Broin, "Deoraíocht:  Réamhchainteanna agus Iarbhreitheanna" ("Deoraíocht:  Preliminary Remarks and Final Judgments"), Feasta 29 (May 1976):  7.

22.   Eoghan Ó hAnluain, "Baile Átha Cliath i NuaLitríocht na Gaeilge" ("Dublin in Modern Gaelic Literature"), <u>Scríobh</u> 4 (1979):  29.

23.   I disagree with Tomás Ó Broin's idea that Ó Conaire contrasts Galway to London, seeing the former as a happy and secure city close to nature.  After all, Ó Maoláin leaves Galway as the result of the snobbishness of his fiancée's family, and when he returns there as a sideshow freak, his sense of alienation is intensified by his fellow Galwegians' callous indifference to his plight.  See Ó Broin's "<u>Deoraíocht</u>: Réamhchainteanna," 7, and especially his "<u>Deoraíocht</u>:  Idéaltacht agus Réaltacht" ("<u>Deoraíocht</u>:  Ideal and Reality"), <u>Feasta</u> 31 (April 1978): 10, 22.

24.   Tomás Ó Broin, "<u>Deoraíocht</u>:   Saothar Eispreisiúnach" ("<u>Deoraíocht</u>: An Expressionist Work"), <u>Feasta</u> 32 (June 1979): 17.  See also Ó Maoldomhnaigh's comment that the namelessness of the novel's characters is a sign of their lack of mutual understanding and sympathy ("Anam ar Strae," 102).

25.   Pádraig Ó Croiligh, "Ní Cung le Duine an Saol: sracfhéachaint ar 'Neill' Uí Chonaire" ("A Person Doesn't Find Life Confining:  A Glance at Ó Conaire's 'Neill'"), <u>Irisleabhar Mhá Nuad</u> 5 (1970): 85, 91.

26.   See Ó Croiligh's discussion of Ó Conaire's symbolic use of houses and rooms in "Go nGoilleann an Bhróg," 61-64.

27.   Ó Conaire, "Neill," in <u>Síol Éabha</u>.

28.   Ó Conaire, "An tSochraid cois Tuinne" ("The Funeral by the Sea"), in <u>Cúr na dTonn</u> (<u>The Foam on the Waves</u>) (Dublin: Comhlacht Oideachais na hÉireann, 1924), 6.

29.   Ó Conaire, "M'Fhile Caol Dubh" ("My Slender Blackhaired Poet"), in <u>Seacht mBua an Éirí Amach</u>, 177.  In this story Ó Conaire again uses window symbolism to bring out the breakdown in love and communication between the two (188).

30.   Ibid., 177.

31.   Ó Conaire, "Ná Lig Sinn i gCathú" ("Lead Us Not Into Temptation"), in <u>An Chéad Chloch</u> (The First Stone), ed. Pádraigín Riggs (Cork:  Mercier, 1978), 99.

32.   Ibid., 104.

33.   Even as perceptive a writer as Seosamh Mac Grianna could see "Nóra Mharcuis Bhig" as rooted in a simplistic opposition between the sordidness of London and the innocence of Conamara; see "Pádraic Ó Conaire" in <u>Pádraic Ó Conaire agus Aistí Eile</u> (Pádraic Ó Conaire and Other Essays), rev. ed. (Dublin:  Oifig an tSoláthair, 1969), 12-13.

34.   Pádraic Ó Conaire, "Ceisteanna a Bhaineas le Buanú na Gaeilge sa nGaeltacht" ("Questions Relating to the Preservation of Irish in the Gaeltacht"), in <u>Aistí Phádraic Uí Chonaire</u> (The Essays of Pádraic Ó Conaire), ed. Gearóid Denvir (Inveran:  Cló Chois Fharraige), 54.

35.   Ó Conaire, "Páidín Mháire," in <u>Nóra Mharcuis Bhig</u>, 38-51.

36.  Pádraic Ó Conaire, "An Scoláire Bocht" ("The Poor Scholar"), in An Scoláire Bocht agus Scéalta Eile (The Poor Scholar and Other Stories) (Dublin: Conradh na Gaeilge, 1913), 1-35.

37.  Ó Conaire, "Rún an Fhir Mhóir" ("The Big Man's Secret"), in Seacht mBua an Éirí Amach, 166.

38.  Pádraic Ó Conaire, "Beirt Bhan Misniúil" ("Two Courageous Women"), in Seacht mBua an Éirí Amach, 95.

39.  Pádraic Ó Conaire, "Fearfeasa agus an Fathach Fada" ("Fearfeasa and the Tall Giant"), in Fearfeasa Mac Feasa (Dublin: Oifig en tSolathair, 1930), 156.

40.  Ó Conaire, "Rún an Fhir Mhóir," 157.

41.  The latter collection includes translations of some of Ó Conaire's finest work:  "Neill" (translated as "The Woman at the Window"), "Nóra Mharcuis Bhig," "An Bhean ar Leag Dia A Lámh Uirthi" ("The Woman on Whom God Laid His Hand"), "An Bhean a Ciapadh" (translated as "Put to the Rack"), and "An Bhean a Gortaíodh" (translated as "Disillusioned").  Poolbeg Press published a collection of translations of many of O Conaire's best-known stories in 1982, under the cumbersome title Padraic O Conaire:  15 Short Stories Translated from the Irish.  The translations are by fifteen different writers.

42.  Pádraic Ó Conaire, "Cuireadh" ("An Invitation"), in An Crann Géagach:  Aistí agus Sceilíní (The Branching Tree: Essays and Anecdotes) (Dublin: Cló na gCoinneall, 1919), 11.

43.  Pádraic Ó Conaire, "Gracie" in Béal an Uaignis (The Edge of Loneliness) (Dublin  Martan Lester, 1921), 45.

44.  Pádraic Ó Conaire, "Amuigh faoi'n bhFásach" ("Out in the Wilderness"), in Béal an Uaignis, 20.

45.  Even in his glowingly positive account of Conamara native speakers in his sketch "Cois Fhairrge," his emphasis is on the toughness and integrity of a people ceaselessly battling against a harsh environment; see "Cois Fhairrge," in Seoigheach an Ghleanna (Joyce of the Glen) (Dublin: An Preas Náisiúnta, 1941), 77-81.

46.  Pádraic Ó Conaire, "Cuireadh," in An Crann Geagach, 11.  It is interesting to note here Ó Conaire's description of the excitement of the world-weary Dublin woman of "M'Fhile Caol Dubh" on hearing the speech of the tramp at the conclusion of Synge's In the Shadow of the Glen; see "M'Fhile Caol Dubh" in Seacht mBua an Éirí Amach, 192.

47.  Pádraic Ó Conaire, "An Fhírinne agus an Bhréag sa Litríocht" ("Truth and Falsehood in Literature"), in Aistí Phádraic Uí Chonaire, 202.

48.  The lines are from Ó Ríordáin's "Do Dhomhnall O Corcora" ("For Daniel Corkery"), in Eireaball Spideoige (A Robin's Tail) (Dublin: Sáirséal ajus Dill, 1952), 51-52.

# 17

# Seumas O'Kelly and James Stephens

*Brendan O'Grady*

In 1917, when Seumas O'Kelly reflected on the place of Dublin in modern literature, he noted two contemporaries both born in February 1882: "James Joyce has put his native city through the stern paces of his frank realism"; "James Stephens in his earlier work—in his 'Insurrections' and his story-book 'The Charwoman's Daughter' made us pleasantly intimate with a domestic life that was the Spirit of Dublin."(1)  Although the relationship between Seumas O'Kelly and James Joyce is tenuous, O'Kelly's ties with James Stephens are more substantial.  Several parallels are found in their lives and works:  there is uncertainity about their exact birth dates; they both had about ten years of formal schooling; both were associated with Arthur Griffith's Sinn Fein movement; and both strongly protested social injustices.  They shared an interest in journalism and in the Irish theater (in fact, under the stage name of Stephen James, Stephens played a role in one of O'Kelly's plays), and they helped to advance the Irish short story.  Both were interested in retelling ancient Celtic legends, and both had a gift for fantasy.  Both were obscured by their brilliant contemporaries, and each has been popularly but unfairly remembered as the author of only one book.

On the other hand, there are many differences between the two: O'Kelly was completely in his element in the country while Stephens was more at home in the city; O'Kelly witnessed the hardships of the West of Ireland while Stephens endured the poverty of Dublin's slums; O'Kelly was Catholic while Stephens was Protestant; and O'Kelly was modest, diffident, and soft-spoken, while his friend was outgoing, a Dublin "character," a celebrated conversationalist.  Although each of these writers shared to some degree the virtues of the other, O'Kelly's literary output, however prolific it was for nearly twenty years, was less extensive than that of Stephens, and his range of emotions and themes was narrower.  O'Kelly possessed a wholesome wisdom, but his mind was not as critical, as intellectual, as Stephens's.  Of the two, O'Kelly may have been the more observant and perceptive, but Stephens was more inventive, more experimental, more daring.  O'Kelly was the traditionalist, Stephens the modernist.

George Brandon Saul concludes his very useful monograph on O'Kelly by saying:

> The fellow author most likely to come to my own mind when reading him is his friend James Stephens:  a fact that seems to me complimentary to each artist and that

is meant to insinuate no indebtedness on the part of
either to the other.  There was clearly, I think, a
greater anguish of genius concentrated in Stephens,
whose mind was also the more nimble of the two; and
there is in O'Kelly (I am of course not now speaking of
him as a political journalist) no evidence of the
occasional fury and desolation of Stephens.  Yet somehow
these men seem to companion each other easily, perhaps
because the capriciousness of O'Kelly's vision may not
be very far removed from that of Stephens.  Then, too,
neither man cursed life, though one recalls that Stephens certainly cursed its cruelty.(2)

Not surprisingly, O'Kelly and Stephens admired one another's work, for
(to borrow a phrase Stephens used elsewhere) they had both "supped on
wonder."(3)   Stephens, in fact, extolled O'Kelly's The Weaver's Grave
in a 1920 letter to Sir Edward Marsh:  "Have you ever read a book
(prose) called 'The Golden Barque', by a lad from here named Seumas
O'Kelly?" he asked.  "There is one short (hundred-page-long) story in
it called 'The Weaver's Grave', and it is about as close to greatness
as anything in our time."(4)   A week later Stephens sent Marsh a copy
of the book and a note saying, "I wonder will you think as highly of it
as we do over here?"(5)  We can only surmise that Stephens perceived in
O'Kelly's novella what readers find in many Stephens pieces:  distinctive imagination, memorable imagery, a skillful blend of respectful humor and grotesquerie, an engaging narrative, a light sprinkling of philosophy, and an aura of romance.
    O'Kelly's gift for fantasy is usually more earthbound, less ethe-
real than Stephens's, and his romanticizing is tempered by a greater
striving after the actuality of the subject.  Stephens more frequently
leans toward allegory or popularized mysticism; often, as Ernest Boyd
notes, "his fantasies are, as it were, intellectual, as would be the
dreams of a city child, as contrasted with the child born in the suggestive atmosphere of the country."(6)  Both authors, of course, risked
lapses into triviality or frivolity--Stephens with his "sophisticated
infantilism"(7) in The Crock of Gold or his diverting "gaminerie"(8) in
The Demi-Gods almost as much as O'Kelly in the mere entertainments
known as the Padna sketches and in The Leprechaun of Killmeen.   There
is a difference here, however:  as Ernest Boyd points out, when Stephens "gambols in naive irreverence about the gravest problems"(9) or
"contemplates the Cosmos with charming familiarity"(10) his imagination
is engaged in a meaningful creative exercise; whereas O'Kelly in The
Leprechaun of Killmeen and its sequel "At the Burning of the Sod" and
similar apprentice tales is mainly exhibiting the "garden variety"(11)
of popular entertainment publishable in the newspapers of his day.
While Vivian Mercier allows that O'Kelly's early novella may be "the
most satisfying reworking of later traditions about leprechauns,"(12)
it is not until Waysiders, Hillsiders, and The Golden Barque collections that O'Kelly's mature gentle humor and his humane understanding
come through.  Although Saul finds the leprechaun stories boring and
the "sociological moralism" overdone,(13) Padraic Colum accepts these
tales as an expression of folk culture and even discerns an important
distinction in the respective genealogies of O'Kelly's and Stephens's
leprechauns.  They "belong to different families," Colum writes:

    James Stephens' leprechaun belonged to the Dublin moun-
    tains.  He was close to the capital and so he was a
    sophisticated leprechaun, and he talked philosophically.

Seumas O'Kelly's leprechaun is as rural as the old thorn
bush that was a landmark for him.(14)

Colum's statement points up a fundamental difference between Seumas
O'Kelly and his Dublin contemporaries. Whatever his relationship with
the city itself or with Joyce and Stephens—or for that matter with
other writers he knew, including Seumas O'Sullivan, Oliver Gogarty,
Thomas MacDonagh, and Arthur Griffith—O'Kelly was preeminently a man
of the country. Not only is The Weaver's Grave essentially rural,
"more conscious of the earth," says Benedict Kiely, "than anything in
Irish literature since William Carleton's people appeared in Traits and
Stories,"(15) but also all of O'Kelly's best works in drama, in poetry,
in the fine novel The Lady of Deerpark, and in short fiction have their
settings and themes in rural Ireland. As much as O'Kelly consciously
appreciated the city of Joyce and Stephens as a cultural and commercial
center, Dublin never penetrated his creative imagination.

If, as David Morton claims, Liam O'Flaherty and Sean O'Casey led
the short story and the drama into town in the 1920s,(16) O'Kelly in
the previous decade, in the dominant trend of the earlier Renaissance
writers, persisted in the belief that the thatched cottage held as much
human drama as any tenement hovel or drawing room or music hall in the
metropolis. What Terence Brown said about Yeats's poetry is true of
O'Kelly's writing: "Implicit throughout is the assumption that Irish
reality, at its most authentic, is rural, anti-industrial, spiritually
remote from the life of the town or city."(17) James Joyce rejected
that assumption, but James Stephens made it part of his philosophy, and
Padraic Colum and Daniel Corkery wholeheartedly embraced it. Regardless of his contemporaries, Seumas O'Kelly built his reputation on his
own approach to rural realism. Historically, to be sure, he had links
with George Moore before him, with Colum, Corkery, Douglas Hyde, and
Lady Gregory in his lifetime, and with successors such as Liam O'Flaherty, Frank O'Connor, Sean O'Faolain, and Bryan MacMahon, all of whom
portray aspects of peasant, Gaelic, Catholic Ireland. Whatever he may
have learned from his countrymen or from his limited access to realistic writing of the Continent or America, O'Kelly imitated no one; he
wrote in his own style and injected his own comments, political views,
humorous asides, and whimsical observations. In effect he was probably
as close to Stephens as to any other writer, though in themes and intentions he was closer still to Colum.

One can say of O'Kelly's accomplishment what Augustine Martin said
of Stephens: that he was able to blend "the mythic and fabulous with
the quotidian and realistic."(18) Readers marvel, for instance, at how
Stephens produced the effect of wonder in The Charwoman's Daughter by
contrasting the seaminess of Mary Makebelieve's surroundings with the
beauty and innocence of her imagination. Such a comment attributes to
O'Kelly and to Stephens parallel powers of imagination: O'Kelly's
ability to transform a dingy barge on the Grand Canal into a marvelous
"golden barque" in "The Golden Barque" is comparable to Stephens's
achievement in elevating a poor city girl's admiration for an ordinary
policeman into an idyllic experience in The Charwoman's Daughter.

The blending of the fabulous and the realistic is also evident in
O'Kelly's and Stephens's leprechaun tales. Stephens was called "the
most popular fantasist of Joyce's time,"(19) for The Crock of Gold—
bringing together leprechauns and philosophers, gods and policemen—is
a classic in its genre. As Martin maintains, however, Stephens is more
than a mere "whimsical lyricist," and The Crock of Gold properly understood is a "serious and subversive" book.(20) The differences, therefore, between Stephens's classic and O'Kelly's entertaining Leprechaun
of Killmeen go much deeper than Colum's genealogical distinction.

O'Kelly's humorous adventure, though it has clear moral implications, has little of the allegorical significance or philosophical speculation abounding in Stephens's Crock of Gold. Each of these books has a distinctive narrative voice, each is a good example of the storyteller's art, and each contains ample good fun, but the genial shanachie of Killmeen focuses on the actions of his characters, while the philosophical narrator of the Dublin hills is more concerned about meanings behind the fantasy. What these books do have in common is lively imagination.

Much the same can be said of O'Kelly's "The Can with the Diamond Notch" and Stephens's The Demi-Gods. Again, these stories demonstrate the art of the storyteller. Again, O'Kelly concentrates on character and action while Stephens infuses his tale with philosophical speculation. Here O'Kelly's picaresque Mac an Ward is at least as well conceived and portrayed as Stephens's clever MacCann, and in the long run, O'Kelly's tinkers are more convincing than Stephens's romanticized characters. O'Kelly is closer to reality, Stephens more ethereal. But the exercise of imagination in these diverse stories is comparable.

Now, tales of leprechauns, fairies, and talking animals as well as tales of matchmaking or of disappointment in love run the risk of sentimentality; similarly, sociopolitical themes as well as legends of heroes and patriots may easily decline into propaganda. In these respects, neither Stephens nor O'Kelly escaped without mishap. Lapses into sentimentality are found even in such professedly realistic works as Stephens's The Charwoman's Daughter and Hunger: A Dublin Story, and more blatantly in O'Kelly's play The Home-Coming, in a story like "Both Sides of the Pond" and in the awkward novel Wet Clay. More positively, Stephens's soaring vision, lyricism, and humor frequently compensate for his sentimentality, explicit moralizing, and overindulgence in epigrams; whereas O'Kelly learned to offset his early tendencies toward triteness, mawkishness, and propagandizing by his later mastery of Hiberno-English speech and a subdued authorial presence.

Ultimately the likenesses between O'Kelly and Stephens are elusive. It is mainly in the spirit and sometimes in the vision of their works rather than in stylistic devices or themes that these writers are frequently kindred. We see this in their mutual affinity for storytelling in the mode of fantasy and fairy lore, in their mutual attraction to the ancient Celtic legends, and even in their depictions of natural happenings. Both writers enable readers to see old things anew, to find the singular in the commonplace, to discover gems instead of stones.


NOTES

1.    Seumas O'Kelly, "Dublin in Modern Literature: The Georgian Spirit and Later Days," Sunday Independent (Dublin), 30 September 1917, 2.

2.  George Brandon Saul, Seumas O'Kelly (Lewisburg, Pa.: Bucknell University Press, 1971), 78-79.

3.    James Stephens, The Demi-Gods (New York: Macmillan, 1930), 18.

4.    James Stephens, Letters of James Stephens, ed. Richard J. Finneran (London: Macmillan, 1974), 247-48.

5.    Ibid., 248.

6.  Ernest Boyd, Ireland's Literary Renaissance (New York: Barnes and Noble, 1968), 268-69.

7.  Vivian Mercier and David H. Greene, 1000 Years of Irish Prose, Part I: The Literary Revival (New York: Devin-Adair, 1952), 606. See also Boyd, Ireland's Literary Renaissance, 416.

8.  Boyd, Ireland's Literary Renaissance, 417.

9.  Ibid., 416.

10.  Ibid., 417.

11.  Saul, Seumas O'Kelly, 68.

12.  Vivian Mercier, The Irish Comic Tradition (London:  Oxford University Press, 1962), 38.

13.  Saul, Seumas O'Kelly, 69.

14.  Padraic Colum, Introduction to The Leprechaun of Killmeen, by Seumas O'Kelly (Dublin:  Gill and Macmillan, 1968), 5-6.

15.  Benedict Kiely, Modern Irish Fiction (Dublin:  Golden Eagle Books, 1950), cited by Eamon Grennan, Introduction to A Land of Loneliness and Other Stories by Seumas O'Kelly (Dublin:  Gill and Macmillan, 1969), 16.

16.  David Morton, "Literature and Life:  A Neglected Talent," The Irish Statesman, 3 August 1929, 511.

17.  Terence Brown, "Dublin in Twentieth-Century Writing:  Metaphor and Subject," Irish University Review 8, no. 1 (Spring 1978): 7.

18.  Augustine Martin, Introduction to Desire and Other Stories, by James Stephens (Swords, Co. Dublin:  Poolbeg, 1980), 8.

19.  Richard Fallis, The Irish Renaissance (Syracuse:  Syracuse University Press, 1977), 153.

20.  Martin, Introduction, 10, 11.

## 18

# Eamon de Valera and the Irish Bond-Certificate Drive, 1919–1921

## *Francis M. Carroll*

In June of 1919, after thirty-four years in Ireland, Eamon de Valera returned to the United States, the land of his birth. The story of his American mission in 1919 and 1920 has not gone unnoticed by historians. The interest shown by writers, however, has generally been focused on two specific aspects of de Valera's trip: the unsuccessful efforts to obtain diplomatic recognition for the Irish Republic from the United States government, and the calamitous split in the Irish-American nationalist movement. De Valera must share part of the blame for these two disasters. Nevertheless, de Valera's mission had one major success which has been ignored by historians—raising money for the Dáil Éireann government. Altogether, between 1919 and 1921, nearly $6 million was raised, which was more money than the Irish-American nationalist movement had ever previously collected for any purpose. This was a signal achievement, for it was accomplished in the face of both the split in the Irish-American movement and the growing disapproval of the American government and sections of the American public.(1)

De Valera presented himself to the American public on June 23, 1919, at the Waldorf Astoria Hotel in New York. He told reporters that Ireland hoped for American aid in the struggle for independence, and he later announced that one of the major sources of aid, indeed one of the most practical, was to raise money to help finance the Dáil government. The question of providing operating revenue for the Republican government had occupied the attentions of the second session of the Dáil, meeting in April 1919. On the 4th of April the Dáil approved a motion to authorize an issue of £250,000 worth of Republican Bonds. Several days later, on April 10, de Valera spoke to the Dáil on the question, pointing out that "It is obvious that the work in order of our Government cannot be carried on without funds." He went on to say that the Minister of Finance, Michael Collins, was doing the preparatory work in order to sell £500,000 worth of bonds, £250,000 at home and £250,000 abroad.(2)

One month later the American Commission on Irish Independence visited Ireland during a lull in their activities at the Paris Peace Conference. Frank P. Walsh, the chairman of the Commission, and members Edward F. Dunne and Michael J. Ryan all supported the idea of a bond issue. As a result of their talks with these Americans, de Valera and Collins sent instructions to the three Dáil members in the United States, Dr. Patrick McCartan, Diarmuid Lynch and Liam Mellows, requesting them to undertake the preparatory work for a $1.25 million Irish bond issue. A suitable bank was to be found to handle the arrangements and to underwrite the issue, and someone of appropriate standing in both the Irish and the financial communities was to be sought out to direct the issue.  After de Valera arrived in the United States and began to confer with Irish-American leaders, the amount to be raised was increased.  Through the urging of Joseph McGarrity of Philadelphia, $5 million was selected as the target, but on August 20, 1919, $25 million was authorized by the Dáil at the request of de Valera.  This enormous figure would have both propaganda and practical value.

The whole matter of selling the Irish bonds in the United States had not been without some formidable difficulties.  First of all there were the objections of the leaders of the Friends of Irish Freedom, the large nationwide organization that had constituted the Irish movement in America since the collapse of home rule during the First World War. The Friends, led by New York Judge Daniel F. Cohalan, had started the Irish Victory Fund at the Irish Race Convention in February of 1919, and the drive to raise money for the Fund was only at mid-course by the summer of 1919.  Furthermore, the use of this Fund was a source of increasing controversy among both Irish-American leaders and Irish leaders.  De Valera and some Irish-Americans, McGarrity and others, wanted most of the Irish Victory Fund to be sent to Ireland for the use of the Dáil; others, such as Judge Cohalan and John Devoy, wanted most of the money to be used by the Friends of Irish Freedom in the propaganda battle in the United States to win support for Ireland and to oppose the Wilson administration and the League of Nations.

Although the disagreement was never completely resolved, the Friends did agree to terminate the Irish Victory Fund by late August 1919, after raising $1,005,080.  They also were willing to finance some of the expenses of the de Valera mission ($26,748), and they did arrange to advance $100, 000 in order to give de Valera's organizers money with which to get the campaign started.  It should also be mentioned that the Friends had financed the American Commission on Irish Independence in Paris earlier in 1919, as well as the Dáil envoys in Paris, and later in the autumn they sent $115,000 in cash to the Dáil.(3)

The second obstacle, about which Judge Cohalan was also particularly sensitive, was the legal problem of an unrecognized government or regime attempting to sell its bonds to the American public.  In legal terms the Irish Republic did not exist, and therefore bonds issued in its name had no standing as an investment.  The sale of such securities under the name of government "bonds" contravened investment protection laws ("blue sky laws") in several states.  Several committees wrestled with the problem of how to sell the issue and still stay within the law, and how to handle the banking arrangements.  Only in late August, after de Valera had returned from his first cross-country tour, did Judge Cohalan, Thomas Hughes Kelly, William Bourke Cockran, Richard F. Dalton, and John D. Moore finally agree on how it could be done.  The solution to the legal conundrum was found by calling the instruments "Bond-Certificates."  The purchaser would receive a certificate that could be exchanged at par for a gold bond issue by the Dáil "one month after the Republic has received international recognition."  The banks would not underwrite the issue at all, but would merely allow the money to be deposited.  This meant that the sale of the issue could not be conducted through the normal securities market, but would have to be done through the efforts of the Irish-Americans and de Valera's staff.

Though briefly told, these several problems were major obstacles for de Valera's objective of raising money in America.  Given the prominence and to some extent the logic of his opposition, it is fair to say that only someone with de Valera's prestige—as senior survivor of the 1916 Rising and as president of Dáil Éireann—and stubbornness could have overcome the resistance and objections to his plan of raising money by this method in the United States.  De Valera and many others felt that the legalistic objections to the sale of Irish bonds did not grow from a desire to protect the investing public or to stay on the right side of the law so much from a desire to keep fund raising, and thus control of the Irish-American nationalist movement, in the hands of the current leadership of the Friends of Irish Freedom.(4)

The difficulties that de Valera experienced with the leaders of the Friends of Irish Freedom raised doubts about how much they could be relied upon to work effectively to sell Bond-Certificates across the United States.  De Valera certainly had a great many supporters, but he could not afford any mistakes in planning if he wanted to raise the money he needed.  The solution was perhaps an inspired one.  De Valera found a perfect compromise in the prestigious American Commission on Irish Independence, which had just returned from France and Ireland and which had earlier discussed the Dáil Loan in America with de Valera. Frank P. Walsh, the chairman, was a lawyer and labor figure of considerable public stature, and equally important, he had the ability to get along with de Valera.  Edward F. Dunne was the former governor of Illinois and Michael J. Ryan was the former president of the United Irish League of America.  The Commission was widely known through its well-publicized, if unsuccessful, mission to the Paris Peace Conference to arrange for an Irish delegation.  These three members attained renewed prominence by their spectacular testimony before the Senate Foreign Relations Committee at the Senate hearings on the Versailles Treaty.  Although there was some hesitation on the part of all of the members, Walsh rallied them with appeals to their sense of duty, arguing that in the circumstances only the Commission could do the job.(5)

By August 23, 1919, the Commission opened its headquarters in New York City at 411 Fifth Avenue and became the national organizers for the Bond-Certificate drive.  In late September work was underway to create a national network to do the selling when the drive would be ready to begin.  State chairmen were appointed across the country and city chairmen in the large metropolitan centers.  These leaders and their staffs were to utilize the manpower of local Irish groups, such as the Friends, the Ancient Order of Hibernians, the Irish Progressive League, the Knights of Columbus, and others, to actually do the canvassing and sales work.  If a separate sales force were needed, it could be created when and where appropriate.  Harry Boland, a member of the Dáil and Irish envoy to the United States, was appointed secretary to the national chairman Frank P. Walsh, and James O'Mara, a member of the Dáil, a Loan Trustee, and a Limerick businessman, directed the sales of the Bond-Certificates and the national campaign.  Handbooks, promotional literature, and letters of advice poured out of the New York headquarters to inform and guide the organizers across the country.  Well-known figures such as Captain Robert Montieth, of Sir Roger Casement's brigade, and Peter Golden, a poet and leader of the Irish Progressive League, were hired as organizers.(6)

De Valera's contribution to all of this was critical.  In July he had made a trip across the northern states to the Pacific coast and back, sounding out Irish-American opinion on the feasibility of raising money for the Irish government.  With many of the structural and organizational arrangements settled, de Valera set out once again.  In late August he went south into Maryland and Virginia and then back to New York, Pennsylvania, Ohio, and Indiana.  By October and November he was ready for another cross-country tour which would take him through the Irish centers of the Mid-west and the Pacific coast.  Sean Nunan, Dr. Patrick McCartan, Harry Boland, James O'Mara, and others accompanied him for parts of his trips.  Once again it was often the prestige of the Irish president that enlisted the support or won the cooperation of the disparate and quarrelsome Irish-American groups.

By early 1920 most of the staff work and organization for the bond-certificate drive was completed. A decision was reached to set a public goal of $10 million, with an anticipated target of raising at least $5 million. The bond-certificates would bear an interest rate of 5 percent, to be paid when they were exchanged for gold bonds drawn on the Irish treasury. The bond-certificates were to be sold in denominations of $10 to $10,000. Fenian bonds would be acceptable for exchange for certificates, which was an ingenious historical touch that linked generations and revolutions, as were United States government Liberty Bonds. The security of all the money was to be protected by the honor of the Trustees of the Dáil Loan--Eamon de Valera, Member and President of the Dáil, James O'Mara, also a member of the Dáil, and the Most Reverend Michael Fogarty, bishop of Killaloe.(7)

By early 1920 the public appeal was ready to begin, and on January 17 the Bond-Certificate drive opened. "An appeal will be made to Americans who love liberty, and who desire to see it triumph in Ireland, for subscriptions to the Bond Certificates of 'The Republic of Ireland,'" in order to assist "the ELECTED government of the Irish people to restore to Ireland her Strength, her Health, her Beauty, and her Wealth." Mayor John H. Hylan of New York bought the first Bond-Certificate from President de Valera in a ceremony in which de Valera was also given the freedom of the city. At that same moment some 40,000 canvassers began soliciting sales across New York City, and according to one spokesman, a million people were ready to sell the Bond-Certificates throughout the United States. De Valera spoke the following day, along with many other Irish-American leaders, at a three-hour meeting in the Lexington Opera House, which got the drive off to a good start. The next week de Valera was invited to Albany, New York, as the guest of Governor Alfred E. Smith, and the New York Assembly passed a resolution endorsing the Bond-Certificate drive.

Within three weeks claims were made that most of the New York quota of $3 million had been pledged, although this would appear to have been an exaggeration. Archbishop Patrick J. Hayes of New York sent $1,000, together with a very gracious letter: "After a very satisfactory conference with Mr. Eamon de Valera, President of the Irish Republic, I am convinced that his program for agricultural, industrial and commercial development of Ireland is entirely practical and constructive." The Archbishop went on to say, "America surely will not refuse her moral support to Ireland."(8) This letter was printed and used by Congressman William Bourke Cockran, the New York state chairman.

Throughout the rest of the country the drive went well, although perhaps not as spectacularly as in New York. But the national effort was spurred on by the visits of de Valera and his staff during 1920. It would appear that over 400,000 people bought Bond-Certificates, the largest proportion buying amounts of $25 or less. About 100,000 New Yorkers bought about $1 million worth, and McCartan recorded that the New York Clan na Gael, whatever its feelings about de Valera, raised $600,000 itself. Slightly more than 1,000 Bond-Certificate subscribers from Massachusetts purchased about $1.25 million worth.(9)

All was not completely easy with the Bond-Certificate drive, however, and several sets of problems developed. The growing antagonisms within the Irish-American nationalist movement could not help but affect the drive. De Valera's unfortunate interview with the Westminster Gazette and the New York Globe in February, in which he suggested that Britain might negotiate for Ireland a kind of foreign policy arrangement similar to that which the United States had for Cuba, caused a storm of protest and did a great deal to bring the faction fight out

into the open.  Through this and several other volatile incidents de
Valera became the central figure in the polarization of the nationalist
movement in America.  The consequence was that the Bond-Certificate
drive was periodically undercut by the split.  James J. Splain, the
Connecticut state chairman, squabbled steadily with the national organizers, de Valera, and his staff.  "He doesn't know America, and apparently some of those who are directing him don't know America," Splain
grumbled to Frank P. Walsh.(10)  The Iowa state chairman, Dr. W. P.
Slattery, held a similar view of de Valera's, staff.  "As for the
choice between Mr. Harry Boland and Judge Cohalan, give me Cohalan," he
wrote to Walsh.(11)  The overall effect of these feelings on the success of the Bond-Certificate drive is difficult to estimate but one
example may be suggestive.  As late as July 23, 1920, the Bond-Certificate drive had not been started in the Detroit area because of the
struggle within the nationalist movement.  "Of course we've known the
split would come," wrote Mrs. Peter Golden on February 16, 1920, "but
too bad it had to come during the bonds."(12)

The sale of Bond-Certificates encountered criticism and obstacles
from outside the Irish community also.  A Boston publisher and booksel-
ler wrote to President Wilson asking if the proposed exchange of United
States government Liberty Bonds for Irish Bond-Certificates constituted
the tacit approval of the American government for the Irish issue.  "If
not," he went on, "how long is this raising of funds for the purpose of
attack upon a friendly government to be permitted."(13)  The secretary
of the treasury, Carter Glass, wrote back that the government discour-
aged any attempts to transfer or exchange Liberty Bonds and other government notes and that the Treasury Department had no knowledge of the
"so-called Irish bond issue."(14)  However, by early February of 1920
the secretary of agriculture, David F. Houston, wrote to Frank P. Walsh
threatening that the campaign to exchange United States securities for
Irish Bond-Certificates would have to stop.(15)  Walsh, for his part,
had already sent specific instructions to all campaign chairmen warning
them to always use the term "bond-certificates" and never say simply
"bonds."(16)  Clearly the technical distinction between the two was
lost on the public, which always referred to them as the Irish bonds.

The extent to which the Bond-Certificates were a financial investment was also a problem.  De Valera wrote to Walsh in September 1919
that he wanted subscriptions "only from those who seek to serve a good
cause, not from those who want immediate pecuniary profit."(17)  This
caveat was echoed by the official announcements of the state chairmen,
such as William Bourke Cockran, but once again it was a subtlety the
public did not understand.  A "government bond" was perceived as a
secured investment.  The Wall Street Journal of February 1920 attacked
the "so-called 'bonds' of the equally so-called 'Irish Republic.'"
"Sold as bonds," the Journal wrote, "the DeValera issue is nothing more
than a swindle."(18)  Ultimately the Bond-Certificate drive became
blended with a number of other Irish issues that provoked a strong
anti-Irish backlash among the Anglophile establishment in the United
States.

Despite the criticism and despite the problems of the split in the
Irish-American nationalist movement, the Bond-Certificate campaign was
a success.  During 1920 and part of 1921, $5,123,640 worth of Irish Re-
public Bond-Certificates were sold in the United States.(19)  It was
the largest amount of money ever raised by the Irish movement in America.  De Valera's contribution to this effort was substantial, and his
determination to raise the money through some form of financial instrument rather than by gifts or contributions was decisive.  The importance of this insistence should not be underestimated.  Ireland failed
to get an audience at the Paris Peace Conference and the hopes of ex-

tracting diplomatic recognition from the United States government through public opinion tactics or Congressional lobbying were wildly unrealistic.  But the Dáil government and its supporters worked diligently to insure that Ireland carried out all of the motions or all of the roles of an international person, a de jure regime, a legitimate nation-state.  For this reason the Bond-Certificate drive and the money it raised were powerful tools in the struggle to convince people in Ireland, Britain, and the rest of the world that the Irish Republic existed and that Dáil Éireann was the legitimate government.  De Valera's travels across the United States as president of the Dáil, also contributed to the success of the drive once a commitment to the Bond-Certificates had been made.  De Valera may have caused bitterness and resentment among the ranks of the leaders of the Friends of Irish Freedom and other Irish organizations, and he may have been imperious and guilty of bad judgment in many instances, but to average Irish-Americans, he was the first president of Ireland and if he asked them to buy Irish-Republican Bond-Certificates, they would.  And they did, over $5 million worth.

Of course the argument can be made that even more money could have been raised for Ireland if de Valera had stayed home or if he had asked for gifts and donations or if he had let the Friends of Irish Freedom raise the money for him.  To be sure, the American Committee for Relief in  Ireland raised for humanitarian purposes $4,907,107.70 in a few months during 1921 without de Valera's participation.  This cannot be seen as conclusive evidence, however, because the circumstances were not strictly parallel.  What can be said is that de Valera did force the sale of Bond-Certificates on the Irish-American leadership and that he rallied a great deal of support behind him from among the rank and file of the Irish community in the United States by virtue of his prestige as president of the Dáil, whatever division he may also have caused in the Irish nationalist movement in America.

By way of an afterword, de Valera returned to Ireland in December of 1920, while the Bond-Certificate drive was still underway.  During the first half of 1921 the drive was closed.  A second loan of  500,000 for Ireland and $20 million for the United States was authorized.  This loan followed the same legal forms and general description in the United States as the earlier one, but because of the peace talks, underway since July, the issue was opened only in Washington, D.C. and in Illinois.  This Bond-Certificate drive ran only from October 15 until the Treaty was signed in December 1921; nevertheless, it raised $622,720 during the several weeks before the drive was called off.  The total amount raised by the two Bond-Certificate drives was $5,746,360, providing a strong finish to this part of the Bond-Certificate story.(20)

NOTES

1.    The most insightful recent examination of this topic is Donal McCartney, "de Valera's Mission to the United States, 1919-1920," in Studies in Irish History:  Presented to R. Dudley Edwards, ed. Art Cosgrove and Donal McCartney (Dublin:    University College Dublin, 1979), 304-23.

2.    Dáil Éireann, Minutes of Proceedings, 1919-1921, 41 and 47. Also see Ronan Fanning, The Irish Department of Finance, 1922-1958 (Dublin:    Institute for Public Administration, 1978), 13-16.

3.    F. M. Carroll, American Opinion and the Irish Question, 1910-1923 (New York:  St. Martin's Press, 1978), 149-55; and Charles Callan

Tansill, <u>America and the Fight for Irish Freedom, 1866-1922</u> (New York: Devin-Adair, 1957), 344-53.

4.     Carroll, <u>American Opinion</u>, 149-55; Tansill, <u>America and the Fight</u>, 344-53.  See also Patrick McCartan, <u>With de Valera in America</u> (Dublin:  Fitzpatrick, 1932), 142-43; Harry Boland to James K. McGuire, 11 September 1919, Daniel F. Cohalan Papers, American Irish Historical Society, New York; Prospectus of the First Issue of Bond-Certificates authorized by Dail Eireann, 1 October 1919, John Devoy Papers, National Library of Ireland, Dublin; and the Earl of Longford and Thomas P. O'Neill, <u>Eamon de Valera:  A Biography</u> (New York:  Houghton-Mifflin, 1971), 100.  It should be mentioned that the sources are by no means clear on how the Bond- Certificate formula was worked out.

5.     Frank P. Walsh to Edward F. Dunne, 12 August 1919, and also Walsh to Eamon de Valera, 2 October 1919, Boxes 124, 115, and Frank P. Walsh Papers, New York Public Library.

6.     Harry Boland to William Bourke Cockran, 20 November 1919, and Instructions on organization for Irish Bond-Certificate campaign, n.d., Box 17, William Bourke Cockran Papers, New York Public Library; Patricia Lavelle, <u>James O'Mara:  A Staunch Sinn Feiner</u> (Dublin:  Clonmore Reynolds, 1961), 141- 47; Katherine O'Doherty, <u>Assignment-America</u> (New York:  De Tanko, 1957), 70-71; Robert Montieth, <u>Casement's Last Adventure</u> (Dublin:  Moynihan, 1953), 239; and McCartan, <u>With de Valera in America</u>, 143-44.

7.     Longford and O'Neill, <u>Eamon de Valera,</u> 101-2; O'Doherty, <u>Assignment-America</u>, 70-74 and 93-112; Lavelle, <u>James O'Mara,</u> 144-46; Prospectus for the Irish Bond Issue, 1 October 1919, Instructions on organization for Irish Bond-Certificate campaign, n.d., and Frank P. Walsh to all state and city chairmen, 8 December 1919, Box 17, William Bourke Cockran Papers, New York Public Library.

8.     Frank P. Walsh, circular letter, 15 January 1920, Cockran Papers; <u>New York Times,</u> 18, 19, and 20 January 1920; "The Irish Bonds," <u>Literary Digest</u> 44, no. 6 (7 February 1920): 16; and Archbishop Patrick J. Hayes to William Bourke Cockran, 17 January 1920, Box 17, William Bourke Cockran Papers, New York Public Library.

9.     John T. Ryan to Senator J. W. Wadsworth, Jr., 3 March 1926, State Department Papers, Record Group 59, 841d.51/60, Roll 243, National Archives, Washington, D.C.

10.    James J. Splain to Frank P. Walsh, 17 September 1919, Bo x 124, Frank P. Walsh Papers, New York Public Library.

11.    Dr. W. P. Slattery to Frank P. Walsh, 3 January 1921, Walsh Papers.

12.    Mrs. Golden to Peter Golden, 16 February 1920, Peter Golden Papers, National Library of Ireland, Dublin.

13.    H. B. Hastings to President Woodrow Wilson, 19 December 1919, State Department Papers, Record Group 59, 841d.51/1, Roll 243, National Archives.

14.    Carter Glass to H. B. Hastings, 22 December 1919, State Department Papers.

15.    David F. Houston to Frank P. Walsh, 7 February 1920, Box 125, Frank P. Walsh Papers, New York Public Library.

16.    Frank P. Walsh to all state and city chairmen, 8 December 1919, Box 17, William Bourke Cockran Papers, New York Public Library.

17.    Eamon de Valera to Frank P. Walsh, September 1919, Box 124, Frank P. Walsh Papers, New York Public Library.

18.    Wall Street Journal, 4 February 1920.

19.    Dorothy Macardle, The Irish Republic (New York: Farrar, Straus and Giroux, 1965), 986; O'Doherty, Assignment-America, 66.

20.    The story of what happened to the money raised through the Bond-Certificates has never been fully told.  Roughly half of the funds were sent to Ireland and a proportion of that was spent by the Dáil; the remainder stayed in New York banks.  After the Civil War started in Ireland in 1922 the Free State government instituted lawsuits in Ireland and the United States in order to obtain possession of the money. In Ireland the courts awarded the money to the government, but the New York courts held that neither the Free State government nor the Republicans qualified for the money, and in 1927 it was ordered that the money be given back to the Bond-Certificate holders.

# JOYCE and his CONTEMPORARIES:

## *A Centenary Tribute*

Thursday, Friday,
Saturday

October 21, 22, 23,
1982

HOFSTRA
UNIVERSITY

HEMPSTEAD, NEW YORK 11550

CONFERENCE CO-SPONSOR:   American-Irish Historical Society
991 Fifth Avenue, New York City

COOPERATING INSTITUTIONS

The Office of the Consul General
of Ireland
New York, New York

Rutgers University-Newark
Newark, New Jersey

Office of the Chancellor
Brandeis University
Waltham, Massachusetts

Viking Press
New York, New York

Division of Special Studies
Hofstra University

Drama Department
Hofstra University

English Department
Hofstra University

Media Services
Hofstra University

Office of Residential Life
Hofstra University

Office of University Advisement
Hofstra University

Special Collections
Hofstra University

Special thanks to·the following people who helped make the Joyce and his
Contemporaries: a Centenary Tribute Conference possible:

Jean Connolly, Mildred McCaw, Constance Mulé and Jane Ogilvie for Conference
preparation; James W. Merrit for publicity; Walter and Lucille Fillin for
sharing their collection of twentieth-century literature; Karin J. Spencer
for photography; John and Patricia Mulrooney for helping to make our exhibit
possible and Marguerite Regan and her staff in Special Collections for helping
to prepare the exhibit.  Special thanks to Prof. Heyward Ehrlich of Rutgers
University-Newark for his advice and generosity in arranging for the loan of
Joyce materials from the Robeson Gallery's James Joyce and Modernism exhibit,
an exhibit made possible by grants from the New Jersey Committee for the
Humanities and the Sealed Air Corporation.

CONFERENCE DIRECTORS:

Diana Ben-Merre
Maureen Murphy

CONFERENCE COMMITTEE:

Karin Barnaby
Robert Lowery

**UNIVERSITY CENTER FOR CULTURAL & INTERCULTURAL STUDIES**
HOFSTRA UNIVERSITY
HEMPSTEAD, NEW YORK 11550

**Joseph G. Astman:  Director**

Thursday, October 21, 1982        Hofstra University Library (South Campus)

10:00 - 11:30 a.m.      Registration:  David Filderman Gallery
                                       Department of Special Collections
                                       Hofstra University Library - 9th Floor

11:30 - 1:00 p.m.       Session I:  Joyce and his Irish Contemporaries

                        Moderator:  Michael Steinman
                                    Nassau Community College

                        "The Function of Biographical Materials in Joyce
                                    and O'Casey"
                                Michael Kenneally, Marianopolis College
                        "Candida and Exiles: the Shaw-Joyce Connection"
                                Rhoda B. Nathan, Hofstra University
                        "Hanna and Francis Sheehy-Skeffington: Reformers in
                                    the Company of Joyce"
                                Bonnie Kime Scott, University of Delaware

2:00 - 3:30 p.m.        Session II:  James Stephens and Pádraic O'Conaire

                        Moderator:  Gareth Dunleavy
                                    University of Wisconsin-Milwaukee

                        "Reincarnated Warriors: The Unpublished Táin Scenario
                                    of James Stephens"
                                Joyce Flynn, Harvard University
                        "The Two Patricks: Galltacht and Gaeltacht in the
                                    Fiction of Pádraic O'Conaire"
                                Philip O'Leary, Yarmouth, MA
                        "Seamas O'Kelly and James Stephens"
                                Brendan O'Grady, University of Prince
                                    Edward Island

3:30 - 5:00 p.m.        Session III:  Joyce: Style and Structure

                        Moderator:  Catherine Shannon
                                    Westfield State College

                        "Symbolic Structures from Early Irish Tradition
                                    in Ulysses"
                                Maria Tymoczko, University of Massachusetts-
                                                                    Amherst
                        "The Stylistics of Regression in Ulysses"
                                Joseph Bentley, University of South Florida
                        "The Ectoplasmic Voices of "The Dead": Some Suggestions
                                    for the Further Study of Narrative Structure"
                                Janet Egleson Dunleavy, University of Wisconsin-
                                                                    Milwaukee

Thursday, October 21, 1982 (Cont'd)

8:00 p.m.                Greetings from the Hofstra University Community

                         James M. Shuart, President

                         Greetings from the Irish Republic

                         Sean O hUiginn, Consul General of Ireland

                         Keynote Address:  The Ireland of Joyce and DeValera
                            Senator/Professor John A. Murphy
                            Seanad Eireann
                            University College, Cork

                         Reception following Professor Murphy's talk.


Friday, October 22, 1982

9:00 - 9:30 a.m.         Coffee, Registration:  David Filderman Gallery
                                                Department of Special Collections
                                                Hofstra University Library-9th Floor

9:30 - 11:00 a.m.        Session IV:  A Portrait of the Artist as a Young Man

                         Moderator:  Marvin Magalaner
                                     John Jay College, Graduate Center-CUNY

                         "The Mediation of the Woman and the Interpretation
                                           of the Artist in Joyce's A Portrait"
                            Julienne H. Empric, Eckerd College
                         "Through a Cracked Looking Glass: The Picture of Dorian
                                     Gray and A Portrait of the Artist as a Young Man"
                            Dominic Manganiello, University of Ottawa
                         "A Portrait of the Artist as a Young Man: Novel as Film"
                            Robert Rhodes, SUNY, Cortland

11:15 - 1:00 p.m.        Multipurpose Room, East - Student Center

                         Film:  Joseph Strick's A Portrait of the Artist as a
                                                 Young Man

Friday, October 22, 1982 (Cont'd)

3:00 - 6:00 p.m.          American-Irish Historical Society
                          991 Fifth Avenue, New York

                          Session V:  Eamon DeValera

                          Moderator:  William Griffith
                                      St. John's University

                          "DeValera and the Irish Constitution"
                                  Alan Ward, The College of William and Mary
                          "The Sow that Eats her Farrow: Gender and Politics"
                                  Jeanne A. Flood, Wayne State University
                          "DeValera in America"
                                  Francis M. Carroll, University of Manitoba
                          "DeValera and the Origin of Development Planning in
                                      Ireland: 1935-1945"
                                  Raymond James Raymond, University of Connecticut

6:00 - 8:00 p.m.          Reception hosted by the Consul General of Ireland,
                          Mr. Sean O hUiginn


Saturday, October 23, 1982

9:00 - 9:30 a.m.          Coffee, Registration:  David Filderman Gallery
                                                 Department of Special Collections
                                                 Hofstra University Library - 9th Floor

9:30 - 11:00 a.m.         Session VI:  Joyce, his Contemporaries and Contemporary
                                                                       Culture

                          Moderator:  Patricia Mulrooney
                                      American Irish Congress

                          "Some Centenary Thoughts on Wyndham Lewis and James Joyce"
                                  Donald Knight, University of South Carolina
                          "Joyce's Favorite Composer: Geoffrey Molyneux Palmer"
                                  Myra Russel, Elizabeth Seton College
                          "Joyce as Historian: Popular Literature and Popular
                                                                   Consciousness"
                                  R. B. Kershner, Jr., University of Florida

11:00 - 12:30 p.m.        Session VII:  Joyce and Contemporary Irish Writers

                          Moderator:  Maureen Waters
                                      Queens College, CUNY

                          "Joyce, Heaney and "that subject people stuff""
                                  Lucy McDiarmid, University of Maryland
                          "Flann O'Brien: Post Joyce or Propter Joyce"
                                  Joseph Browne, West Chester State College
                          "Non Serviam: James Joyce and Modern Poetry"
                                  Robert F. Garratt, University of Puget Sound

Saturday, October 23, 1982 (Cont'd)

2:00 - 3:30 p.m.          Session VIII:  Finnegans Wake

                          Moderator:  Diana Ben-Merre
                                      Hofstra University

                          "Joyce and Popular Culture: The Wake Sermon"
                                  Cheryl Herr, Virginia Polytechnic and
                                                State University
                          "Anna the Almaziful"
                                  Suzette Henke, SUNY Binghamton
                          Comments:  Alison Armstrong, James Joyce Broadsheet

3:30 - 4:30 p.m.          Session IX:  James Joyce: the Next Hundred Years

                          Moderator:  Morris Beja
                                      Ohio State University

                          Panelists:  Alison Armstrong, James Joyce Broadsheet
                                      Edward Epstein, Queens College
                                      Lucy McDiarmid, University of Maryland
                                      Robert Rhodes, SUNY Cortland
                                      Bonnie Kime Scott, University of Delaware

7:00 p.m.                 Private Dining Room A - Student Center
                          Conference Banquet
                          Banquet Speaker:  Denis Donoghue
                                            Henry James Professor of English and
                                                        American Letters


                    *      *      *      *


CONFERENCE EXHIBIT:

                          David Filderman Gallery
                          Hofstra University Library - 9th Floor, South Campus

                          "Joyce and his Contemporaries: a Centenary Tribute"

                          October 15, 1982 - October 27, 1982

                          Gallery Hours:  Monday - Friday, 9:00 a.m. - 5:00 p.m.

                                    *      *

                          American-Irish Historical Society
                          991 Fifth Avenue, New York

                          "Eamon DeValera"

                          October 22, 1982 - January 30, 1983

                          Gallery Hours:  Tuesday - Saturday, 10:00 a.m. - 6:00 p.m.

# Irish Literary Supplement

ISSN: 0733-3390

Published by Irish Studies, 114 Paula Blvd.,
Selden, New York 11784 (516) 698-8243

*Postmaster: Please send address change to above address.*

**Robert G. Lowery, Editor and Publisher**
**Maureen Murphy, Features Editor**

**Contributing Editors**
Alison Armstrong, James Joyce Broadsheet
Audrey Eyler, Pacific Lutheran University
Donal O Cathasiagh, SUNY at Oneonta
Kevin McEneaney, Facsimilie Bookshop

The *Irish Literary Supplement* publishes reviews of
Irish-interest books. Publishers should send books to:
Book Review Editor, P.O. Box 333, Holbrook, New York 11741
Editorial, advertising and other correspondence should be
sent to the editor at  114 Paula Blvd., Selden, New York 11784
Advertising rate card available on request.


U.S. Subscriptions: $5.00
Libraries and Other Countries: $6.00
*(U.S. Funds or I.M.O. only*

Frequency: Twice yearly, April and October
Printed in the U.S.A.

**HOFSTRA UNIVERSITY**

HEMPSTEAD, NEW YORK 11550

# Index

# About the Editors and Contributors

DIANA A. BEN-MERRE received her Ph.D. from the Graduate Center of the City University of New York. She is a Teaching Fellow at New College, Hofstra University, where she directs the Writing Program. She has written about Joyce and Yeats.

JOSEPH BENTLEY received his Ph.D. from Ohio State University and is Professor of English and Director of Graduate Studies at the University of South Florida. He is the author of several studies of Aldous Huxley, James Joyce, and T. S. Eliot.

JOSEPH BROWNE is Professor of English at West Chester University. He has also taught at Temple University and was visiting professor at the University of New Hampshire. His articles on a wide range of Irish and Irish-American subjects have appeared in *Eire-Ireland, Canadian Journal of Irish Studies, The New Republic, The CEA Critic,* and *College Literature.* He has coedited a collection of essays on George Orwell and has just completed a collection on Flannery O'Connor.

FRANCIS M. CARROLL is Professor of History at St. John's College, University of Manitoba, and was the Mary Ball Washington Professor of American History at University College Dublin in 1984-1985. His interest in Irish history centers on the interplay between Ireland, the United States, and Great Britain during the period of Ireland's struggle for independence and the formation of the Irish Free State. He is the author of *American Opinion and the Irish Question, 1910-1923* and several other works.

JANET EGLESON DUNLEAVY is Professor of English at The University of Wisconsin–Milwaukee. The recipient of a Guggenheim Fellowship with Gareth E. Dunleavy for a biography in progress of Douglas Hyde, she has published widely on diverse subjects in Irish literature and Irish culture. She edited *The O'Conor Papers* with Gareth Dunleavy in 1977.

JULIENNE H. EMPRIC is Professor of Literature and Drama at Eckerd College in St. Petersburg, Florida. She has written a book on the image of woman in Joyce's *A Portrait of the Artist as a Young Man* and other scholarly articles and reviews on Old and Middle English literature, Shakespeare, and Poe.

JEANNE A. FLOOD is an Associate Professor of English at Wayne State University. She has written on Irish literature and history. The research for the present chapter was done on fellowship at the Bunting Institute of Radcliffe College.

ROBERT F. GARRATT is Professor of English at the University of Puget Sound, where he teaches modern literature. He is the author of *Modern Irish Poetry: Tradition and Continuity from Yeats to Heaney* and coeditor of *The Uses of the Past: Essays on Irish Culture*.

SUZETTE HENKE is Professor of English at the State University of New York at Binghamton. She is author of *Joyce's Moraculous Sindbook: A Study of "Ulysses"* and coeditor of *Women in Joyce*. Professor Henke has recently completed a book entitled *James Joyce and the Politics of Desire* and is presently working on a study of "Feminist Fabulation and Women's Life-Writing." She has published numerous articles in the field of modern literature, including essays on Virginia Woolf, Samuel Beckett, Anais Nin, Dorothy Richardson, Frances Farmer, John Cage, W. B. Yeats, E. M. Forster, and Linda Brent.

CHERYL HERR is Associate Professor of English at the University of Iowa and was formerly a member of the faculty at Virginia Tech as well as a Visiting Assistant Professor at Swarthmore College. She is the author of *Joyce's Anatomy of Culture* and numerous articles on subjects ranging from Olaf Stapledon to the films of Cheech and Chong.

MICHAEL KENNEALLY is Professor of English at Marianopolis College in Montreal. He is President of the Canadian Association for Irish Studies and the Literature Representative on the Executive of the American Conference for Irish Studies. His principle research interests are Irish literary autobiographies and contemporary Irish writing. His book *Portraying the Self: Sean O'Casey and the Art of Autobiography* was scheduled to appear in January 1988. He is the editor of *Studies in Con-*

*temporary Irish Literature,* a four-volume series of critical essays, the first of which will appear in 1988. He is the coeditor, with Wolfgang Zach, of *Studies in English and Comparative Literature,* and the Canadian editor of the *Irish Literary Supplement.*

R. B. KERSHNER, JR., is Associate Professor of English at the University of Florida. He has published widely on Joyce, Murdoch, Bowen, and other figures in modern British and Irish literature. He is the author of *Dylan Thomas: The Poet and His Critics* and of a forthcoming work on Joyce and popular literature.

LUCY McDIARMID is the author of *Saving Civilization: Yeats, Eliot, and Auden Between the Wars* (1984) and a book on Auden's poetics (forthcoming). She has also published many articles on modern British and Irish poetry. A former Fellow of the Bunting Institute at Radcliffe, she has taught at Swarthmore College, the University of Maryland, Baltimore County, and the Yeats International Summer School, and is Associate Professor of English at Villanova University. Her current research involves the study of Mozart comic opera and the traditions of New Comedy.

DOMINIC MANGANIELLO is Associate Professor of English at the University of Ottawa. He has published articles on Wilde and Walter Miller, Jr., and is the author of *Joyce's Politics* (1980) and a forthcoming work, *T. S. Eliot and Dante.*

MAUREEN MURPHY is Dean of Students at Hofstra University. The editor of *A Guide to Irish Studies in the United States* and coeditor with James MacKillop of *Irish Literature: A Reader,* her work in progress is a study of Irish domestic servants in the United States. She has published on Irish literature, folklore, history, and Irish-American literature.

RHODA B. NATHAN is Associate Professor of English at Hofstra University. She has published *The American Vision* (1973), *Nineteenth-Century Women Writers of the English-Speaking World* (Greenwood Press, 1986), and *Katherine Mansfield: A Critical Biography.* Her articles on Henry James and George Bernard Shaw have appeared in *The Journal of Narrative Technique, The Shaw Review, Modern Drama,* and *The Shavian.* A widely published Shavian, Professor Nathan is also vice-president of the Bernard Shaw Society.

BRENDAN O'GRADY is Professor of English at the University of Prince Edward Island, Canada, where he conducts seminars in Irish fiction. He has prepared a collection of the plays of Seumas O'Kelly, and his studies in the history of Irish settlements in Prince Edward Island are now being edited for publication.

PHILIP O'LEARY is a member of the Executive Committee of the American Conference for Irish Studies and the Irish Language editor of the *Irish Literary Supplement*. He has published numerous articles on medieval and modern Irish literature on both sides of the Atlantic.

BONNIE KIME SCOTT is Professor of English at the University of Delaware. She has written two feminist books on James Joyce, *Joyce and Feminism* (1984) and *James Joyce* (1987). She is also the editor of the collection *New Alliances in Joyce Studies* (1988), and has written numerous articles on Irish writers, women writers, and feminist theory. She is currently editing an anthology, *The Gender of Modernism*, which offers primary texts and feminist introductions that encourage a revised definition of literary modernism.

MARIA TYMOCZKO is Associate Professor of Comparative Literature at the University of Massachusetts, Amherst. She is a specialist in early Irish literature, and is the translator of *Two Death Tales from the Ulster Cycle: The Death of CuRoi and The Death of CuChulainn*. Her principal fields of research are early Celtic literature, medieval romance, and translation theory. Her most recent work includes explorations of the ways in which James Joyce translates the themes and poetics of early Irish literature into an English literary context.